# GET CLARK SMART

## THE ULTIMATE GUIDE FOR THE SAVVY CONSUMER

Clark Howard and Mark Meltzer

LONGSTREET PRESS
Atlanta, Georgia

# GET
# CLARK SMART

## THE ULTIMATE GUIDE
## FOR THE SAVVY
## CONSUMER

Published by
LONGSTREET PRESS
2140 Newmarket Parkway
Suite 122
Marietta, GA 30067

Printed in the United States of America

1st printing 2000

Library of Congress Catalog Card Number: 00-105058

ISBN: 1-56352-629-8

Cover photo by Bita Honarvar/*Atlanta Journal-Constitution* photo staff

Book design by Megan Wilson
Cover design by Burtch Bennett Hunter

For Lane, Rebecca, Stephanie, Nancy and Connie,
who inspire us to do our best.

# ACKNOWLEDGMENTS

Putting together a book like this requires a lot of help, and I'm grateful to the many people who were so willing to provide it.

More than a dozen people and organizations provided their expertise and ideas, particularly those listed below. My thanks to them all.

Joni Alpert

Amela K. Bell

Dan Blake

Kim Curley

Nancy Deubell Meltzer

Christa DiBiase

Deb Elvin

Jim Guthrie

Steven L. Hale

Neal Howard

Jerry Hunt

Gary E. Jackson

Mike Kavanaugh

Daniel H. Kolber

Mac the Mechanic

Elizabeth Manley

Todd Mark

Robert G. Martin

Michael Perling

Joe Turner

Jack Sawyer

Also, a special thanks to Mary A. Burt and Allison Price, who supplied the winning entries in my contest to name this book. Thank you both for being dedicated listeners.

# CONTENTS

# A NOTE FROM CLARK

*Get Clark Smart* is my fourth book, and I think it's my best effort yet at helping you take control of your financial future.

You and I have tons of choices that didn't exist a generation ago. People used to work for one company for thirty years, then receive a pension. There was one phone company, one electric company, and one gas company, and their rates were set by the government. Airline routes and prices also were established by the government.

Almost all cars came from three auto makers, General Motors, Ford, and Chrysler, which introduced new models every three years on the same day. When one raised prices by 3.5 percent, the others did the same. You could watch any channel you wanted on TV for free — as long as it was ABC, NBC, or CBS. The three introduced their new shows on the same day in September each year. Central control and predictability were a big part of our lives. Choice was not part of the picture.

But now we have endless choices in almost every area — which brings opportunities to save money as well as lose it. That's where *Get Clark Smart* enters the picture. I hope you find this book to be a great guide to making wise choices each day as you try to avoid the pitfalls and take advantage of the fantastic deals offered by a free, open, competitive, and chaotic marketplace.

Should you buy a new car or a used car, and how much should you pay? Should you buy an extended warranty on your new refrigerator or VCR? What's the best way to save for your child's college education? How much should you pay for long-distance service?

I've put many of my best answers to those questions into this book. I've also listed some of the best money-saving sites on the Internet, nearly 150 of them. You can use them to find out what's likely to go wrong with your car (www.alldata.com), get the best rate on a new credit card (www.cardweb.com), and shop for wireless phone service (www.point.com). And while you're surfing, look for more great tips on my Web site, www.clarkhoward.com.

Things have changed a lot since my last book, *Clark Howard's Consumer Survival Kit III*, was published in 1998, and so have my strategies for getting the best deal. *Get Clark Smart* has all-new information on what to do if your identity is stolen, how to buy a computer, and how to save money on airfare and hotels. It contains the best and most up-to-date advice I can give.

I love all the competition and choice we have today, but I know how confusing it can be. I hope *Get Clark Smart* helps you get the most for your money.

Clark Howard
July 2000

# GET CLARK SMART

## THE ULTIMATE GUIDE FOR THE SAVVY CONSUMER

# CARS

**The most** difficult calls I take on my radio show involve cars. We call them "razor blade" calls, which means the situation is awfully bad. A typical call involves someone who's recently purchased a used car, sometimes for several thousand dollars, only to find it is ridden with problems. They're faced with impossible choices. The vehicle often can't be repaired properly, and the dealer won't take it back. That could mean scrapping it, absorbing an expensive loss, and trying again.

It's even worse if the buyer is making car payments on a useless vehicle. These situations are very sad, because in many cases nothing can be done to help the caller. It's simply too late.

What I hope to do is educate you so that you can avoid the most common mistakes, and at the same time buy a car more effectively, with less stress, and probably get a better deal than you ever have before.

I want to teach you the right way to buy a new car or a used car, finance that purchase, and get it fixed if something goes wrong.

# 2 🚗 BUYING A NEW CAR

There are a lot of tools available today to help you buy a car. Unfortunately, most people don't take advantage of them, because they get caught up in the emotion of buying. If money matters to you, put that emotion aside and be smart about your car purchase.

First, go to your bank or credit union and prequalify for a car loan, or apply online. Once you prequalify, you'll know how much car you can afford and what type of monthly payment you will have to budget. It also means your purchase won't collapse because you can't get financing.

Once your financing is set up, decide what kind of car you want. One of the best times to go look at cars is when a dealership is closed. If the dealership isn't open, there's no salesperson there to pressure you. You're free to look around the lot at vehicles. It may sound strange, but a shopping mall parking lot also is a good place to look at a lot of different vehicles.

Everyone wants a car that will run dependably and stay out of the repair shop. The best way to improve your odds of getting a trouble-free car is to check out the repair records of the models you like. *Consumer Reports* magazine is the best place to find repair data on cars. Each year, the magazine's April issue is devoted to car buying, and it contains detailed ratings and data on a variety of models

for several model years. Consumers Union, which publishes *Consumer Reports*, also publishes a car-buying guide that is available year-round in bookstores. *Consumer Reports* is available online for a monthly fee at www.consumerreports.com.

Of course, no repair data is available on newly introduced car models. I don't recommend buying a new or radically redesigned model, because if you do, you are the guinea pig for any problems the vehicle might have. After a few model years, you have a better idea if a car is well-made and worth purchasing.

Once you've narrowed your search to a couple of different models, call your insurance agent to find out how much it would cost to insure those vehicles. There may be a significant difference between your choices, even between two versions of the same model. The size of the cars' engines, for example, could be one reason for a cost difference.

Become familiar with the various versions of a car. The Honda Accord, for example, might come in a DX, LX, EX, and SE version. Each version comes with a different package of options and standard equipment. You'll find that the most expensive version of the car will cost several thousand dollars more than the least expensive version. It's to your advantage to buy the least expensive version of the model that meets your needs. That's because, over time, the value of those two vehicles converges. An initial gap of $8,000 between the cheapest and most expensive versions might dwindle to $1,000 in the resale value of the two cars after a few years of ownership. If you buy the most expensive version, you pay a higher price both up-front and at resale time.

I don't recommend test-driving a car at a dealership. You'll only have a short time to check out the car, and the salesperson will be right there. The best way to test-drive a car is to rent it for a day or two. Car rental companies make most of their money on business rentals, so they offer great specials on the weekends, when volume is light. I actually check out cars this way on business, since I travel so much. I've rented cars I thought I might want to buy and changed my mind after driving them for a few days. It's the ultimate test drive and it's not expensive. After all, considering that you might spend $25,000 to buy a car, spending $25 to $40 to rent it is rather inexpensive.

If you do a test-drive at a dealership, a representative may ask for your driver's license. If you turn it over, make the dealership give you a signed release saying they will not pull a credit report on you. Dealerships like to check your credit while you're on a test drive, and if you visit several dealerships, the number of credit inquiries could damage your credit rating.

The Internet has put consumers completely in control of the car-buying process. To get the best deal, you have to have Internet access. If you're not online, find a friend who is and enlist their help, or go to a local library. It's that important. In fact, using the Internet will save you so much on the car purchase that, even if you don't have a computer or an Internet-only appliance, spending a few hundred dollars to buy one would be a bargain.

First, go to www.edmunds.com and look up the actual dealer cost on the base vehicle and options you're interested in. Add the dealer cost for air conditioning, automatic transmission, whatever you want, and calculate the total dealer cost for the car. Any negotiating you do with the dealer should start from the dealer's cost, not the manufacturer's suggested retail price. The price you pay will depend upon the popularity of a particular model, and it could range from thousands of dollars above dealer cost for the most popular cars to below dealer cost for unpopular models.

You can get an instant price quote for the model you want to buy at a number of Web sites. Some of the biggest are www.carorder.com, www.carsdirect.com and www.greenlight.com. There will be many others. With these sites, you enter the model, equipment and color you want, interior and exterior, and within 15 seconds, they give you a guaranteed price for which they will sell you the car. It's amazing. If you wish, you can then go through that process, as I

**4**

have, and buy a car online. I did it at www.carorder.com for my mom, and I was able to buy her car at $6,000 less than she had been quoted from two dealers.

The process was so easy it was startling. There's no delivery charge, and you have the option of picking the car up at a nearby dealer, or having it delivered to your home or office. You sign the papers and hand them the money and they hand you the keys. Buying a car via the Internet is so superior to the traditional process that dealer groups in state after state are trying to outlaw Internet car shopping. If they're successful, you may have to accept delivery at the home of a friend or relative in another state.

If you decide not to buy online, you still can use the Web sites to get a feel for fair market value. Use the online price as a guideline when you call local dealers. See if they'll match or beat the price you found on the Internet. If the dealer agrees and then reneges, walk out.

You'll find big differences in price at different Web sites, just as you would from different dealers. So don't assume any one Web site will be the cheapest for any car. It will depend on their sources of supply.

However, beware of the many supposed Internet car-buying services that actually are glorified referral services paid for by the dealers. These simply are a form of advertising for the dealers, and you won't benefit by using them.

If you choose to buy a car the old-

fashioned way, by walking into a dealership and talking with a salesperson, be prepared for a difficult process. Some dealers still use a variety of tactics to snare you. They know you're excited about buying a new car and will use that to their advantage. One strategy they'll employ is delay. Dealers know that the longer they can keep you at the dealership, the more likely you are to buy a car. So they'll try to keep you there for several hours.

One common tactic to delay you is to make your car unavailable. When you show up at a dealership, they ask to have the used-car manager check out your car, to evaluate its trade-in value. While you're test-driving a new car, they send somebody to look over your car and make sure you don't get it back too quickly.

I recommend that you discuss any trade-in only after you've negotiated the purchase of the new car. I'll talk more about why in the next section. But if you keep the transactions separate and stay close to your car, you won't be kept in the dealership any longer than you want to be there.

One of the most despicable practices in the industry is "roofing," in which the used-car people literally throw the keys to your car onto the dealership roof, then report that they somehow can't find the keys. The purpose is to get you to drive home in the new car while they look for the keys. The best way to protect yourself in a dealership is to be willing to walk out.

## TIPS ON BUYING A NEW CAR

◉ Go to your bank or credit union and prequalify for a car loan, or apply online. That tells you how much car you can afford and what type of monthly payment you will have to budget.

◉ Look at cars when a dealership is closed, so there's no salesperson to pressure you.

◉ The best way to test-drive a car is to rent it for a day or two. It's the ultimate test drive and it's not expensive.

◉ Use the Internet to buy a car for incredible ease and price savings.

◉ Start your research with at least two different vehicles in mind. Then check out the price, reliability, and cost to insure each of the cars you're considering.

◉ Find out the dealer cost of the vehicle and options you want and begin negotiating from that cost.

◉ When you've narrowed the search to one or two vehicles and have the actual dealer cost for each, shop online for instant price quotes.

◉ If you prefer not to buy online, use the online quotes as a guideline and call local dealers to see if they'll match the best online price.

◉ If you go into a dealership to sign the paperwork and pick up a car, make sure the purchase agreement shows what you've agreed to pay. If it's not the same, walk out.

◉ If you choose to negotiate in the traditional manner with a car dealer, be prepared for a difficult process.

## REFERENCE

*Consumer Reports*' April Auto Issue or Car Buying Guide

## INTERNET

www.edmunds.com
www.carorder.com
www.carsdirect.com
www.greenlight.com

# 6 TRADE-INS, FINANCING, AND EXTENDED WARRANTIES

If you have a trade-in, the time to discuss it with the dealer is after you've completed the purchase of the car. Do it as a completely separate transaction, because if you mix the trade-in with the purchase, you'll never know whether a dealer is offering you a great price on the new car and making up for it by giving you a poor value for your trade-in.

Start by finding out what your trade-in is worth. One of the best places to do that is www.edmunds.com. If you're not Internet-active, ask a friend to help. Edmund's also has books, available at most bookstores and libraries.

There are two prices: the trade-in price, which is what you can expect a dealer to pay you, and the retail or market price, which is the price at which a dealer may sell it to someone else. By selling the vehicle yourself, you'll get a price about halfway between average trade-in and average retail. Once you've measured that gap, you can figure out whether it's worth the bother of selling the car yourself.

Once you've shopped around and the dealers realize you're a good shopper, their prices will be similar. You can help decide which dealer to buy from by seeing how much they'll give you for the trade-in. Take the car to each dealer for a trade-in quote and use that as the decision-maker.

I always skip the trade-in process and sell my cars myself. A large number of people do sell privately, and they are able to get a better price. But most prefer to trade their car to the dealer because they don't want to deal with the hassle of a private sale — classified ads, phone calls, and test drives.

## FINANCING THE CAR

It's critical to finance the purchase of a car in advance at a bank, credit union, or an online lender and not at the dealership. By doing this, you'll know the financing is set, and you can proceed to buy.

An alternative to the bank or credit union is to do Internet financing of a car purchase, with rates equivalent to what a credit union charges. A few to consider are www.carfinance.com, www.carsdirect.com, and www.carorder.com. There are dozens of sites available.

When you allow the dealer to arrange financing, all kinds of terrible things can happen. If you drive your new car home and give the dealer your trade-in, you're in trouble if, as happens more and more, the financing later collapses.

Here's what happens when the dealer calls you a few weeks later with the sad news that your loan didn't go through. Because the loan and purchase are done separately, you may not be able to undo the sale. Even if you can, your old car may be long gone. So you either have to come up with a lot more money for a down payment, or pay an exorbitant rate of interest, so that a lender will accept the loan. You can try to get the dealer to undo the sale and give you the value of your used car in cash. But depending on the laws in each state, you may have to fight to reverse the deal.

I got an incredible call from a woman who financed with a dealer. She went to see a salesman she had bought a car from a few years earlier, this time to ask about buying an extended warranty. The salesman quickly convinced her to buy a new car, and roll the old loan into a new car loan. According to the salesman, she could turn the car in after three years if she didn't want it any longer. The bad news was that, without realizing it, she had signed her name to a seven-year auto loan with a $6,000 balloon payment due at the end of the seven years. She wound up owing $10,000 more than the car was worth. When I get these calls, it's like trying to fix a train wreck. The damage is already done.

You also can end up paying a higher interest rate on a dealer-arranged loan, because dealers will sell a loan to a customer at whatever rate they can get the customer to pay. A disgruntled finance manager told me the dealership may get the loan at 8 percent and mark it up to 14 percent or 18 percent if they can get the customer to pay that much. The spreads are scary. The finance manager gets the car buyer to pay a higher

rate by pointing out blemishes on their credit report, scaring them into thinking they might not be approved. When they're done psyching the customer out, the customer is ecstatic to get the loan at the high rate.

Dealers want to do the financing, because that's where most of the profit is in car sales today. If you take the extra effort to prequalify with your bank or credit union, you will steer clear of a lot of financial danger. If the dealer offers a better interest rate than your bank or credit union, it's okay to go ahead and take the dealer loan, just as long as you have a back-up lender.

Car buyers care mostly about their monthly payment, and are more and more likely to opt for long loans. But you should finance a car for 48 months or less. The 60-month loan is a poor financial choice because under it, the value of the car declines much faster than the loan balance. So, for much of the five-year period, you're "upside down" in the loan — you owe more than the vehicle is worth.

Being "upside down" can be a major problem. Let's say you decide after a couple of years that you can't stand your car. Selling it won't generate nearly enough money to pay off the loan. Unless you can come up with several thousand dollars to pay off the balance of the loan, you're stuck in the vehicle. If the vehicle is totaled in an accident, you could end up owing the lender thousands of dollars. You have to cover the gap between the amount the insurance

**8**    company pays and what you owe.

The beauty of a shorter loan, particularly 42 months or less, is that the loan amount tracks the value of the vehicle. For most people, 48 months is a good compromise. I know this sounds harsh, but if you go in for a car loan and the payments for a 48-month loan are too high, you're trying to buy too much car. Stretching it to 60 months is the wrong response.

## EXTENDED WARRANTIES

I don't like service contracts or extended warranties for computers or consumer electronics, but I'm neutral when it comes to cars. Automobiles cost so much money and many people feel better having one.

However, it's more important to buy a car with a record of reliability than to worry about an extended warranty.

If you do buy, choose only the manufacturer's extended warranty or one sold by your insurance company. Don't buy any third-party warranty. Many third-party warranty companies go out of business before they ever pay a claim, and even if that doesn't happen, the language in these contracts is so full of holes it will be virtually worthless.

I've had case after case of extended warranty companies selling cheap contracts to dealers and then going out of business without paying claims.

These ripoff companies sell service contracts to dealers for $90, and the dealers resell them to car buyers for $1,100. The pitch is that the dealer will make a fortune even if they sell the warranty for $600. After a few years, claims start coming in and there's not enough money in the pool to pay the claims. The company collapses or vanishes, and the consumer ends up with a worthless service contract.

The price on extended warranties is highly negotiable. One of the manufacturer's contracts that retails at $795 costs the dealer $180. The dealer may make little profit on the sale of a car, but on an extended warranty the markup may be 400 percent to 1,000 percent, depending on the type of warranty.

The best way to negotiate is to call your auto insurance agent for a quote on an extended warranty. Then, compare the costs and coverages to those offered under the manufacturer's contract.

It's very important not to make a decision on an extended warranty from the dealer or anyone else until you've had time to think about it. This is not a decision that has to be made at the moment you're buying your vehicle. In fact, that's the worst time to decide because you're not thinking clearly. You're excited about buying a new car and you want to be done with the paperwork.

With most extended warranty providers, you have at least 12 months from the date you purchase the car to make the decision. One of the advantages to waiting is if the car turns out to be a lemon and you're always having problems with it, then you know you should buy an extended warranty. During the first year, the manufacturer's warranty protects you.

## Clark says

### TIPS ON TRADE-INS, FINANCING, AND EXTENDED WARRANTIES

- If you have a trade-in, the time to discuss it with the dealer is after you've negotiated the purchase of the car.

- Find out what your trade-in is worth at www.edmunds.com, or ask a friend to look for you. By selling the vehicle yourself, you'll get a price about halfway between average trade-in and average retail. A dealer will give you the trade-in price.

- After you've negotiated a price for a new car, you can decide which dealer to buy from by seeing how much they'll give you for the trade-in.

- Finance a car for 48 months or less. With a 60-month loan, the value of the car declines much faster than the loan balance. So for much of the five-year period, you owe more than the vehicle is worth.

- Keep the financing separate from the car-price negotiation, too. When you allow the dealer to arrange financing, all kinds of terrible things can happen.

- Buy a manufacturer's extended warranty or one from your own auto insurer. Don't buy a third-party contract.

- Don't buy an extended warranty from an automobile dealer or anyone else until you've had time to think about it and shop prices. You don't have to make this decision at the moment you're buying your vehicle.

## INTERNET

www.edmunds.com
www.carfinance.com
www.carorder.com
www.carsdirect.com

# 10 🚗 LEASING

It's almost impossible to talk to an auto salesperson without hearing a pitch for you to lease, rather than buy, a vehicle. That's because leasing is a very profitable method of selling vehicles for dealers.

Car buying can be complicated enough. Leasing is much more complicated, and that makes it very difficult for you to compare prices, even if you're a savvy consumer. With the sky-high financing costs built into most leases, you'll almost certainly end up with a bad deal if you agree to lease.

One of the most popular tricks of the trade is for manufacturers and dealers to advertise incredibly low monthly lease payments — $169, $199, or $249 a month. But what they don't tell you, except in the fine print, is you'll have to pay a large, non-refundable fee up-front. This fee, sometimes called a capital cost reduction, or a capital acquisition fee, often amounts to $2,000 to $4,000. Essentially, you're getting that low monthly payment by paying part of the lease in advance. The idea is to sell low payments, because a lot of consumers buy a car today by figuring out if a particular payment will fit into their budget.

The low monthly payment makes it seem as if you're getting a good deal, but on the typical lease, you're not. Let's say you pay a $3,000 up-front fee for a 36-month lease at $249 a month. If you spread the $3,000 over the 36 months,

it amounts to more than $83 a month. So the actual cost of the deal to you is $332 a month, not to mention that you give up the use of the $3,000 right away. Clearly, not as good a deal.

Whenever you lease, you're giving away your future. If you buy a vehicle and pay it off in four years, you own a vehicle that still has value. You can keep it and avoid making car payments for a while, or sell it and use the money to help buy a newer vehicle. But after four years of leasing a vehicle and making payments, you own nothing.

A lot of people use leasing to get more car than they can afford. The monthly payment for two similar cars will be cheaper for someone who leases than for someone who buys, so people will lease, foolishly, so they can have a more expensive car. Let's say you buy an $18,000 vehicle with no down payment. Over four years, you'll pay $18,000 plus interest, and your monthly payment will be based on the cost of financing $18,000. If you lease a vehicle, you may finance $8,000 and have a residual value of $10,000. Your monthly payments will be based on the $8,000 being financed, so the payments will be much lower. You'll have the option of paying $10,000 to buy that car at the end of the four-year lease.

You also may owe sizable mileage penalties at the end of a lease. Most leases allow you to drive an average of

15,000 miles per year. If you exceed the limit, you have to pay a penalty of 8 to 15 cents per mile. If you lease a car for four years and drive a total of 80,000 miles, you might owe as much as $3,000.

Too often, people are not realistic about how many miles they're going to drive each year. Or they may end up changing jobs and find themselves driving much farther than they originally intended. Before they know it, they're near the end of the lease and tens of thousands of miles over the limit. If you owe a big mileage penalty, the best thing to do is buy the vehicle at the predetermined price specified in the lease. Then you won't have to pay the penalty.

I had a call from one fellow who turned in his Mercedes-Benz at the end of his lease, not realizing he was way over the mileage limit. He wasn't asked to pay any penalty. But two years later, he was told that he owed $8,000 in excess mileage costs. It would have cost him just $2,000 more, a total of $10,000, to buy the car outright. But the car had been sold long before and he no longer had the option to buy it.

If you're going to pay a mileage penalty or buy the car, you'd better have some cash on hand. If the car has a lot of miles on it, a bank won't lend you the money to pay off its residual value. You avoid all these problems if you just buy the vehicle in the first place.

A lot of people are getting hit with surprise fees over the condition of the car when they turn it in. One of my callers turned in her car and received an inspection report saying the car was in good condition. But later she got a bill from a bank for $1,850 for what the bank considered to be excessive wear and tear on the vehicle. The bank claimed the dealership was not officially charged with determining the condition of the car.

I have essentially the same recommendation here as I do when people leave an apartment. Before you turn in a leased car, hire an auto detailing service to get the car as clean as possible. If there's something damaged on the car, get it fixed yourself. You'll pay a lot less to have the repair done than you'll be charged by the leasing company if you let it go. Then document what you've done by taking pictures of the interior and exterior of the car. Shoot a roll of film or more if needed. Then, make sure you're turning it in to the official source who determines the condition of the car.

Short-term leases can be bad enough, but a four- or five-year lease is a recipe for disaster. Many customers end up married to a vehicle they hate. Even if they like the car, most don't keep it the full four or five years. Instead, they frequently end up paying severe early termination penalties.

If you lease for five years and your car is totaled in an accident, you may have big problems. You could be responsible for a giant gap between the amount the insurance company will pay and the stated residual in the lease.

**12** 🚗 It's not unusual in these cases for the gap to be as much as $8,000. Some leases contain an automatic gap clause, which states that, if the vehicle is totaled in an accident, the manufacturer's financing arm accepts the insurance company payment and releases you from any further responsibility. Be certain any lease you sign covers this gap provision. Some car dealers, if you raise this issue, will offer you a separate insurance product called gap insurance. They should provide gap insurance for free as part of the deal.

You can tell how bad an idea leasing is by how good a deal you can get buying a vehicle someone else has leased. My wife and I bought a three-year-old car with just 16,000 miles on it for half the retail price. The people who leased it paid for all that depreciation.

There are two circumstances in which leasing a vehicle makes sense. The first is when someone likes to have a new car every two to three years. If that's your goal, to always have a new car and get rid of it before the warranty is up, you're a candidate for a short-term lease. You won't have to deal with getting rid of the car.

The other circumstance in which leasing can be okay is when there's factory-subsidized financing on the lease. If the manufacturer offers no-interest financing, your total cost to lease for two years and then buy the vehicle might be lower than if you bought it outright.

If the manufacturer subsidizes the lease by stating an unrealistically high residual value on the vehicle, you can lease for two or three years at a great price, but then you should walk away. In any case, don't lease for more than three years. You can tell if the lease if factory-subsidized because the advertisement will be from the manufacturer, not the dealer.

## TIPS ON LEASING

◉ It's hard to compare prices on a lease, and the financing costs built into a lease are very high.

◉ Leasing may seem cheaper than buying, but you're mortgaging your future when you lease. After a few years of leasing a vehicle and making payments, you own nothing.

◉ Manufacturers and dealers like to use up-front fees to create ultra-low monthly payments that mask the actual cost of a lease.

◉ Most leases allow you to drive an average of 15,000 miles per year. If you exceed the limit, you have to pay a penalty of 8 to 15 cents per mile.

● Before you turn in a leased car, have it detailed inside and out, and make any needed repairs. Then find out what company is officially responsible for determining that the car is in acceptable condition.

● A four- or five-year lease is a recipe for disaster. Many customers end up married to a vehicle they hate or end up paying severe early termination penalties.

● If you lease for five years and your car is totaled in an accident, you could be responsible for a giant gap between the amount the insurance company will pay and the stated residual in the lease.

# BUYING A USED CAR

Buying a used car is a lot easier than it used to be. The supply of high-quality used cars is way up, thanks to the popularity of leasing and America's growing love of travel, making available a lot of former leased and rental cars.

It's really smart to buy a used car because of the tremendous savings you get. Because new cars depreciate so quickly, a high-quality two- or three-year-old car might cost 40 percent less than a new car, which is a tremendous savings.

Just as with buying a new car, the Internet is your biggest friend in buying a used car. It can help you figure out what make and model to buy and how to finance it.

If you know the general amount you'll need to borrow, go ahead and set up the financing first. See the section on trade-ins, financing, and extended warranties in this chapter for more information.

To help you decide what make and model to buy, check *Consumer Reports'* April car issue. You can look at it at the library, or access it online at www.consumerreports.com. You'll have to pay a subscription fee for the online service, but it may be worth the convenience. *Consumer Reports* has lists of the best and worst used cars. Don't buy any car if it's on the list of cars to avoid. Buying a used car always is riskier than buying a new car. Don't do anything that worsens your odds.

The used cars on the recommended list are grouped by general price category: $10,000 to $12,000, $12,000 to $15,000, and so on. That can help you narrow your choices to fit your budget. But just because a make and model of car is on the list, don't assume that an individual car you're thinking of buying is going to be good. More about that later.

Once you have a make and model

**14**  in mind, it's time to figure out the price. Several Web sites can give you the average trade-in value of the car and the average retail price. You should pay between average trade-in and average retail, adjusting up or down for equipment and mileage. Pricing guides on the Internet and the bookstore will show you how to do that. Two to try are www.edmunds.com and www.kbb.com (Kelly Blue Book). In the used-car market, price quotes may vary widely. Check multiple sources to get a good idea of likely prices. Another good source is www.autotrader.com, which tells you not what cars are selling for, but what prices owners are asking. Do nationwide searches first, then look for prices in your own area.

Many dealerships now have what they call "certified used car programs," under which they allow you to return a vehicle for a full refund up to three, five, or seven days after you purchase it. The vehicle also may come with a manufacturer's or dealer's warranty, ranging from three months to two years. The manufacturer's warranties are preferable. And a used car also may have some of the original new-car warranty remaining. You won't get as good a price on the car if you buy one of these reconditioned, certified vehicles, but it gives a lot of buyers assurance that someone is standing behind the purchase, and I like that.

But even if you buy a "certified" car, it's very important that within the three-, five-, or seven-day period, you have the vehicle inspected by an independent diagnostic mechanic. Look for someone with an ASE certification, an indication that the mechanic has the expertise needed to do a comprehensive evaluation. It's well worth the $100 or so you'll spend to make sure the vehicle has no major defects and hasn't been in an accident. A wreck can cause a car to have tremendous operating problems as well as suffer a huge loss in value. The only way to know whether it's been in an accident is to have it inspected.

The diagnostic tests aren't pass or fail. Sometimes, the mechanic will report that a part is worn, and you'll have to make the decision whether to buy the car. You can also use the disclosure of certain problems as leverage to lower the price. Then you can use the savings to pay for repairs.

If you buy at a traditional dealership that doesn't offer you the opportunity to return the car for a refund, make your deal for the purchase contingent on it passing an inspection by a diagnostic mechanic. Then have it inspected before you complete the purchase. If a seller refuses to allow the vehicle to be inspected, don't buy it.

In the past, I recommended that people look at buying a car at one of the used-car superstores. Many of them have gone out of business, not because of the cost of selling cars that have been reconditioned and guaranteed, but because they put too much money into building fancy facilities and putting too many vehicles on the lot. I still believe the public wants companies that sell a car and stand behind it, but the used-superstore concept as defined by AutoNation and CarMax did not work.

Another company, iMotors.com, has what I think is the most innovative way for you to buy a used car. But there's no way of knowing if what they're doing is going to work. They carry no inventory at all. You go to their Web site and tell them what used car you want to buy — make, model, year, color, and equipment — and they give you a guaranteed price for the car. Then they go out and find a car that matches your description and take it to one of their reconditioning centers. If they aren't happy with its condition, they re-wholesale it. But if it inspects well, they recondition it fully and deliver it to you. Imotors then gives you seven days to return the car, if you decide for any reason that you don't want it.

It's a low-cost process for iMotors, because the company avoids the expense of carrying a huge inventory of cars that people may not want.

Most used-car sales in the United States still are as-is sales, with no warranty to protect you. If you buy from an individual, as happens in 20 percent of used-car transactions, you don't expect any warranty. But if you pay more to buy from a dealer, you have a right to expect some protection if the car doesn't work.

The law is of minimal help. Only a handful of states provide any legal protection for used-car buyers. In many other states, you own the car as soon as you sign the papers.

Some unethical dealers still sell worthless cars salvaged from wrecks. The paperwork is washed, and you could buy a vehicle that actually is two or three cars sewn together. I once got a call from a couple who spent $2,800 on a used Honda Civic, only to find that they couldn't get a title for it. The car had been wrecked in another state and shabbily repaired. The frame was bent in the crash and a plate was welded to the undercarriage in a halfhearted attempt to fix it. When my staff and I interceded, the dealer offered to buy the car back, but they wanted a $600 fee for eight months of use.

An inspection almost certainly will find a wrecked car. But if you want to be absolutely sure, pay about $20 to run a history of the car's title instantly. There are several sources for this. The one that's best known is www.carfax.com, which also will do a free check to see if the car has been part of a Lemon Law buyback. Paying to run the title history also can determine if the car's odometer has been rolled back or disconnected.

To minimize these kinds of dangers, do not buy vehicles from old-style dealers who sell only used cars. When a new-car dealer takes a trade or a return from a rental company, it keeps the best vehicles on its lot and sells the rest through auction. The most problem-ridden cars end up at used-car lots.

The worst used-car lots are the "Buy

**16**  Here, Pay Here" lots. Almost always, the cars are incidental to the purpose of these places. They make their money on the loans they extend to you on your vehicle. They're in the loan business, not the car business.

### TIPS ON BUYING A USED CAR

◉ Arrange your financing first.

◉ Check *Consumer Reports*' listings of car models that have performed well. Don't buy any car on the magazine's Used Cars to Avoid list.

◉ Find out what you should pay by checking prices at www.edmunds.com or www.kbb.com, or ask a friend to look for you.

◉ Have a used car inspected by a diagnostic mechanic, to see if it has been wrecked or has any major defects.

◉ Don't buy from an old-style used-car-only lot.

### INTERNET

www.edmunds.com
www.kbb.com
www.consumerreports.com
www.carfax.com
www.imotors.com

# CAR REPAIRS

Cars have become a lot more reliable over the years, but they've also become far more complex. The proliferation of car models, the advancement of technology in cars, and a lack of people who are properly trained to repair those vehicles has made car repair much more difficult.

So often when I hear complaints about car repair, the problem isn't a repair shop trying to rip you off — it's a lack of competence on the part of the mechanic. We fear the crook, but the reality often is that the mechanic doesn't know enough about your car to fix the problem.

One of the best safeguards you can use when you take your car in for service — and especially if you have to return a car for the same problem — is to control what is written on the work ticket. Don't let the mechanic list a cure on the ticket, but rather a description of the symptoms. If the car is stalling out at 30 miles per hour, that's what should be on the ticket. You don't want the ticket to say, "Do a tune-up," because if the problem isn't corrected, they will be able to say correctly that they did a tune-up.

How you prepare the service ticket is a key strategy if you want to assert your rights under your state's Lemon Law (see also the Lemon Law section). To claim benefits under most of these laws, you have to produce service tickets that show you attempted to repair the vehicle. Make sure the shop writes a service ticket and make sure you keep a copy. If the service tickets you receive do not show clearly the vehicle was brought in several times to repair the same problem, you may not be able to provide the proper documentation in order to force the manufacturer to buy back or exchange your vehicle.

If you're going to have an estimate done on the car, make sure the work ticket says it has been authorized only for an estimate. If you're authorizing specific work, write down the exact dollar limit you are authorizing and don't permit any work to be done beyond that dollar limit.

If the estimate is large, don't accept it as the final word. Even if your car is not driveable, it would be wise to have it towed to another repair shop for another estimate of what is wrong and how much it would cost to repair. If the repair is $2,000 or more, it would not be overkill to bring it to three places for repair estimates.

Obviously the best circumstance is when the vehicle is still driveable. You'll feel like the worst kind of sitting duck when the car isn't driveable and you think you're married to the first repair shop to which it is towed. But a $50 tow charge is money well spent when the alternative might be hundreds of dollars in unneeded repairs.

Estimates may vary because two different mechanics can come up with two different explanations for what is wrong, or different ways to fix it. One summer, my air conditioning went out when a $550 computer module failed. I could have paid for a new module, but my car was four years old at the time and had 60,000 miles on it and that sounded like an expensive answer. But the mechanic had a great idea. The module's job was to turn off the air conditioning compressor temporarily when the car was started. The mechanic suggested a simple rewiring of the air-conditioning to bypass the module. I just had to remember to turn off the air conditioner before I started the car. Getting a second opinion in that case saved me hundreds of dollars.

If your car is towed to a mechanic,

**18**

don't allow the tow-truck driver to choose the repair shop. Quite often, he or she will be paid to steer your vehicle to a particular shop. You have no way of knowing if that shop is legitimate, honest, or competent. Make your own decision about where to take the car.

Don't rely on a nationally famous name when you go for a car repair. Too often at a franchise location, the parent company fails to accept responsibility for a problem. A common response is, "We're not responsible, but we'll see if we can talk to them about an accommodation." That doesn't mean the national company is behind you. Make sure you know who backs the warranty. If the warranty is good only at that location, then taking your car to a chain or franchise means nothing.

Over the years, I've received a lot of complaints from people who've had their cars repaired at Goodyear and Firestone service centers. The regional offices for these companies have become infamous for backing away from anything their independent dealers do. Go to these centers only if you're confident in the work of the individual dealer, because the company isn't likely to help you if there's a problem.

No matter which repair shop you use, always ask for the return of parts being replaced. That's one of the best ways you can prove later that a repair shop didn't make a repair it was supposed to make. At the very least, it gives you peace of mind that the shop made the promised repair. There's

always the risk they can dig out some old parts. If you're dealing with true crooks, these precautions don't really matter. That's why word-of-mouth is so important in car repair. If you know someone who has been thrilled with a certain service facility, consider taking your car there.

I've taken my cars to an independent shop that works on nothing but my brand of car. They've seen all these problems hundreds of times, so it's easier for them to make the correct diagnosis. Even if a specialty shop charges more for a repair, it's valuable to know the repairs are done right. My mechanic knew about a potential engine failure on my car that could be avoided by replacing a belt. He recommended this preventative maintenance to make sure there was no catastrophe.

That's a real benefit of using an independent shop. A dealer knows your make and model of car, but may side with the manufacturer and not disclose those kinds of problems. However, using an independent mechanic is no fail-safe method. You still have to make sure you're happy with the work the shop does.

Another problem with dealer repairs is that you often don't get to speak with the mechanic who works on your car. You speak to a service writer, who writes a note describing the problem to the mechanic. If you need to go to the dealer because your car is under warranty, or if you like going to that particular dealer, insist upon speaking personally to the mechanic if a repair is unsatisfactory. If you can talk to him directly, you can often explain the problem more completely.

I once had a Chevy Prism that was stalling out at any speed, and the dealership couldn't repair it after two tries. On the third trip, I demanded to speak to the mechanic and explained what was wrong. He hadn't been able to understand the scope of the problem from a few perfunctory notes on the service ticket. But after I explained it to him, he realized what was wrong and fixed it in 15 minutes.

There are two schools of thought on the shops that specialize in particular components of a vehicle. Some like to go to a quick-lube place for oil changes, a tune-up shop for tune-ups, or a brake repair place for brake work. Others like to go to one mechanic for all repairs. I tend to do the routine things like oil changes at a place that does just those, but have anything significant done by a shop that specializes in my brand of vehicle. The most important thing about oil changes is to have them done regularly, not where they're done.

I have a built-in skepticism about general repair centers that claim to be able to repair all components of all vehicles. You're asking a lot from a mechanic if you throw any number of different vehicles at him or her and say, "Fix this." I don't think that's possible; specializing by component or by vehicle are the two wisest methods.

Whichever place you choose, try to find a reputable, qualified service center before your car is in trouble. Then you'll know where to go when repairs are needed. Ask people who have the same brand of car as you where they go, and whether they're happy.

Most car owners have only rare encounters with an auto body shop, so they have no idea what to expect when they need body work. First, get an estimate of the cost to repair the vehicle. Many insurers require two estimates, so they can be sure the estimate is accurate. Some use their own adjuster.

Most insurers figure into their estimate the cost of new, brand-name parts. Unless you insist upon new parts, some body shops will sneak in a used or generic door panel or fender, and charge you the same amount. If you have an older car, you may not mind used parts. But if you're paying for new parts, you ought to get new parts.

The insurance company check may be sent to you or the body shop you select. If you have a collision deductible, usually $250 or $500, you may have to pay that as well. Some body shops will agree to do the repairs for the amount paid by the insurer, so you won't have to pay the deductible. Check with a few body shops and see what kind of deal you can cut. If you don't mind generic or used parts, you can agree to let the body shop install used parts to reduce the cost.

You can have repairs done by any body shop you choose, even if the

**20**  other driver's insurer is paying for them. Ask friends or your insurer for a referral, or try a new-car dealer's body shop. Since the dealer is likely to be a stable business, you know its body shop won't be a fly-by-night operation. More on this in the Accidents section.

## TIPS ON CAR REPAIRS

◉ Every time you take a car to the mechanic — and especially if you have to return a car for the same problem — you should control what is written on the work ticket.

◉ If you're going to have an estimate done on the car, make sure the work ticket says it has been authorized only for an estimate. If you're authorizing specific work, write down the exact dollar limit you are authorizing and don't permit any work to be done beyond that dollar limit.

◉ If the estimate is large, don't accept it as the final word. If your car is not driveable, have it towed to another repair shop for a second estimate.

◉ If your car is towed to a mechanic, don't allow the tow-truck driver to choose the repair shop. He or she may be paid to steer your vehicle to a particular shop.

◉ Don't rely on a nationally famous name when you go for a car repair. Too often at a franchise location, the parent company fails to accept responsibility for a problem.

◉ No matter which repair shop you use, always ask for the return of parts being replaced.

# RECALLS

If your brakes don't work or your ignition system fails, it's possible the trouble is due to a design or manufacturing error. Other car owners may have had the same trouble, perhaps prompting the manufacturer to issue a general recall or send a service bulletin to dealers detailing the defect. Unfortunately, the public usually receives no such notification.

The dealer often won't know if a service bulletin has been issued or won't disclose it to you. That's where a great Web site, www.alldata.com, really comes in handy. Alldata has a centralized database that includes service bulletins and recall notices for most cars. Service bulletins are how-to notices to dealers and independent repair shops, telling them how to repair certain problems.

If your car has a serious problem and is in the shop, check alldata.com to see if there's a technical service bulletin or a recall notice about that problem. If there is, you might not have to pay for a repair. A good time to check alldata.com is before your manufacturer's warranty expires. If you see there's a bulletin or a recall notice on your transmission, you'll have a much better chance of getting it fixed, for less or no money.

I got a call from someone who paid $1,600 to have a transmission problem repaired, then heard me talk about alldata.com and found a description on the site of the exact transmission problem he had just paid to fix. He was angry, and was planning to go after the manufacturer for reimbursement. But it's a lot easier to get the manufacturer to pay for the repair up-front than trying to be reimbursed later.

Even if your car is out of warranty, alldata.com can tip you off to common problems. You may be able to prevent a much larger repair by being aware of a small modification your car needs. Or it may help you keep alert for symptoms.

The Center for Auto Safety, www.autosafety.org, is another good resource. It can tell you what other drivers have said are consistent problems with specific models. Combining that information with what you learn from alldata.com can help you develop a pattern that you can bring to the manufacturer.

Even if a manufacturer does its job well, many consumers are going to be unhappy. After all, things do break and need to be repaired. The manufacturer's representative talks to unhappy people all day long. To get satisfaction, you have to stand out from the pack and justify what you want. You don't want to be viewed as just another complainer who doesn't like having to spend money.

Callers have told me for years about a tendency for the paint to flake on several car models. If you know the paint has flaked in certain paint colors on specific vehicles, you'll have a lot more leverage if the same thing happens to your car. You might be able to convince the dealer to repaint the car for free, or for less than $100. If you don't know about the paint defect, you may have to pay the full cost of a paint job, more than $1,000. Or you may be able to negotiate some sort of cost-splitting deal with the manufacturer. Knowledge here is so important. If you know a particular vehicle has had a problem, you're going to win.

The only way vehicle defects become widely known is because consumers are willing to stand up and complain. You can do that by contacting the Center for Auto Safety or the National Highway Traffic Safety Administration.

**22**

### TIPS ON RECALLS

- A breakdown in your vehicle may be part of a defect in the model that affects other car owners.

- You may be able to negotiate a lower repair price or receive a reimbursement for repair work if the vehicle has been cited in a recall or in a service bulletin.

- www.alldata.com posts service bulletins and recall notices for your vehicle.

### CONTACT

Center for Auto Safety
www.autosafety.org

National Highway Traffic Safety Administration
800-424-9393
www.nhtsa.gov

### INTERNET

www.alldata.com

# THE LEMON LAW

A lemon is a new car that breaks down repeatedly for the same reason and cannot be repaired. They're not nearly as common as they once were, but it's still a major headache if you get one.

Every state now has a Lemon Law to protect consumers by allowing the car buyer to exchange the flawed vehicle for a new one or have the manufacturer buy it back.

Lemon Laws vary widely by state, but in most, if the defect involves the major safety systems of steering and braking, the dealer will have one chance to fix the vehicle. If the dealer cannot fix it, the manufacturer will have one chance to make the needed repairs. In other safety-related systems, the law will allow two repair attempts for the dealer and one for the manufacturer.

With any other component of the vehicle, it will be three repair attempts for the dealer, one for the manufacturer.

In most states, the Lemon Law applies to problems that arise during the first year or 12,000 miles of ownership. If you have a new vehicle with a serious problem, your best bet is to document everything. Keep records of every phone call, every repair attempt. That's why it's so important that the repair work tickets are written correctly. If they don't show a persistent defect, you may have a hard time invoking your rights under your state's Lemon Law.

You must follow other specific procedures in order to make a Lemon Law claim. For example, you might have to notify the manufacturer by certified mail. You can obtain the specific procedure in your state by calling the administrator of the state's Lemon Law. Ask for a copy of the rules governing the law.

Under Lemon Laws in most states, the manufacturer figures out how much to pay to buy back your car by assuming it has a useful life of 100,000 miles. It takes your purchase price, and divides it by 100,000 miles, to come up with how much money it will charge you for each mile you've driven the car. Let's say you buy a typical $18,000 car and drive 20,000 miles on it by the time the man-

ufacturer agrees to buy it back. The manufacturer will charge you 18 cents a mile for each mile, or $3,600, for the miles you've driven, and give you $14,400 for your car. That seems like a big hit financially, but it really isn't, mainly because of how much value your car loses in the first year of ownership. The manufacturer's deal is better than you'd get by trying to sell it. In some states, you may be able to negotiate the mileage charge with the car maker.

You'll have to pay the manufacturer to exchange your lemon for a newer model of your car. To figure a fair amount, take the dealer cost for the new model and subtract the dealer cost for the model you have. Generally the manufacturer will ask for the difference between the suggested retail price of each vehicle, which will be a larger sum.

If you follow the steps under the Lemon Law and keep good records, the manufacturer often will offer to buy back your vehicle before you go all the way through the arbitration process. And the sooner you execute the buyback, the less of a mileage charge you'll incur.

The best way to guard against getting a lemon in the first place is to buy a car that has a good repair record. That won't always work, but it will certainly improve your odds.

TIPS ON THE LEMON LAW

● Every state now has a Lemon Law to protect consumers. It allows the car buyer to exchange the flawed vehicle for a new one or have the manufacturer buy it back.

**24**

- In most states, the Lemon Law applies to problems that arise during the first year or 12,000 miles of ownership.

- You can obtain the rules and procedures to make a claim under the Lemon Law in your state by calling the administrator of the state's Lemon Law.

- Once you've established the manufacturer is going to buy back your car, the battle will be over the vehicle's value. You want the per-mile charge to be as little as possible.

- The best way to guard against getting a lemon in the first place is to buy a car that has a good repair record.

### INTERNET

www.carlemon.com
www.autopedia.com

# ARBITRATION

If you are unable to resolve a dispute with a car manufacturer, you have an option other than a lawsuit. Most manufacturers agree to participate in arbitration to help resolve disputes over cars still under warranty. The arbitration programs may be independent of state-sponsored Lemon Law programs or a provision of the laws.

Call the Council of Better Business Bureaus' Autoline for details on how to file for arbitration in your area.

Arbitration in most cases is binding on the manufacturer but not the consumer. You still have the right to sue if you are unhappy with the arbitration decision. But you don't want to sue. You want to solve it either through negotiations with the manufacturer or through arbitration.

Interestingly, just filing for arbitration often is enough to get the manufacturer to make a settlement offer.

As a consumer, you have to weigh what you might gain in arbitration versus what you might lose by not settling. If you believe your case is well documented, you might want to take your chances with the arbitration panel. If you think it could go either way, the best approach might be to file for arbitration, then cut the best deal you can before your case is heard. That's really no different from what lawyers do.

You will not appear before the arbitrators. They will decide the case based on written arguments submitted by both you and the manufacturer. So you want to give a short, clear, and detailed explanation of what has gone wrong with your vehicle, what efforts you and the manufacturer have made to repair the problem, why you believe the problem has not been solved, and what

remedy you believe is fair. You want to appear to be eminently reasonable and have strong documentation. It's a good idea to organize your presentation carefully and make it easy to read. Include a short summary and then an index, with tabs that guide the reader to each area of specific documentation, such as your work tickets. It's very frustrating to get a car problem fixed, but writing a novel won't get you anywhere with an arbitration panel.

## TIPS ON ARBITRATION

- ◉ If you are unable to resolve a dispute with a car manufacturer, arbitration may be an option. Most manufacturers agree to participate in arbitration to help resolve disputes over cars still under warranty.

- ◉ Arbitration in most cases is binding on the manufacturer but not the consumer. You still have the right to sue if you are unhappy with the arbitration decision.

- ◉ Just filing for arbitration often is enough to get the manufacturer to make a settlement offer.

## CONTACT

Council of Better Business Bureaus
800-955-5100
www.bbb.org/ (online complaint form)

Ford Consumer Assistance Center
800-392-3673

# 26 🚗 ACCIDENTS

I hope you're never in a car accident. But if you are, even if it seems to be the most minor fender bender, don't just drive away. Having the patience to take a few simple steps can save you some big headaches later.

First, wait for a police officer to write a report. It will be vital to you in case any claims are filed. Second, exchange information with the other driver about yourselves and your insurance companies. You'll have about a two-thirds chance that the other person actually will be insured. If the person is not, you'll file the claim with your insurer.

Third, as soon as possible after the accident, report it to your insurance company, even if you don't plan to make a claim. I realize this sounds like strange advice, particularly if the amount of damage is too small to make a claim. People rarely want to tell their insurance company about minor accidents, but you have to guard against the possibility of a lawsuit, even if the accident was only a fender bender. Many times drivers will consider an auto accident a chance to get rich. They'll see a TV commercial for a lawyer who claims they can get a lot of money for accident victims. A lawsuit may seem absurd, but that doesn't make it less serious. Normally, your insurer will defend you in a lawsuit. But if you failed to notify them, the

company might not have to defend you or pay a claim if you lose.

On the other hand, if you have soreness or any injury following an accident, unless you're sure it's very minor and temporary, do not negotiate with an insurance company on your own. I sometimes make fun of personal injury lawyers, but if you have been injured, it's very risky, financially and legally, to try to negotiate without a lawyer.

Most often, accidents cause some damage to a vehicle but no injuries. When that happens, getting your car fixed and being reimbursed properly is a real trick. In most cases, insurers will maintain that their insured driver was not at fault and try to force you to make a claim against your own insurance company. The best way to avoid being wrongly blamed for an accident is to get the names and telephone numbers of as many witnesses as you can at the time of the accident. That's going to be very difficult in a highway accident. But most accidents occur on surface streets, and in many cases witnesses will be blocked temporarily by the accident and unable to scatter. While the accident is fresh in your mind and you're waiting for the police, draw a sketch of the accident scene. If you think it was the other guy's fault, it's essential to have a police report. If the officer gives the other driver a ticket, it's a very strong piece of evidence in proving fault.

Establishing fault is even more important if you have an older vehicle and no longer find it worthwhile to carry collision coverage. If you're ruled at fault, you will have to pay for the repairs to your vehicle. Sadly, some insurers try to take advantage of drivers who don't have collision protection. Be prepared to document every single phone call you have with that insurance company. Write down the date and time, who you talked with, and what was said. Be prepared to sue the company in small claims court, if necessary.

If you have no collision coverage and the other driver has no insurance at all, your only recourse is to sue the driver. But the odds are if the person doesn't have any insurance, he or she probably doesn't have anything worth getting. When you choose not to carry collision coverage, you agree to live with the risk.

Contact both your insurance company and the other driver's insurance company after an accident. Even in situations where there isn't a shadow of a doubt about who was at fault, some unethical insurance companies will attempt to avoid you or avoid responsibility for the accident. Be persistent and use your state insurance department as a resource when another insurer fails to act in good faith. The state insurance department may not want to get involved in questions of fact, but they can help push an insurer

to discuss the accident and try to reach some accommodation. If there's a dispute about who is at fault, file the claim with your own company. The two companies will duke it out later over the amount each will pay.

I heard about one case in which a car was damaged in a collision and the other insurance company initially accepted responsibility for the claim. The car was fixed, but poorly, and the insurance company tried to duck out of its responsibility to pay for additional repairs. The victim was worried that she would have to pay for thousands of dollars in new repairs herself. But there was no reason at all to do that. Instead, she made a claim against her own insurance company and paid her deductible. Then her company went after the other company for the bill.

You pay premiums to your insurance company so you will have protection when you have a problem. When you buy insurance, see if your state insurance department can tell you which insurers do the best job of handling claims. You should expect your insurance company to provide speedy service and fair treatment, to make sure the body shop does the job correctly, to track down the other insurer if the company is eluding you, and to defend you if you are sued. You are their customer. I'm always disappointed when I hear callers say their insurer is treating them like the enemy, rather than as a valued customer.

*Consumer Reports* has evaluated

**28**

insurers three times in a 10-year period, and in each of the studies, rated the same insurers as the best in providing service: Amica Mutual Insurance, USAA, and Cincinnati Insurance. For a fee of $12 for the first car, $8 for each additional car, the magazine will send you a report on the lowest-cost auto insurers in your area.

If your vehicle is going to require some repair, insist upon being supplied with a rental car or reimbursement for a rental car. If it will take 10 days to repair the vehicle, make sure the rental car is authorized for at least 10 days. Don't agree to release the body shop or the insurer of final responsibility until you're comfortable that the repairs are complete and the vehicle operates properly. It's typical with major body work that the first repair isn't the final one and that more work will be required to finish the job.

Many insurers now have preferred-provider body shops, just as health insurers now have a network of doctors in their managed-care networks. In return for the volume they provide to a body shop, the insurer gets a lower price on repairs. But you have to make sure the lower price the insurer gets isn't to your detriment. The shop may use inferior or used parts. Before you agree to take your car to the insurer's preferred facility, insist that the insurer provide you with a lifetime guarantee on the repairs. USAA provides such a guarantee if you go to a preferred facility. That's a win-win for me, because I

don't have to worry that they're going to use an inferior shop or parts, and stick me with a car that doesn't work. In fact, I had a bumper replaced for free when the parking lights integrated into an aftermarket bumper didn't work right.

Another thing you can do to make sure the work was done correctly is hire an independent company to evaluate the repair and recommend changes that may be needed. The cost of using such services varies dramatically ($80 to $250). Even though you pay it out of your own pocket, it's cheap compared to the cost of having your car repaired again later on.

Insurers and drivers sometimes disagree about whether a car is a total loss. One caller insisted her car was not damaged badly enough to be totaled. She had it towed to another body shop, who gave her a reasonable estimate to fix the car. She ended up saving the insurance company money and got her car back.

More often, the dispute is over how much the insurer is required to pay for a vehicle that has been totaled. No matter which insurance company you're dealing with, this is an area of great frustration. Insurers tend to offer approximately 70 percent of the amount it would cost to buy your vehicle on the used-car market. But the initial offer is negotiable. To improve your odds of getting the best price, check www.edmunds.com, or look at a used-car price guide to see what your car was worth.

If you don't know any better, you'll take too little money for your car. Once the company realizes you've done your research, the negotiating usually gets to be more fair and honest. If the insurance company won't budge, accuse them of failing to act in good faith and request a face-to-face meeting with the adjuster and the adjuster's supervisor. Your state insurance department won't get involved in determining fair market value of your car, but it will push the insurer to meet with you.

With many insurance contracts, you also have the option of hiring a third-party appraiser, or public adjuster to be your advocate. That's usually someone who has worked for an insurance company adjusting claims, and they know how to talk the insurance company's language. Look for them in the Yellow Pages under Insurance Adjusters or Public Adjusters. If you're arguing about enough money, it's worth the several hundred dollars to hire somebody.

If the insurer still won't budge, talk to them about "substitution of vehicle," under which your car loan or lease remains in force and the insurer finds you a similar vehicle as a replacement. If they think the car is worth so little, let them find you a replacement vehicle for that price.

Substitution of vehicle is critical for people who have a long-term lease or loan. It may be the only way to keep a lease in force without being subjected to extremely large termination penalties. With a loan, it may prevent you from being left with a sizable loan balance and no car, because you owed more than the vehicle was worth. As I've said, it's very common for drivers with five-year loans to be "upside down" in a loan, because with relatively small monthly payments, the car's value drops much faster than the loan balance.

## TIPS ON ACCIDENTS

⦿ Don't just drive away from an accident, even a minor fender bender. Wait for a police officer to write a report.

⦿ Exchange information with the other driver. Get the names and telephone numbers of as many witnesses as you can.

⦿ As soon as possible after the accident, report it to your insurance company, even if you don't plan to make a claim. If you believe the other driver was at fault, contact his or her insurance company also.

⦿ If there's a dispute about who's at fault, file the claim with your own company. The two companies will fight it out later over the amount each will pay.

**30**

- If your vehicle is going to require some repair, ask for a rental car or reimbursement for a rental car.

- Don't agree to release the body shop or the insurer of final responsibility until you're comfortable that the repairs are complete and the vehicle operates properly.

- If you agree to take your car to an insurer's preferred body shop, insist that the insurer provide a lifetime guarantee on the repairs.

- To ensure collision work was done correctly, consider hiring an independent company to evaluate the repair.

- If your vehicle is totaled, don't accept your insurance company's first settlement offer. Check www.edmunds.com or look at a used-car price guide to see what your car was worth.

- If you have a five-year lease or loan and owe more than the car is worth, ask for "substitution of vehicle," in which the loan or lease remains in force and the insurer finds you a similar vehicle as a replacement.

# MONEY

**People used** to be afraid to make their own financial decisions, but the Internet sure has changed that. In fact, the Internet has created an investment monster.

Too many people now look at long-term investing as investing for several months, rather than many years. Because people can make their own stock trades and monitor their investments daily, and because many have made extraordinary gains in the stock market, many have come to look for the quick gain. They've become speculators, rather than investors, steering away from the diversification and relative safety of mutual funds for the potential of big gains in individual stocks. People who used to brag about the size of their car now brag about owning a hot stock.

That's great for a lucky few, but it's not a sound investment strategy. If you like that kind of casino mentality, what I have to say isn't for you. I want to show you how to develop wealth as safely as possible.

In this chapter, I'll give you tips about investing, dealing with debt, protecting your money in a divorce, and why you need a will.

# 32 💰 CLARK'S RULES FOR INVESTING

I've had a number of experiences with investments in my own life, both good and bad. I invested in a video rental concession in a major supermarket and lost all my money when the general manager embezzled from us and skipped town. I also was involved in an experimental car company in which I lost my investment.

I've had other ventures that have been very successful. I invested in a commuter airline that went from being privately held to publicly traded. I did quite well as one of the original investors in a community bank. And I've done extremely well buying troubled real estate, including foreclosures, relocations, and even estate sales of real estate.

Here are a few of the things I've learned:

1) Don't invest in businesses you don't know anything about.

2) Don't buy individual stocks unless you just think it's fun to do or you widely diversify your holdings. It's too risky to place your money in just a few companies.

3) If you're going to take a major stake in a business, don't do so without having some voice in how that business is operated.

But my most important advice on invest-

ments is the simplest — if you do not understand an investment, do not buy it. Just because a friend, a relative, or an investment counselor tells you to invest in something, don't do it unless you fully understand the investment. People violate this investment rule often, even though it makes the most basic sense. Then they're shocked when their money disappears. People get seduced by risky, trendy, and confusing investments such as oil and gas limited partnerships, wireless communication limited partnerships, futures, and commodities trading. Don't rely on the promotional literature for such investments. Investigate further before you buy.

The most important time to be conservative with your money is when you win the lottery or receive an inheritance or a large settlement of a lawsuit or claim. People who are lucky enough to come into a large sum of money have a tendency to want to gamble with it. That's the opposite of what you should do. The best approach is to be as conservative as you possibly can. If you receive a large amount of cash, you shouldn't increase your spending or change your lifestyle dramatically, or that money soon will disappear. If others know, everybody's going to be at your door trying to sell you the greatest new business venture, the greatest new investment, or a resort property you don't need. So batten down the hatches.

That's the one time when it's okay to lock the money in the bank and let it earn the market rate of interest.

One fellow I met seemed determined to give away a large amount of cash. He just won the lottery and came to talk to me at a trade show about the three-wheel car company I was involved with. He told me this was a business he wanted to invest in because he believed it was the fuel-efficient car of the future. Here I was, one of the owners of the company, and we needed money. But while I would have loved to have had his money in the company, I told him it was a risky venture and that he should

rethink his plans. He didn't appreciate the advice, but it was the best advice I could have given him. I've long wondered what ever happened to that man and whether he blew all his money.

  **33**

Now the reverse sometimes happens. I've heard of people who have invested their winnings in a business and wound up with 10 times the original sum. But that doesn't happen very often. For every one entrepreneur who successfully invests his or her new money in a start-up business, there are probably 100 who fail and wind up with nothing.

# INVESTING

The secret to building long-term wealth remains basic — put money aside regularly. Whether you deposit money in an investment account once a month or have a deduction made from every paycheck, you'll create a strong financial resource for your future.

I still believe one of the best places to invest your money is in no-load (no-commission) mutual funds, which allow you to own a piece of corporate America with less risk than owning individual stocks. In a capitalist society such as ours, the wealth goes to those who own companies — the stockholders — not to those who work for them.

Your No. 1 investment priority

should be funding your own retirement, because you can't rely on the traditional vehicles that may have helped fund your parents' or grandparents' retirement. Their generations had a strong Social Security system and pension plans that were fully funded by their employers.

Today's working Americans will get only a small portion of the funds they need for retirement from Social Security, and the employer-paid pension is a thing of the past. Without the government or a paternalistic corporation to fall back on, you have to be much smarter and more aggressive in planning for your retirement.

**34** ⑤

Despite the increased interest in investing, most people are still under-saving for retirement. That upsets me because, while most people probably won't starve in their old age, if they haven't saved sufficiently they probably will have to work until they die.

To properly fund your retirement, you'll need to save about 10 percent of your pay throughout your working life. If you start saving in your 20s, you'll be leaps and bounds ahead of everyone else. But if you're 45 and haven't saved anything for retirement, don't be fatalistic and do nothing. Just start now.

There are several investment vehicles that you should consider when putting aside money for retirement, including the 401(k) plan, the Roth IRA, the traditional Individual Retirement Account, and the Simplified Employee Pension (SEP). All charge a 10 percent penalty if you withdraw the money before age 59½.

No matter which of those investment vehicles you select, you have to choose a specific investment. That list of choices includes fixed-income investments like a bank certificate of deposit, purchases of individual stocks or bonds, or mutual funds, which buy hundreds of stocks or bonds for you.

I'll describe the investment vehicles first, then the specific investments and how to buy them.

## THE 401(K) PLAN

The principal retirement vehicle is the 401(k) plan. It's a tax-sheltered investment account, set up by your employer, to help you accumulate money for retirement. The 401(k) is the best way to build a retirement nest egg, because you can painlessly set aside money for your future, and you can take the money with you if you switch jobs.

The 401(k) provides several significant advantages. Most importantly, many employers match or partially match the money you contribute to your 401(k) plan. So if you contribute $100 per month to the plan, they'll contribute either $25, $50, or $100. With most investors trying hard to get a 6 to 10 percent return on their money, a vehicle that gives you an automatic return of 25, 50, or 100 percent, thanks to the employer contribution, is sensational.

The money you put into your 401(k) plan is deducted from your gross (before-tax) income, so participating in the plan lowers your tax bill for the year. In addition, you don't have to pay taxes on the interest or dividends your money earns until you withdraw the money at retirement. Sheltered from the corrosive effect of taxes, your investment can grow faster than money in a traditional savings or investment account.

Since 401(k) contributions are deducted from each paycheck, making the contributions is easy to do. Participating in a 401(k) plan is an incredible deal for those who are lucky enough to have the opportunity.

To best take advantage of the benefits of a 401(k) plan, you should put as much money into the plan as your employer will match. The more you put in, the bigger the annual tax deduction, the faster your retirement nest egg grows, and up to a point, the more your employer contributes.

Each company's plan is different, but many will match your contribution up to 6 percent of your pay. Let's say your company will invest 50 cents for each dollar you invest, up to 6 percent of your pay. If you earn $35,000 a year, you can put up to $2,100 into the 401(k) plan, and your employer will add in $1,050. Your total contribution for the year will be $3,150. In most cases, you may put in more of your pay, usually up to 15 percent of your salary. The extra money won't be matched, but it still will grow tax-deferred.

Many 401(k) plans permit employees to borrow against their accounts, but I don't recommend it. It's true that you borrow the money from your own fund, and pay it back with interest to the same fund. But the money you pay back gives you a lower rate of return than if your money was fully invested in a stock mutual fund. So borrowing diminishes the size of the pot of money that will be available when you retire. It's an especially bad idea if the purpose of borrowing is for something unnecessary, like a vacation.

There's also a danger if you quit your job or are fired. When that happens, the borrowed money is due immediately. If you can't pay it back,

the IRS treats the loan as an early distribution of your retirement money. You'll have to pay a 10 percent federal penalty on the total, plus ordinary state and federal income tax, for that tax year. On average, you'll have to pay 46 percent of the money you borrowed in taxes and penalties. If you've already spent the money, you may not even have what you need to pay the taxes.

## THE ROTH IRA

I used to tell people to put as much money into their 401(k) plan as their company permits. But the Roth IRA has forced me to change that advice, because the tax advantage of the Roth IRA is superior to that of any other retirement vehicle.

Here's how the Roth IRA works. If you deposit money into a Roth IRA account and leave it there until retirement, you never pay taxes on the earnings. Never. With a standard IRA, the money grows tax-deferred — you pay federal and state income tax on it as you withdraw funds in your retirement years, which can eat up a quarter to a third of your money. But with the Roth, the earnings grow tax-free. If you build a nestegg that 30 or 40 years from now contains $1 million, it's yours free of income taxes.

One thing you don't get from a Roth is an income tax deduction in the year you make the contribution. So you pay taxes on it up-front. But the tax-free compounding over the years makes

35

**36** 💰 that tradeoff more than worthwhile. It's the best savings deal we've had since the income tax went into effect.

If you start a Roth account, or any retirement investing, while you're in your 20s, you will be sitting pretty at retirement. In fact, if you set aside $150 a month beginning at age 25, and earn a conservative 8 percent on your money, you'll have nearly $1 million at age 65. If that money is in a Roth account, you'll get it tax-free. If it's in a 401(k), the employer match probably will make the total larger. If you want to do some retirement calculating on your own, visit www.vanguard.com or www.rothira.com.

I recommend that you put as much money into your 401(k) as your employer matches, then put whatever else you can afford into a Roth IRA, up to the limits allowed. Each person can put up to $2,000 a year into a Roth IRA, or $166 a month. Married couples can each deposit $2,000 a year into a Roth IRA, as long as they don't exceed certain income limits.

So if you earn $30,000 a year and your employer matches your 401(k) contribution up to 6 percent of your income, try to put $1,800 into your 401(k) and $2,000 more into a Roth IRA. If you earn $40,000, put $2,400 into the 401(k) and $2,000 into the Roth.

If you're still in a position to save more money, go back and put as much into the 401(k) as your employer allows, even though the employer won't match any of the additional funds. You still get the tax deduction and the tax-deferred earnings growth.

Let's say you and your spouse both work and each of you earns $30,000. Each of you should put 6 percent into the 401(k), or $1,800, for a total of $3,600. (The employer match, at 50 percent, raises the contribution to $2,700 each, or $5,400.) Putting another $2,000 each into a Roth IRA increases the amount your family is saving for the year to $7,600, or 12.6 percent of your $60,000 family income. That's without the employer match on the 401(k). You could effectively stop there and do nothing else. If you want to go beyond that, take the 401(k) up to the maximum amount the employer matches.

If you work for a company that doesn't offer any kind of retirement plan, your first priority for retirement investing would be to put the maximum $2,000 into a Roth IRA.

One of the advantages of a 401(k) over a Roth is that the 401(k) comes out of your paycheck before you see the money. I encourage you to set up an automatic payment plan for a Roth, because even with the best of intentions, people forget.

## THE SIMPLIFIED EMPLOYEE PENSION (SEP) AND SIMPLE IRA

If you're self-employed, or have some freelance or self-employment income, you have the right to take advantage of one of two fantastic retirement plans, either a SEP, or Simplified Employee

Pension, or a Simple IRA. Both are kind of super-IRAs, tax-sheltered plans which allow you to invest a much greater amount of money than an IRA allows.

With a SEP, you can contribute up to 13.08 percent of your net earnings from self-employment for the calendar year, up to $30,000 a year in most circumstances. You figure your net income at tax time, after deducting expenses, and calculate your maximum SEP contribution from the net. You figure the amount you may contribute, deposit the money in your SEP account, and note the SEP contribution on your tax form.

A Simple IRA allows you to put aside up to $6,000 a year, even if you earned only $6,000 in self-employment income. You can contribute 100 percent of your self-employment income, up to the $6,000 maximum. So if you have a lot of self-employment income, choose the SEP. If you have moderate earnings from self-employment and you want to maximize what you put aside for retirement, choose the Simple IRA.

Let's say you earn $50,000 annually as a full-time, self-employed individual. You can contribute up to $6,540 to the SEP. If you work part-time for yourself as a landscaper and earn $10,000 after expenses, you can contribute $1,308 to a SEP or $6,000 to a Simple IRA. That's true even if you have a 401(k) plan at your regular job. In most cases, you're not eligible to open a

deductible IRA if you have a 401(k) plan — your eligibility decreases as your income rises.

The short application form to start a SEP or Simple IRA can be obtained from any broker or mutual fund company.

People who earn all of their income through self-employment should put their first $2,000 of retirement savings into a Roth IRA, and the rest into a Simple IRA or SEP.

## THE INDIVIDUAL RETIREMENT ACCOUNT (IRA)

Another option for retirement is the traditional Individual Retirement Account, although it's not really a very attractive investment option anymore. IRA accounts allow you to shelter up to $2,000 a year from income tax. The law also allows your non-working spouse to deposit up to $2,000 into a separate IRA. Just as with a 401(k), the money is deducted from your gross income and grows tax-deferred. However, there is no employer match and you must pay federal and state income tax on the money as you withdraw it in retirement.

## VARIABLE ANNUITIES

This is another investment vehicle that doesn't make much sense anymore, since Congress lowered the tax on capital gains in 1997. A variable annuity is like an IRA without any limit on the amount you put in, but without any current deduction

**38** ⑤ from income. It works only if you make a lot of money and you've already exhausted the other tax-advantaged ways to save for retirement. It makes sense only if you are 25 or more years from retirement, and you pick an ultra-low-cost variable annuity, such as those from TIAA-CREF or Vanguard. If you pick a higher-cost annuity, your investment will net you less than if you put it into a no-load mutual fund in a traditional, taxable account.

If you do make a great deal of money and are in one of the highest tax brackets, a better alternative is to invest in a tax-managed portfolio. These are regular taxable investments whose managers use special strategies to limit your tax obligation. When you decide to spend the money, not necessarily in retirement, you're taxed at much lower capital gains tax rates, rather than regular tax rates. Once again Vanguard is the leader in tax-managed portfolios.

## SAVING FOR COLLEGE

The biggest change in how you should save for a child's college education is a plan known by its IRS code, the 529 plan. The 529 plan is a state-sponsored, tax-advantaged college savings plan that allows a parent, a grandparent, or even a nonrelative to contribute money towards a child's college education. And it solves an age-old problem in college savings strategy. The parent, grandparent, or nonrelative retains control over the account, so the child can't take his

college nest egg and buy a motorcycle. But the money, if spent for college, is taxed at the child's income tax rate, which is nearly nothing while they're in school. You get to grow the money tax-free and spend it nearly tax-free.

The money can be used for any qualified college expense, which goes way beyond tuition and books. It includes housing and food costs, and other expenses directly and sometimes indirectly related to college.

Another thing that's great about the 529 plan is you choose how much you put aside. Some states will allow you to put aside as little as $15 per paycheck or $20 per month, to as much as a lump sum of $50,000 up-front. So a grandparent who is aging and wants to contribute can do something unrestricted by the normal $10,000 gift-tax limit and also keep control of the money if the child ends up being irresponsible.

If you save the money and the child ends up getting a full scholarship, or decides not to go to college, you can transfer the money to another child in the family, tax-free. Or, if there are no children that are going to college, you can take the money back and pay a federal tax penalty, plus income tax.

With all that good, there has to be some bad. So here it is. Your money has to go into a state-sponsored plan. Unfortunately, some of the states have made poor choices in appointing plan administrators. In two states, bribery was discovered, and state decision-makers went to prison. The states had to shut down their plans, and the money was returned to the people.

Fortunately, you can put your money in many state plans, no matter where you live. There are two good Web sites — www.savingforcollege.com and www.collegesavings.org — that show you which state has the lowest-cost plans, and which has a plan that may suit you. Savingforcollege.com rates the plans from one to five graduation caps. Pick one that is rated four or five graduation caps. I live in Georgia, and the best plan I found for my needs was California's plan, called the Golden State ScholarShare program. You should check your own state's plan first, because there may be some state tax advantages to choosing that plan, if your state plan is rated highly. Be careful. *Forbes* magazine found the worst plans had costs six times higher than the lowest-cost plans, which had costs of less than 1 percent per year. If your state plan has high costs or corruption, take your money elsewhere.

The state decides how conservatively your money is invested and who manages the plan. Generally, while the child is young, the money is invested heavily in the stock market. As the child gets closer to college age, the money is moved into safer and safer investments. At the end of the process, almost all of the money is in money-market funds.

I still consider your retirement plan far more important than saving for your children's college. That's because there

are so many different ways to pay for college, but you can depend only on yourself to pay for your retirement.

I had a call once from a couple who were leaving the hospital with a two-day-old baby, and wanted to put money aside for their child's college education. I was gratified to hear that they were thinking ahead. Unfortunately, they hadn't yet started saving for their own retirement.

Your first investment priority should be to put as much money aside as possible into a tax-deferred plan. If you've reached the limit of saving in these plans, and you still have money you wish to put aside, the next priority is to develop a safety net for you or your family, in the event that you suddenly find yourself with unexpected expenses or a loss of income.

Any form of periodic savings plan will help you build a rainy-day account. You can use a payroll deduction plan or an automatic transfer from your checking account. It doesn't matter if the money goes into a savings account, the purchase of savings bonds, or into shares of a mutual fund. The most important thing is to put aside a certain amount of money each month. Money you'll need within five years should be parked, not exposed to the short-term risk of investments. Next is saving for college, and the 529 plan is by far the best method.

## WHERE YOUR INVESTMENT DOLLARS GO

Once you've selected your investment

**40**  ⑤  vehicle for retirement — 401(k), Roth IRA, SEP, Simple IRA, IRA, or annuity — you need to choose a specific investment within the retirement fund. The best choice is stock and bond mutual funds, which give you the safety of diversity and the growth potential you must have to build a sizable retirement nest egg.

Stock mutual funds are the most efficient way for you to own companies, far better than investing in individual stocks. Mutual funds limit your risk by giving you a small part of a big basket of companies. So if one company fails or encounters trouble and suffers a sharp decline in its stock price, it barely affects your diversified holdings. In that way, you benefit over time from the natural growth of corporate America and the profits it generates.

The problem for so many people is that they fear the short-term loss that can be generated from investing in stocks. Any mutual fund can have a bad year or two. But over periods of 10 years and longer, most good funds will easily beat "safe" fixed-rate savings vehicles. In fact, when you look at any 10-year period from the 1920s to today, stock market investors have received an average annual return of more than 10 percent. That includes the huge market losses in the Great Depression and the 1987 market crash.

The last decade has brought some huge run-ups in the value of stocks, and also some scares about declines in value. I've gotten scared too, from time to time. But that is an irrational fear if your investment is for a long-term goal. I've made a pact with myself to review my investments only every 24 months. That reminds me that I'm investing to meet long-term goals. And it qualifies me under the law for lower taxation on capital gains. Under the current tax law, money outside of retirement accounts qualifies for lower capital gains taxes only if it has been invested for 12 months or longer. By reviewing my portfolio every two years, I'm ensuring that my investments will always qualify as long-term investments.

For money inside retirement accounts, I try to force myself to keep a long-term outlook, even if there's a calamitous decline in the short term. I know that long-term in a capitalist society, stocks, and preferably stock mutual funds, are the place to be.

Having said that, don't expect the market to perform as well as it has over the past decade. Be realistic. A well-diversified stock portfolio should grow an average of 10 percent a year. Not in every year, but over the years that's likely to be your average gain.

If you see your investments take a tumble and you can't sleep at night because of it, switch to a more conservative investment strategy, such as a balanced fund, a lower-risk combination of stocks and bonds. It's not worth the potential reward if investing is going to scare you to that degree.

You can enhance your chances of investing safely with a simple technique called dollar-cost averaging, which eliminates the dilemma of trying to time the market's peaks and valleys. You make regular contributions to a mutual fund, perhaps $50 a month, or divide a lump sum into 12 or 18 monthly deposits.

Without dollar-cost averaging, market dips are a real danger. If you invest $12,000 in stocks and the market plunges the next day, you're in trouble. But if you invest the same $12,000 over a 12-month or 18-month period, it doesn't matter what the market does. If prices go down, your $1,000 a month buys you more shares of stock. If prices rise, your portfolio increases in value. Over the long haul, given the historical tendency of the stock market to climb, you should do quite well. Dollar-cost averaging dramatically reduces risk.

Here's a great example of why you should use dollar-cost averaging. My brother invested $100,000 in a stock partnership in September 1987. The October 1987 stock-market crash occurred a few weeks later, and when it did, he lost 40 percent of his money in three days. It took years for prices to climb to the point that he made back the $40,000 he had lost. If he had used dollar-cost averaging to invest over a 12-month period, he would have put $8,333 into the market in September 1987 and lost $3,333 — instead of $40,000 — when the market crashed. The second $8,333 he put in would have bought him a great many more shares, as would subsequent deposits, because

the crash made each share of stock cheaper. When the market eventually took off again, he would have made a fortune. It's too hard to guess where the market is headed, and with dollar-cost averaging, you don't have to try.

Your 401(k) plan may offer anywhere from three to 10 investment options, including a money-market investment, some form of fixed-income investment, a bond mutual fund, and one or more stock mutual funds. The worst thing you can do when you're saving for retirement is put any of your money in the fixed-income investment. Fixed-income investments, like a bank certificate of deposit or a 401(k) plan's Guaranteed Income Contract, grow too slowly to meet your retirement goals. They're good places to keep money that you're going to need within a few years. But they will not be able to far outpace inflation and are a poor choice for a long-term investment. The best strategy is to choose several of the stock funds or combined stock and bond funds that are available in the plan. There's nothing wrong with having a bond fund in your retirement portfolio, but the proportion should be 20 percent or less.

People often put a lot of their 401(k) money into the stock of their own company, and that's a mistake. If your company hits hard times, its stock could drop and you could lose your job. It's a double risk. Don't put your retirement money and your salary in the same basket.

Your options in a Roth IRA, SEP, or

**42**  💰

traditional IRA are nearly unlimited. So you'll need some background to help you sort through the myriad of mutual fund choices. My best advice is to go to a bookstore and buy one of several excellent, comprehensive guides to mutual fund investing. Two of my favorites are *The Handbook for No-Load Mutual Fund Investors*, by Sheldon Jacobs, and the *Guide to Mutual Funds* by The American Association of Individual Investors.

But if you feel intimidated or overwhelmed by the prospect of reading an entire book on mutual funds, let me offer some basic strategies. These aren't the only right answers, but they are the kind of things that have worked well for people and keep them from being frozen by investment fear or apathy.

## INDEX FUNDS

Most mutual funds have a professional manager, whose goal is to outperform the broad market by carefully buying top-performing stocks. For that professional management, mutual fund investors pay an annual management fee, which usually ranges from 0.5 percent to 2.0 percent of their investment in the fund.

One interesting kind of mutual fund, an index fund, operates with a different strategy. Instead of using a professional manager to pick stocks, the index fund aims for safety and growth by buying a very broad range of stocks or bonds, usually 500, 1,000, or 2,000 individual stocks or bonds. Instead of guessing where to put the fund's money, they own everything.

Some index funds aim to match the performance of the Standard and Poors 500 or other widely followed market indexes. Bond index funds often mix long-term and short-term government and corporate bonds.

The management costs for index funds are very low, and their performance often is very good to excellent. Buying a mixture of index funds is an easy, low-cost investment strategy.

Here's one idea that will give you a widely diversified portfolio as to the number of stocks and the type of investments you own. Put 30 percent of your money into a 500-stock index fund, 30 percent into a broad-market index fund (it will usually own 2,000 to 4,000 stocks), 20 percent into an international index fund, and 20 percent into a bond index fund. With that portfolio, you've bought the world; you've bought the biggest companies in the country; you've bought virtually all the publicly traded companies in the U.S., and you've balanced some of your equities with ownership of corporate debt, or bonds.

With this strategy, you can buy all your funds from one mutual fund company. You'll probably want to pick the company with the lowest costs. Vanguard is my favorite. Buying is as simple as calling one of the mutual fund companies and asking for a catalog of their funds. Or you could ask for a prospectus on their 500-stock fund, their international index fund, their broad-market index fund, and one of their bond index funds. If there are several bond index funds, ask for a prospectus on the intermediate-term fund. That would be a fund that buys bonds with maturities from three to 10 years. I think an intermediate-term fund works best for people who are buying bonds just to balance their portfolio. Short-term bonds (less than three years) don't make sense in a long-term retirement portfolio.

You can put as much effort into assembling an investment portfolio as you want. Using an assortment of index funds is a low-tech answer for people who want to invest but are fearful or uninterested in making a lot of decisions.

Another kind of low-cost fund, exchange-traded funds, are becoming very popular. These are the equivalent of an index mutual fund, but with even lower costs and lower taxes. They're traded on the stock exchange. A number of companies, including Barclay's and Vanguard, have established exchange-traded funds.

Exchange-traded funds are about half the cost of the lowest-cost index funds and are even more tax-efficient. But you pay commission when you buy or sell these funds, and the fact that you can buy and sell them may encourage investors to over-trade. The very reason I like people to invest in index funds is so they can allow their money to sit and

grow, while they add to it.

To set up any mutual fund portfolio, just call the mutual fund house you choose and they'll send you an application form. Fill it out and you're in business. If your money already is in an IRA account, you may be able to shift it into the investments you select by telephone.

If you have to transfer money from a bank IRA or roll it over from a 401(k) account, put the money into the mutual fund company's Money Market fund while you're deciding on your portfolio mix. Then call them and move the money into the funds you choose.

You can move a lump sum directly into the investments you choose, but that carries some risk. Instead, use dollar-cost averaging. Put the lump sum into the company's Money Market fund, then transfer a portion every month into the specific investments you've selected.

You're not necessarily giving up anything in performance by choosing an index fund, because the fees associated with an index fund are so low. Investment experts believe that an actively managed fund must outperform the market by 2 percentage points in order to compensate for the transaction costs and higher management fees. So a brilliant fund manager would have to achieve a 9 percent return just to keep up with an index fund that gains 7 percent, after fees are considered. However, some experts believe that a managed fund might be a better choice

**43**

**44** $

if your investment window is less than five years.

However, because index funds directly mimic the market, they're perfect in an "up" market" and perfectly bad in a "down" market. That's one potential advantage of a professionally managed fund.

If you want to invest in mutual funds but are afraid to make any decisions, you can choose one of the catch-all "multifunds" available from several mutual fund houses. Vanguard's version, Vanguard Star, has 62.5 percent stocks, 25 percent bonds and 12.5 percent in Money Market funds. T. Rowe Price's fund is called Spectrum fund. Several other no-load fund companies have similar products.

There are a lot of choices in mutual funds — Fidelity itself has hundreds of funds — and if you like to read about all of them, have fun. But I want to caution you about becoming so overwhelmed by the choices that you do nothing.

If you want to spend a few hours getting some background, *The Handbook for No-Load Mutual Fund Investors* is very readable and will help you make decisions. But here are some basic things you should know.

The primary fees associated with mutual funds are sales loads, a hidden sales fee called a 12b-1 charge, and a management fee.

I don't think it ever makes sense to pay a significant load charge to buy a mutual fund. There's a vast selection of

no-load funds, and your chances of doing well with them are as good as with a fund that carries a load.

You should never buy any mutual fund from a commission salesperson, such as a stockbroker. If you buy a professionally managed fund, you'll pay a management fee to the fund. Don't pay a second fee to a stockbroker for his advice. That goes double for an index fund. You get no professional advice with an index fund, so you certainly shouldn't pay a commission.

The loads you would pay if you bought from a stockbroker or financial planner could be as high as 8.5 percent. So if you invest $1,000, $85 comes off the top as a sales commission and the remaining $915 goes into your account. That's a lot of money to pay. Fidelity has low sales loads on some of its funds — 3 percent or below — and no loads on most.

Some brokers and financial planners will misrepresent a fund as a no-load fund when it has hidden loads through something called a 12b-1 charge, which is a hidden sales charge that's collected each year on your funds. This fee, which might be 1 percent of your investment, could turn out to be more costly than an up-front charge, because you pay it every year. Plus, you pay not only on your initial investment, but on your investment gains.

Over a 10-year period, a $10,000 investment in a mutual fund growing at 10 percent would be worth $25,937. The same investment in the same fund, but with a 12b-1 charge of 1 percent, would grow to $23,674. That's a difference of $2,263, about the same as investing in a fund with an 8.5 percent up-front sales load.

Some brokerage houses have said that they have "no-load" mutual funds, but the fine print in their ads shows an annual account charge or service fee of 1.25 percent. That's not a no-load fund.

Finally, all mutual funds have a management fee, which is the money you pay to have a professional money manager buy and sell stocks for your mutual fund. You'll pay this fee annually on the total amount invested. But it will be lowest with an index fund, for which management duties are insignificant. The management fee for index funds generally is less than 0.5 percent.

In addition to having low fees, index funds are very tax efficient, and are a good investment choice for people who are investing outside of a retirement plan. In many mutual funds, professional managers who are trying to produce strong results trade actively, and those trades create short-term capital gains on which investors have to pay income taxes. Index funds avoid that pitfall.

Paying more for a professionally managed fund could be worth it if the fund delivers. If over both a five-year period and a 10-year period, a fund with a high expense ratio has outperformed greatly a fund with a lower expense ratio, it may be worth paying the higher expenses.

Fidelity's heralded Magellan fund,

managed for many years by Peter Lynch, has a 3 percent upfront sales load and a 1 percent annual management fee. But the fund was such a great performer — it grew at an annual average of 27.4 percent for nearly 20 years — that investors happily paid the charges.

**45**

However, Magellan points out the risk of choosing a fund for a name-brand manager like Lynch, who retired in the late 1980s. Since he retired, the fund has had many managers and its performance has been questionable. If the manager of your fund leaves, there's no guarantee that the fund's performance will be similar to its past results.

If you choose your own mutual funds, it's a good idea to choose an assortment of funds that have different investment goals. So while you might want some money in an international fund, don't put all of your money into one. Putting some money into several different types of funds will give you better long-term growth.

If your goal is to build a personal savings fund, for personal use or for a child's college, a good strategy is to put a set amount of money each month into a mutual fund. For this kind of investment plan, a good choice is one of the all-purpose "multifunds." Some mutual funds have a minimum monthly payment that's too high for many budgets. TIAA-CREF, which allows you to put in as little as $25 a month, is a great choice.

USAA has a terrific plan that helps

**46** 💰 you teach your children about investing. You put a minimum of $25 a month into an account. Then, each month, your child receives a statement that's geared to their age. Very young children get coloring books to teach them about money. As they grow older, the material becomes more sophisticated. Stein Roe has a similar account that has a minimum of $50 a month, and it has been even more popular.

If you understand the basics I've discussed here, you won't be intimidated by anything you see in a prospectus or a book on mutual funds. If you want to study mutual funds in intricate detail, subscribe to Morningstar, an information service that will provide you with all you ever wanted to know about mutual fund investing. Or check Morningstar's Web site, www.morningstar.com.

## TIPS ON INVESTING

◉ Your No. 1 investment priority should be funding your own retirement.

◉ Put money aside regularly, in a variety of stocks and mutual funds.

◉ Consider several investment vehicles when putting aside money for retirement: the 401(k) plan, the Roth IRA, the Individual Retirement Account (IRA), the Simplified Employee Pension (SEP), and the Simple IRA.

◉ When you're investing for retirement, the growth potential of stocks is a better bet than conservative investments such as certificates of deposit, which barely keep up with inflation.

◉ To minimize the risks of investing in stocks, consider stock mutual funds. Mutual funds limit your risk by giving you a small part of a big basket of companies.

◉ Saving for a child's college education is a lesser priority than saving for your retirement.

◉ One low-tech investment strategy is to invest in an assortment of index funds. Some index funds aim to match the performance of the Standard and Poors 500 or other market indexes.

◉ Don't expect huge gains each year and don't worry about huge losses in the short term. Keep your eye on the target, which is long term, 10 years or longer.

⦿ If you see your investments take a tumble and you can't sleep at night because of
it, switch to a more conservative investment strategy, such as a balanced fund, a
lower-risk combination of stocks and bonds.

## CONTACT

American Century
800-345-2021

Fidelity Investments
800-544-6666
www.fidelity.com

INVESCO
800-525-8085
www.invesco.com

Janus Capital
800-525-3713
www.janus.com

Morningstar Inc.
312-424-4288
www.morningstar.com

Charles Schwab Corp.
800-648-5300
www.schwab.com
The Scudder Funds
800-225-2470
http:\\funds.scudder.com

Stein Roe
Young Investors Fund
800-338-2550
www.steinroe.com

T. Rowe Price Investor Services
800-638-5660
www.troweprice.com

USAA First Start Growth Fund
800-841-6489

**47**

**48**  The Vanguard Group
800-662-2739
www.vanguard.com

## REFERENCE

*The Handbook for No-Load Mutual Fund Investors*
by Sheldon Jacobs
800-252-2042
www.sheldonjacobs.com

*Guide to Mutual Funds*
The American Association of Individual Investors
312-280-0170

## INTERNET

www.morningstar.com (Mutual fund information)
www.quicken.com (Investments, mortgage calculator)
www.fundalarm.com (Links to dozens of other investment sites)
www.investorama.com (Stocks, general)
www.hoovers.com (Business information)
www.bloomberg.com (Business information, mortgage calculator)
www.fdic.gov (To see if online banks are legitimate)
www.bankrate.com (CD rates)
www.sheldonjacobs.com (Investment strategy)
www.sec.gov (Securities and Exchange Commission)
www.freetrade.com (Trade stocks for free)
www.rothira.com (Roth IRA information)
www.aaii.org (American Association of Individual Investors)
www.mfea.com (Mutual Fund Investors Center)
www.ici.org (Mutual fund information)
www.investingonline.org (Guide to discount brokers)
http://finance.yahoo.com/?u (Yahoo Finance)
www.steinroe.com (Stein Roe Young Investors Fund)
www.calcbuilder.com (Financial calculators)
www.indexfunds.com (Index fund information)
www.savingforcollege.com (College savings: 529 plans)
www.collegesavings.org (College savings: 529 plans)
www.tiaa-cref.org (College savings)
www.collegeboard.com (Estimate costs of college)
www.fastweb.com (Scholarship information)
www.nasfaa.org (National Association of Student Financial Aid Administrators)
www.finaid.org (Guide to financial aid)

# SHORT-TERM INVESTING

Investing for retirement is a low-risk proposition, because an investment window of 10 or more years smooths out the ups and downs of many growth-oriented investments.

Short-term investing is trickier. You need investments that fluctuate very little in value, so the money will be there when you need it. Let's say you put $5,000 into a mutual fund and, in the third year, the value of your investment drops 10 percent. That's no problem in a retirement portfolio, because the fund's value in 2002 is far less important than its value in say, 2022, when you retire. But you could get burned if you have to cash in the investment in 2002 and take a substantial loss.

If you have an investment window of five years or less, stay conservative and consider yourself a saver, rather than an investor. Three good options are bank certificates of deposit and short-term Treasury securities, both of which are fully guaranteed, and money-market mutual funds.

Bank CDs, which used to be a dull investment and one in which a good deal was hard to find, have become more interesting and lucrative thanks to the Internet. You can shop instantly for CDs online, and find rates that are significantly higher than those at your local bank or credit union.

The Internet provides two great resources. One is access to Internet-only banks. They're federally insured, just like any other bank, and pay much higher rates than traditional bricks-and-mortar banks. Second, the Web offers shopping services to find you the best deals on CDs. The one I find easiest to use is www.bankrate.com. By shopping this way, you'll generally find rates at least one percentage point higher than at the local bank.

For run-of-the-mill, federally insured money-market accounts, the difference can be as much as five percentage points in interest. As I write this, most of my local banks are paying 1 percent or less on money market accounts, and one online bank is paying 6 percent. That's a monster difference.

If you find a great deal online, it's important to make sure it's a real bank. That's easy to do, but please do it, because there have been some terrible tales of people who have invested in what appeared to be banks but turned out to be con games. Just go to www.fdic.gov and check to make sure the bank is federally insured. Whether you put your money in a bank locally or nationally, limit the amount you invest to $90,000. Federal insurance protects you up to $100,000 if the bank were to fail, but holding your investment to $90,000 will safeguard both your principal and interest.

You can get the best return on CDs by "laddering" your savings. If you're

**50** 💰 investing $5,000, use $1,000 to buy a one-year certificate of deposit, $1,000 for a two-year CD, $1,000 for a three-year CD, $1,000 for a four-year CD, and $1,000 for a five-year CD. When the one-year CD matures, use the $1,000 to buy a five-year CD, and do the same the next year when the two-year CD matures. If you continue this process, each of the CDs will be for five years, giving you the best interest rate on your money. But instead of having all $5,000 locked up for five years, you'll have access to one-fifth of your money each year.

Another alternative I like is money-market mutual funds. Unlike the money-market accounts at a bank, money-market mutual funds are not federally insured. But they're regulated in a way that makes it virtually impossible for your money to be at risk. These accounts require a minimum of $1,000 to $10,000 to open, and their interest rate changes daily. Your money is available to you all the time, free of any penalties. You get a checkbook just like you would with any checking account, except you typically cannot write a check for less than $100 or $250. This is a great way to park money if you're saving for a downpayment on a house, and don't know exactly when you're going to need the money. It's also a great place for a rainy-day account. Money-market mutual fund accounts are issued by discount and traditional stockbrokers and mutual fund companies. You can find the best deals nationally in each Thursday's edition of *The Wall Street Journal*, in the Money & Investing section.

A third alternative is U.S. Treasury bills, which you can buy direct from the U.S. government. Treasurys compete with banks for your money. There are times when Treasury investments will pay more than banks, and there are times when Treasurys will pay less than banks.

You can buy Treasurys online, by phone, or in person. For information, go to www.publicdebt.treas.gov, or call the Federal Reserve Bank at 1-800-943-6864. If you live in a city with a Federal Reserve branch, walk in, fill out a short form, and hand it to a teller with a check.

The beauty of buying Treasurys direct from the government is that you pay no commission. People who don't know about this program might needlessly pay a commission to a stockbroker or a bank to invest in Treasurys. That could eat up most of the advantage of buying them.

Treasurys of one year or less have a $10,000 minimum. Two-year and three-year Treasurys have a $5,000 minimum, and Treasurys with maturities of five years or longer have a $1,000 minimum.

If you think Treasurys are for you, buy *The Wall Street Journal* and check the approximate interest rates. They're listed in a daily chart called the Treasury Yield Curve.

Investment decisions are more difficult if you want to put money aside for a moderate period of time — five to 10 years. People with an investment window of five to 10 years often will do well with short-term bond funds or "balanced" funds, which own both stocks and bonds. But you still have more risk than with a long-term investment horizon.

I see a lot of advertisements for tax-free municipal bonds, but I'm not at all sold on them for most taxpayers. A lot of people buy municipal bonds because they hate to pay the government taxes. It's fine to feel that way, but disliking taxes shouldn't be the basis for an investment decision. If you're in the 15 or 28 percent tax bracket, you may be better off with a taxable investment than with a tax-free investment. You get a lower yield on a tax-free municipal bond than with a taxable corporate bond, and the tax advantage often isn't sufficient to make up the difference. Tax-free municipal bonds are a good choice if you're in the top tax bracket and want an investment that produces a steady, current income. But the top tax bracket includes less than 2 percent of all taxpayers.

If you're 60 to 70 years old, you have several factors to consider when making investments. You have a short investment window, because you might need access to your money in less than

10 years. You also want your investments to generate income. But you need growth too, because there's a good chance you could live another 20 years.

The solution is to invest a portion of your money to generate income, through high-dividend stock or bond funds, and a portion with an eye towards the future. In *The Handbook for No-Load Mutual Funds*, mutual funds expert Sheldon Jacobs suggests that even someone in retirement should have 60 percent of their investment portfolio in stocks (and 40 percent in bonds). You might find that too aggressive for your taste.

Jacobs suggests a retirement portfolio with 35 percent in a variety of stock funds, 25 percent in internationally oriented stock funds, and the remaining 40 percent in bond funds.

In a portfolio for investors within 10 years of retirement, Jacobs suggests a more aggressive approach, with 50 percent in stock funds, 25 percent in international stocks, and 25 percent in bonds. And in a younger person's "wealth-builder" portfolio, he suggests 65 percent in stock funds, 30 percent in international and 5 percent in aggressive-growth stock funds.

51

**TIPS ON SHORT-TERM INVESTING**

◉ If you may need your money in a few years, it's more important to choose less volatile investments.

◉ Good options for people with an investment window of five years or less are bank certificates of deposit, short-term Treasury securities and money-market accounts.

**52** 💰

- For a great deal on CDs, shop online.

- A good strategy with certificates of deposit is "laddering," buying certificates of different maturity and constantly rolling over the funds.

- Money-market accounts from online banks, or money-market mutual fund accounts from brokerage houses, pay significantly more than money-market accounts at traditional banks.

- If you have an investment window of five to 10 years, try short-term bond funds or "balanced" funds, which own both stocks and bonds.

- Tax-free municipal bonds generally are a good idea only for investors in the top tax brackets.

## CONTACT

Bureau of the Public Debt
800-943-6864
www.publicdebt.treas.gov

## INTERNET

www.fdic.gov
www.bankrate.com (CD rates)
www.sheldonjacobs.com

# BUYING AND SELLING STOCK

I used to talk about stockbrokers in different categories: discount brokers, retail brokers, and more recently, Web brokers. Now they're all mixed together, creating both a great opportunity for investors and a lot of confusion. With almost any firm, you can choose to save money on trades by using the Internet, save money by doing the trades yourself, or pay a significant amount of money for stock buying and selling and advice from a broker, and following his or her recommendations. The price differences are staggering. On some Web sites, you can trade stocks for free. If you have a brokerage account with American Express of $100,000 or more, the purchase and sale of stock is free. If you put $25,000 or more in the account, buying stock is free; sales cost $15. Another site, www.freetrade.com, allows you to buy and sell for free, and it requires only a $5,000 minimum to open an account.

In a traditional brokerage relationship, which some people still choose to use, the commission on the sale or purchase of stock could be $200 to $400.

In the self-service model, the key issue isn't price, because virtually everyone is going to be ultra-cheap. The real issue is customer service. If you're considering a broker, try its customer service number in the middle of a busy trading day, and see how easy it is to reach someone. Talk to other investors, and see who they've had good and bad experiences with. I mentioned a broker once called T.D. Waterhouse Securities that has a business model I like: very inexpensive Web trading combined with retail offices you can visit to resolve a problem. But I've been getting a lot of complaints from my listeners about poor customer service at T.D. Waterhouse. *Barron's* magazine, in a review of discount brokers, said it had received a lot of complaints about Waterhouse. So it's not enough to be cheap and offer what looks like a full menu of services. The caliber of customer service must be top-flight. After all, you're dealing with your savings or your retirement money.

If you want to hire somebody to provide you with advice, you have to be very, very careful. Stockbrokers, and people who refer to themselves as financial planners, may seem like unbiased investment advisors. In truth, they are commission salespeople, who may get you to buy and sell investments that generate higher commissions for them. There is an inherent conflict of interest between the investment products that would be most suitable for you and the ones that generate big commissions.

A lot of my listeners now are dealing with quasi-independent or independent financial planners, as opposed to traditional stockbrokers. And lots of stockbrokers are now calling themselves financial advisors or planners. In many cases, they're charging an annual fee, rather than a fee for each transaction. But in addition to the annual fee, they may put you into investments that get them extra payments.

If you choose to do business with a financial planner, or with a broker who provides advice, make certain to state your investment objectives very clearly on the brokerage agreement you will be asked to sign. If you're a conservative investor who does not like risk, state it. If you like a moderate amount of risk, state that. And if you have no fear of risk, indicate that you're willing to try risky investments. If you fail to state very clearly in the brokerage agreement what level of risk you're willing to take, you can get burned later.

If you ever notice transactions you didn't authorize, write a letter to the financial planner or stockbroker stating that the activity in your account is unauthorized and all trading activity should stop immediately. Make sure someone at the company signs to acknowledge receipt of the letter.

53

## 54 ⑤ CONTACT

National Association of Securities Dealers (Investments)
Disciplinary History: 1-800-289-9999
Licensing Information: 301-590-6500
www.naspr.com

## INTERNET

www.investorama.com (Stocks, general)
www.sec.gov (Securities and Exchange Commission)
www.freetrade.com (Trade stocks for free)

# 401(K) PAYOUTS

I get so excited by people who save for retirement through their employer's 401(k) plan, but then get so disappointed over how many of those people blow their 401(k) money when they quit their job or get fired.

The majority of people spend the money, instead of rolling it over into their new employer's 401(k) plan, or transferring it to an IRA. And that's a big mistake, because the average consumer loses 46 percent of their 401(k) money to state and federal taxes and penalties when they spend it prematurely. It's a double loss. You lose almost half your money and you have nothing saved for retirement.

Instead of spending the money, do a trustee-to-trustee transfer. That means you send your money directly from your old job to your new job, or to the place you set up an IRA account, without the money ever coming to you. If you want to put it into a 401(k) plan where you've gone to work, ask your benefits manager if the company will accept transfers from your old plan. Most will, and they'll have a form for you to fill out to do that.

If you aren't allowed to move the money to your new employer, or don't want to, you can set up an IRA account — a mutual fund house or a stockbroker are the two best places — and put the 401(k) money there.

If you do either of those things, there's no tax and no penalties.

If you elect not to do a trustee-to-trustee transfer and you instead accept a check from your old employer's 401(k) plan, the rules really mess with your wallet. In that case, 20 percent of your 401(k) money will be withheld to cover your potential tax liability. With 20 percent withheld, it's very difficult to put the full amount into an IRA.

Let's say you've had $10,000 in a 401(k) plan. You have 60 days to roll over the full $10,000 into another retirement plan. Because $2,000 of your $10,000 was withheld by the government, you have to redeposit not just the $8,000 you received, but write a check for $2,000 to make up the full balance. If you don't, the $2,000 you haven't rolled over will be considered a withdrawal and will be subject to a 10 percent early withdrawal penalty ($200 of the $2,000) plus normal federal and state income tax. The withdrawal penalty doesn't apply if you are 59½ or older.

If you don't roll over any of the 401(k) payout into a retirement plan, then all $10,000 is subject to tax and the early withdrawal penalty. For most of us, that means $4,000 to $5,000 of the $10,000 would be eaten up.

If you get fired and you're afraid you might need money, transfer the 401(k) money directly from your employer's 401(k) plan into an IRA. Make sure the IRA account is totally liquid, that is, money can be withdrawn from it at any time. If you use a mutual fund account, choose a money-market mutual fund. Then, if you find you must have some of that money to live on, pull out what you need and leave the rest in the plan. If

you do it that way, only the portion you've withdrawn will be subject to tax and penalties.

Here's another trick. If you lose your job late in the year and you expect to have a lengthy period of unemployment in the following year, try to leave your money in an IRA until at least January 2. There are two advantages to that. First, your tax rate will be much lower if you don't earn much that year, so getting your retirement money won't cost as much in taxes. Also, the tax won't be due until the following April 15, almost 16 months later. So you'll have some time to get back on your feet. But make every effort not to spend more than half of your retirement money if at all possible. That way, you'll always have the other half to cover you in case you end up with a huge tax bill. Someone I know was unemployed and spent all her retirement money during her unemployment. She ended up having to borrow the money to pay the IRS.

When you roll the retirement money into an IRA, I recommend you do it using a procedure I outlined earlier called dollar-cost averaging. First, deposit the money into a money-market account inside the IRA. Then, with all the money safely under the IRA umbrella, divide it into roughly equal amounts and transfer portions of it from the money-market account into the stock mutual funds you've picked, over a 12- or 18-month period. If you have $12,000 to invest, you transfer

**56**  $

$1,000 on the same day each month from the money-market account into the stock mutual funds, or $667 a month for 18 months. That way, you're protected from the sudden ups and downs of the market.

I got a pension fund distribution once and deposited all the money with Charles Schwab, which allows purchase of certain no-sales-commission mutual funds. Schwab's plan is called the Mutual Fund OneSource. Customers buy without any sales cost, just as if they were buying directly from the mutual fund house. But they have the convenience of dealing with a brokerage house.

I transferred my money to Schwab's money-market fund and I periodically bought into nine different mutual funds. My plan was set up so that I made an initial investment in each of the nine funds and put the rest in the money-market fund. Each month for 18 months, a portion of my money was transferred into the nine funds. The minimum amounts to invest in this way are very low, but there are some perks for putting a larger sum in. Under Schwab's plan — and these things are subject to change — if you transfer $10,000 from a 401(k) plan or IRA, you pay no IRA custodial fees for life. And with OneSource, I can keep my account with one institution but buy mutual funds from a number of different mutual-fund families.

Another strategy is to do a trustee-to-trustee transfer of your retirement money and instantaneously buy the same holdings you had in the company-sponsored plan. You don't even have to worry about dollar-cost averaging because you've already done that by making payments out of every paycheck into the company's mutual fund.

One word of caution: If you transfer a 401(k) payout into an IRA, you might want to keep it separate from any previous or future IRA you may have. If you keep the 401(k) money separate, you are permitted to move it later into another company's 401(k) plan. If you mix funds, you lose that option.

Finally, many employers will continue to manage your retirement money for you even after you leave. If you don't want the hassle of investments, it may be a smart thing to leave your 401(k) money in the care of your former employer.

If you have company stock in your 401(k) plan, there are special tax rules that may make it better not to transfer the stock to an IRA, but instead take it as a distribution. If you have a lot of company stock inside your plan, meet with a CPA before you make a decision. One hour of a CPA's time could save you thousands of dollars in taxes.

## TIPS ON 401(K) PAYOUTS

 **57**

- ◉ If you leave your job and spend your 401(k) money, you'll lose nearly half in taxes and penalties.

- ◉ Instead of spending the money, transfer your money directly from your old job to your new job, or to the place you set up an IRA account.

- ◉ If you take a check for your retirement money, 20 percent of the money will be withheld to cover potential federal taxes, making it difficult to redeposit 100 percent of the money into an IRA account or another 401(k) plan within 60 days.

- ◉ If you think you may need the money, put it in an IRA, then withdraw only what you need.

- ◉ Use dollar-cost averaging if you're going to put your money into a stock or bond mutual fund. Put the money into a money-market IRA account, then transfer the money gradually into other funds over 12 or 18 months. This protects you from the ups and downs of the market.

- ◉ If you transfer a 401(k) payout into an IRA, keep it separate from any previous or future IRA you may have. If you do, you are permitted to move it later into another company's 401(k) plan.

- ◉ If you have company stock in your 401(k) plan, meet with a CPA before you make a decision.

# TAXES AND INVESTING

It's a huge mistake for the primary emphasis of an investment to be its tax value. You never know when such a decision will come back to bite you.

In 1993, I bought a variable annuity, which was the smartest tax move I could make at the time. Then in 1997, Congress changed the tax law, and the economic benefit of the variable annuity disappeared. What seemed like a smart move in 1993 became a stupid move four years later.

This was yet another lesson that the underlying investment should first be sound. Then, if it has tax advantages, that's a bonus. Making an investment decision solely for tax reasons leaves you exposed to loss.

The purchase of a home is another instance in which the tax advantage of

**58** $

the investment is frequently overstated. Home ownership is part of the American dream and part of the measurement of our success. But from a financial standpoint, buying a house is not always the smartest decision. Houses sometimes lose value, and they are expensive to sell. The standard deduction is so large now that the benefit of itemizing deductions on your tax return — the main financial benefit of home ownership — has been significantly reduced.

Let's take the example of a family that earns $60,000 a year and owns a $120,000 house. Say they put $10,000 down and borrowed $110,000 on a 30-year, 7.25 percent fixed-rate mortgage. By itemizing their deductions, the family would owe about $6,388 in federal income tax. If the family took the standard deduction, they would pay $7,907 in federal tax. So the federal income tax savings in buying a house, for this family, is just $1,519 annually. There would be additional savings on state income taxes. But that's not a huge amount of money compared to the cost of the purchase.

Until Congress changed the law a few years ago, you faced potential tax consequences when you sold a house. Now you can sell your house and the proceeds are tax-free, up to $250,000 for an individual and $500,000 for a couple. So if you paid $80,000 for a house and sell it years later for $150,000, the money you earn from the sale will not be taxed. Before the

change, you had to put the proceeds from a home sale into your next house, usually a larger, more expensive house, or pay tax on the price increase in your house since the day you bought it. Now you can use some of your profit as a down payment on the next house — a smaller house if you prefer — and invest the rest however you choose.

This tax treatment also makes a house a great way to build savings for the future. But as I've warned, tax laws are subject to change.

Many banks encourage people to borrow against their house, through a home equity loan, for a vacation, a boat, or a car. They pitch it as a smart loan, because you can deduct the interest paid on the loan from your income tax. On consumer loans, there is no interest deduction.

But home equity loans have grown way out of control. Home equity — the difference between the market value of your house and the amount you owe on the mortgage — is the best way for most Americans to build wealth. If your house is worth $150,000 and you owe $100,000, you have $50,000 in equity. If your house continues to grow in value and you pay down the mortgage, your equity could grow to $75,000 or $100,000 in the future. But that won't happen if you spend your equity away.

I was shocked to find out that, nationwide, because of home equity borrowing, the amount of equity people have in their homes actually is shrinking instead of increasing. If you use your house like a short-term piggy bank, you damage your future.

There's another risk in home equity loans. If you use your house as collateral for a loan and you're unable to pay back the loan, you lose your house. It's unwise to put your house at risk because of a tax advantage. It's even worse if you're borrowing against your house for something that retains no value, like a vacation. The only reason to borrow against your house is to increase the worth of the house, say for a bathroom addition or kitchen renovation.

The worst circumstances I'm hearing about are people who are taking out home equity lines that exceed the value of their home. These loans, known as 125s, allow a person whose home is worth $100,000 to carry $125,000 of debt against it. This is leading to a massive increase in foreclosures around the country.

One of the most troubling tax decisions people make when April 15 rolls around is not filing their tax return because they don't have the money. If you can't pay, you should file your return anyway and attach an explanation. You're treated much differently if

you fail to file than if you filed but can't afford to pay. Those who don't file can face potential criminal charges.

If you do file and can't pay, you should enter into negotiations with the IRS and your state for a payment plan. Generally, they will be reluctant partners in this process, so you need to give a complete explanation as to why a payment plan is justified. You will have to give a lot of information about your finances, but this is far preferable to burying your head in the sand.

Once people don't file one year, they become afraid and they don't file in subsequent years. If you find yourself in that situation, you can go to the IRS and turn yourself in. They will help you re-create your tax return for those years. Surprisingly, people fail to file in many cases when they are due a refund. So you may not be facing the financial albatross you suspect, and there is a tremendous feeling of relief when you do settle up.

If you have a problem with the IRS, try the IRS Taxpayer Advocate. If that doesn't work, call or write your congressman or U.S. senator's constituent service office for help.

**59**

### TIPS ON TAXES AND INVESTING

⊙ In choosing an investment, the investment itself should be sound. If it has tax advantages, that's a bonus.

⊙ Don't use home equity loans. They damage your ability to build wealth. And if you're unable to pay back the loan, you lose your house.

**60** $

- From a financial standpoint, buying a house is not always the smartest decision. The standard deduction is so large now that the benefit of itemizing deductions on your tax return — the main financial benefit of home ownership — has been largely negated.

- You no longer have to reinvest the proceeds of a home sale into a new house, so a house has become a good, tax-advantaged way to save money.

- If you can't pay your income taxes on April 15, file your tax return anyway and attach an explanation.

- If you have problems with the IRS, try the IRS problem resolution office. If that doesn't work, call or write your congressman or U.S. senator's constituent service office for help.


## CONTACT

IRS Taxpayer Advocate
800-829-1040
www.irs.gov

# CREDIT CARDS

I feel a lot better lately about the way many consumers have been dealing with credit card offers and debt.

For much of the 1990s, consumers were showered with offers for credit cards, and many were taking the cards and using them to build up massive debt. But times have changed and more people are throwing the offers in the trash. In fact, the response rate for credit card solicitations is down to less than 1 percent.

People are using credit cards more wisely as well. More than 40 percent now pay their balance in full each month, rather than paying expensive finance charges. Credit card companies refer to them as "deadbeats," people who don't generate any income for the lender.

Because consumers are better borrowers, the industry has changed. Many of the credit card companies have sold their portfolios to other companies and gotten out of the business, or stopped soliciting new customers for cards. As a result, the offers to new customers aren't as good as they used to be, which I think is great, because there's less temptation for people to be lured in by extra-low "teaser" rates. Instead, the credit card companies have become very gimmick-oriented. I got a solicitation offering me a free duffel bag if I would apply for the card. Another was a British heritage card, with a Union Jack on the card. That's fine, but I'm not of British heritage.

But while things are better for many, a lot of people still have serious credit problems. The number of bankruptcies has declined, but is still about 1.3 million families per year, about one in 75 families in the country filing for bankruptcy, and almost always because of credit card debt or medical bills. If you're among the almost 60 percent of consumers who aren't paying your credit card bill in full each month, I want you to start thinking about debt as a disease, and credit cards as one of the easiest ways to get sick. Nobody ever got wealthy borrowing money for gifts, clothes, restaurants, entertainment, or travel. When you purchase lifestyle with credit, you end up with huge obligations and no tangible assets. The meal is eaten, the trip is taken, and most of the clothes you bought at the mall end up sitting in your closet.

If you've been using credit this way, start thinking about your credit purchases as if you were buying with cash, where the bill comes due in 25 days. If you can't pay it in 25 days, don't buy it.

It's never too late for you to change the way you use credit. If you're only paying monthly minimums and you

feel discouraged, know that you can dig your way out.

It's so heartening to hear from people who have been fortunate enough to emerge from overwhelming debt and are determined not to make the same mistake again. A few years ago, I met a fellow at a convenience store who told me a remarkable story. Two years earlier, when he started listening to my show, he had $26,000 in credit card debt and he hated answering his telephone. In those two years, he completely changed his lifestyle, wiped out all his credit card debt, and bought his own home. That made me feel great. In two years, someone whose life had been out of control wiped out the debt and reclaimed his life.

Credit cards are okay if you use them for safety or convenience. In high-crime cities, it's good to carry a credit card rather than cash because, if your card is lost or stolen, the maximum cost to you is $50. Having been a victim of crime, I almost always use credit cards and carry only a minimum of cash. But I use credit cards only as an alternate method of payment, and I pay the bill in full every month.

Some experts say you should pay for everything with cash. But if you track what you buy it doesn't matter how you pay. If you feel your spending is out of control, take a little notebook along with you and record every expenditure you make for two weeks. Then put a code by each item. Put an "A" next to things you absolutely had to

**62**  💰  spend the money on. Put a "C" down when you're not really sure if you had to have it or not, and put an "F" by anything that you truly didn't have to have. The reason I use those codes is because people can relate them to school grades. You get an "A" for spending money correctly and an "F" for spending money incorrectly.

If you can discipline yourself to use credit cards only for convenience, choosing a card is easy. All you need to do is get a card with no annual fee and a 25-day grace period between the day of the purchase and the day the interest meter starts running. That way, you can have the convenience of credit cards with no cost at all.

However, if you frequently carry a balance, the annual fee matters very little. Far more important is the interest rate, which will cost you a lot more money on a high balance than will any annual fee. Certain banks now specialize in credit cards with variable interest rates. Those cards tend to have high annual fees and the rates are not fixed at a certain level, but the interest rates tend to be lower than those of most cards. If you can't avoid carrying a credit card balance, at least make it less expensive by paying a lower rate to finance that balance.

A lot of people still carry too many credit cards in their wallet. It makes sense to carry a VISA and a MasterCard, but skip department store cards and gasoline credit cards. Department store cards have very high

interest rates and are primarily a tool to get people into the stores to spend money. These cards are really an invitation to build debt for yourself.

Gasoline cards are similarly useless. Generally a business that takes a gasoline credit card will also take a VISA or MasterCard. Using a gasoline card or a department store card means there's an additional bill you have to pay, and if that card gets stolen, you're liable for the same $50 on it as any other card. If your wallet is stolen and you have two credit cards in it, your maximum risk is $100. If you have seven cards, your maximum risk is $350.

You don't want to carry just one card because if, for some reason, that company decides to lift your card, you are without credit. No two banks use the same credit standards, so you're better protected if you carry a VISA and a MasterCard, each from different institutions. I carry a Southwest Airlines VISA card to earn free miles, a Diner's Club card for travel, and a fee-free American Express card from Costco, which doesn't take any other cards.

I have a love-hate relationship with a type of VISA or MasterCard known as a debit card. I call them fake cards because they look like a VISA or MasterCard but work very differently. The reason I love them is the same reason I hate them. There's no credit involved, so you can't spend money you don't have, which is very useful for people who are having credit trouble. The money comes right out of your

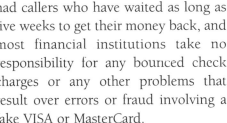

checking account, so if you don't have money in your checking account, you can't buy something. That eliminates the consequences of buying something you can't pay for in 25 days.

The problem with debit cards is they directly attack your checking account, and if a criminal gets your card, or even just your number, they can take money right out of your account. Or, as we've had in many cases from callers, the wrong amount can easily be deducted from your checking account and you're left with no money. You have nothing in your checking account to pay your own bills, and you have to fight with your own bank to get your own money put back into your account. Although both VISA and MasterCard both say your money should be returned in a week, we've had callers who have waited as long as five weeks to get their money back, and most financial institutions take no responsibility for any bounced check charges or any other problems that result over errors or fraud involving a fake VISA or MasterCard.

Another big problem is you have no right to dispute an item with a fake VISA or MasterCard. I had a caller who purchased a ticket on Priceline.com with a debit card. Priceline had a computer error and issued the ticket for the wrong date, which Priceline admitted. But instead of having a credit immediately issued to their credit card, the caller waited 10 weeks and still didn't have their money back. With a real credit card, no money would ever have left the customer's account. They simply would have put the charge into dispute.

## TIPS ON CREDIT CARDS

◉ Debt is a disease, and credit cards are one of the easiest ways to get sick. Nobody ever got wealthy borrowing money for gifts, clothes, restaurants, entertainment, or travel.

◉ If you've been using credit this way, start thinking about your credit purchases as if you were buying with cash. If you can't pay it in 25 days, don't buy it.

◉ Credit cards are okay if you use them for safety or convenience.

◉ If you don't carry a balance, get a card with no annual fee and a 25-day grace period between the day of the purchase and the day the interest meter starts running.

◉ If you frequently carry a balance, get a card with a low interest rate. The annual fee matters very little.

**64**  $

- Don't carry more than two or three credit cards. They're unnecessary and can cost you up to $50 per card if they're lost or stolen.

- Don't use debit cards, particularly for online purchases. They may help you avoid using credit, but thieves or errors can drain money directly from your checking account.

## CONTACT

CardWeb.com Inc.
800-344-7714
www.cardweb.com
(For a comprehensive guide to low-interest credit cards, no-fee credit cards, and secured credit cards)

# CREDIT PROBLEMS

If you misuse your credit cards, trouble is inevitable. Eventually, you'll be heavily in debt and just making the minimum payment on your credit card bills. By paying the minimum, you never work off the balance. All you're doing is paying interest on the early debt you took on.

Some advisers say you can tell you're in credit trouble if your debt payments exceed a certain percentage of your take-home pay, but I don't think anybody ever figures out those ratios, except when they're applying for a mortgage. You know how you feel. You need help if you're afraid to answer the phone or open the mail, you have trouble sleeping at night, or you're eating too much or too little.

I've seen more credit trouble over the years, not because people are making less money, but because they're taking on more debt. Because couples have come to need both spouses' income, if either loses a job or gets sick, or if there's a divorce, a money crisis may soon follow.

When you get into financial trouble, you need to create a pyramid of priorities. The most important thing to pay is your mortgage or rent. The next priority is your car loan and the third is to pay your utilities, which keep your house functioning. After that you pay your unsecured creditors — credit card and loan companies.

Ironically, the most ferocious and frequent phone calls you'll receive when you fall behind on your bills will be from the credit card and small loan companies. The mortgage companies tend to react more slowly because their loans are secured by your home. The car loan people are a little quicker but not real quick because their loan is secured by your automobile. Because of these calls, people in credit trouble often throw money at the wrong source. The credit cards should always come last.

You have strong rights under federal law to prevent collection agencies from harassing you, although the law does not apply to the creditors themselves. The Fair Debt Collection Practices Act bars collectors from threatening to harm you, your reputation, or your property, and from using profane language or falsely claiming to be an attorney or a government representative. The law also prohibits claims that you will be arrested or imprisoned if you don't pay, and it prohibits late-night phone calls and repeated phone calls intended to harass you.

You can stop collection agencies from contacting you at home, at work, or at all by sending them a "drop-dead" letter. You'll find a prewritten drop-dead letter in the Workbook chapter of this book. It's a good idea to send it by certified mail, and don't forget to keep a copy. Once a collection agency receives it, the company can contact you only to acknowledge that it won't contact you again, or to notify you that it is filing a lawsuit. Under the law, if a company continues to harass you, you can sue it for actual damages and punitive damages of

up to $1,000. The law is enforced by the Federal Trade Commission.

Beware of companies who say they'll help you get out of debt. A caller told me she was considering such a service. She was supposed to send a check each month to this company. The company would then subtract its fee — $15 a month plus $5 per credit card or loan — and distribute the rest to her creditors. The red flag was a line in the contract saying she wouldn't hold the company responsible if the company didn't send the money to her creditors.

A legitimate consumer service is available to help you when you can't keep the wolves from your door. It's called Consumer Credit Counseling and it is available in most areas. Consumer Credit Counseling is provided by a network of nonprofit organizations. They're funded, ironically enough, by the credit grantors, to offer people a method to honor their debts.

Call the National Foundation for Consumer Credit Counseling to find a location near your home.

Many Consumer Credit Counseling services now will do counseling by phone, or even via the Internet. I prefer that you do it face-to-face if you can, because I think that commits you more to following up.

People who go to credit counseling generally fall into one of three categories. A third of the people who walk in the door are so far in debt or have such little income that credit counselors cannot be of help to them.

65

**66**  💰  These are the people for whom bankruptcy becomes a real option. The next third are not in nearly as bad a shape as they think they are and really just need help in setting up a budget and new spending priorities. These folks are helped through counseling at little or no cost to them.

Consumer Credit Counseling is best known for the way it helps the third group of people, those whose debts have grown beyond a manageable size but have the ability to repay them within three years, with some help. A repayment plan negotiated by Consumer Credit Counseling requires some give on both sides. It requires the consumer to cut spending or increase income through a part-time job or more work hours. It requires the department stores and other lenders to reduce the amount of money owed or create more favorable terms for repayment.

Some people worry that going to credit counseling will hurt their credit rating. Most of these people already have a flawed credit report, and credit counseling really has a neutral impact. Plus, once you've completed a repayment plan, most Consumer Credit Counseling chapters will work to help you obtain one mortgage loan, one car loan, and one credit card. So, rather than being a negative, credit counseling has a reward at the end — the establishment of a responsible level of credit with the service's assistance.

If you have had credit problems and are trying to reestablish credit, I suggest you get a secured credit card. That's a credit card you get by posting a deposit with the lender, say $500. Then you're able to charge up to the $500 you have on deposit. The money you have on deposit earns interest and you have a credit card you can use like any other VISA or MasterCard holder. There are a lot of organizations that offer secured cards with very unfavorable terms and a precious few that offer secured cards at reasonable terms. The best ones tend to have a moderate annual fee, $35 a year or less, no application fee, and a grace period from the purchase date until interest charges begin. For a list of lenders who offer reasonable terms on secured cards, go to www.cardweb.com.

Perhaps you haven't reached the point of going to Consumer Credit Counseling and things have begun to improve. Maybe you got a job or a raise. Start digging out of debt this way. Take your unsecured debts and rank them by interest rate. Pay the monthly minimum on all credit cards and credit lines, except for the one with the highest interest rate. Throw every penny you can at that one each month until you've paid it off, then go to the second highest and extinguish that one. If you have six lines of credit, motivate yourself to cut it to five. That's much easier and more satisfying than trying to get rid of all of them at once. Try to set a realistic time period, within three years, to get rid of your debt.

### TIPS ON CREDIT PROBLEMS

- By paying the minimum payment on your credit cards, you never work off the balance. All you're doing is paying interest on the early debt you took on.

- When you get into financial trouble, create a pyramid of priorities. The most important thing to pay is your mortgage or rent. The next priority is your car loan, and the third is your utilities, which keep your house functioning. After that you pay your unsecured creditors — credit card and loan companies.

 **67**

- If you need help, don't immediately file for bankruptcy. The best option is Consumer Credit Counseling, which can help you work out a debt repayment plan.

- If you've had credit trouble and want to reestablish credit, try a secured credit card, which lets you charge up to an amount you place on deposit with the lender.

## CONTACT

Federal Trade Commission
Publications Division
202-326-2222
www.ftc.gov
(Ask for a copy of the brochure "Fair Debt Collection Practices Act.")

National Foundation for Consumer Credit Counseling
800-388-2227
www.nfcc.org

CardWeb.com, Inc.
(For a comprehensive guide to low-interest credit cards, no-fee credit cards, and secured credit cards)
800-344-7714
www.cardweb.com

# CREDIT REPORTS

Your credit report may be one of the most important documents with your name on it. The information on the report affects whether you can qualify

**68**  💰  for a home mortgage, whether you can get a car loan, whether you can rent an apartment, or whether you are hired for a new job. So a mistake on your credit report can be a very big problem.

Getting a credit report corrected is one of the most difficult and frustrating things consumers ever face. There are three major credit bureaus — Equifax, Experian, and Trans Union — and they don't share information. So even if you correct an error with one, you will have to do the same with the other two. After a four-month-long battle to get an item removed from your Equifax credit report, Experian and Trans Union may still show you to be a deadbeat.

Congress changed the Fair Credit Reporting Act to force credit bureaus to be more responsive, but the effect has been minimal. Even though you now have a right to talk to a human being, the Federal Trade Commission discovered that the credit bureaus were openly refusing to talk with people. It's very frustrating.

My wife has a very confusing name, K. Lane Carlock Howard, and all three credit bureaus show her name differently. One shows her as Howard K. Carlock. We discovered there was a real problem when she was turned down while trying to buy a wireless phone. While her credit report was excellent, her name didn't match the one on the report, so she was denied. As I write this, she is going on her seventh month of trying to get all three credit reports corrected. It's as frustrat-

ing for her as it is for other consumers.

The credit bureaus make it very clear that you are not their customer. You are just trouble. The customers are the people who pay them for the reports, and these errors actually are advantageous for the customers, because a lender might charge you a higher interest rate for a loan if there's a problem on your report. That's why nobody on the lending side cares about the inaccuracy of a credit report. It actually makes them more money.

But you can't let the system deter you from your mission, which is to get your credit report right. If you don't get it right, it's going to mess with your ability to get car loans, home loans, and whatever type of credit you want. If you're persistent in challenging errors on your report, you will set things right.

After you contact the credit bureau to notify it of an error, you also should contact the lender or source of the negative information, and document that you've done so. When you challenge an error, credit bureaus generally will contact the lender, who often will say that the information is accurate. That's where documents are key. You have to be able to prove you're right, and provide that information both to the lender and the credit bureau. Then make it clear that if they don't fix the error, you're going to use your right under federal law to sue. Neither the credit bureau nor the lender wants to end up in court.

If you do sue, the damages depend

on the amount of harm you suffer. In most cases and in most states, you sue in small claims court. But if the harm you suffer is major and you're going to seek a great deal of money in damages, you'll need a lawyer.

One of the ways to determine damage is to see how the credit error has harmed your ability to get a loan. Because credit grantors now use a scoring system to evaluate you, based on your credit payment history, it's easier to measure the costs of a credit reporting error.

I get calls from people who have 10.5 percent mortgages because they've had a great deal of credit trouble in the past. Even though their credit isn't completely clear, they may be able to refinance their mortgage to 8.75 percent when the lowest rate in the market is 7.25 percent. The lower score people get, the more fees will be involved in closing the loan, because people who have bad credit tend not to shop as much for a loan. They're happy they can get one at all, and they're not as worried about having to pay fees.

Credit card lenders have a sophisticated technique called predictive analysis they can use to determine whether you're likely to file for bankruptcy. If they decide you're a big risk, they can send you a notice raising your interest rate, in one case to as high as 34 percent, even if you haven't done anything wrong. Or they'll close off your account privileges, leaving you with no available credit and a balance left to pay.

One reason mistakes have been hard to fix is the way information is supplied to the credit bureaus. Let's say a credit card company incorrectly says you're a deadbeat, but you convince Equifax to remove the error. A month later, the credit card company may send a new report to the credit bureau and the error reappears on your credit record. If that happens, you have to ask the credit bureau to use something called "suppression technology," which will prevent an item from ever reappearing on your report once it's been cleared up.

I've had many callers tell me their credit report listed a loan they knew nothing about. Someone else borrowed the money and didn't pay it back, and somehow it wound up on their credit report.

I strongly recommend that you spend the money to get all three of your credit reports six months before you apply for a home loan. Federal law now sets an $8 limit on the amount you can be charged for a copy of your credit report. Some states allow you to get a copy for free.

Because errors take so long to clear up, a mistake you discover while purchasing a house very likely will cause you to lose that house. With a car loan, time is not as important. Go into your bank or credit union and get preapproved for a car loan just before you're ready to buy. You'll know immediately if there is a problem. It's not as much of an earth-shattering crisis if there's a reason you can't buy a new car. When

69

**70** $

you get knocked out of the housing market, it's traumatic.

I receive so many distressing phone calls from people who are trying to get approval for a home loan and are stymied by a credit report problem. I had a call from one fellow whose credit report was so messed up that he had to take two weeks off from work to straighten it out. He discovered, while refinancing his house, that someone he didn't know had used his Social Security number to obtain 10 credit cards. The crook had fraudulently rolled up several thousand dollars in charges.

One way to avoid this potential disaster is to guard your Social Security number. Consider leaving your Social Security card at home, rather than carrying it in your wallet, in case your wallet is ever lost or stolen.

## TIPS ON CREDIT REPORTS

⦿ There are three major credit bureaus that issue credit reports to lenders — Equifax, Experian, and Trans Union — and they don't share information. So even if you correct an error on one credit report, you will have to do the same on the other two.

⦿ You have the right under federal law to challenge items on your credit report. But the process of correcting your report can take months and is very frustrating.

⦿ If a credit bureau refuses to correct a mistake, you can sue them.

⦿ Get copies of all three credit reports six months before you apply for a home loan. If a credit report error keeps you from getting a loan, you'll lose the house.

## CONTACT

Equifax Information Service
800-685-1111
www.equifax.com

Experian
Experian National Consumer Assistance Center
888-397-3742
www.experian.com

Trans Union
800-888-4213
www.transunion.com

INTERNET

www.fairisaac.com (Explains credit report scoring)

# DIVORCE

People often get so caught up in the emotions of a divorce, they forget the financial aspects. I think that's human nature. I can tell you from personal experience that divorce is one of the most painful experiences you can go through.

Still, during this period when you are vulnerable emotionally, you are also vulnerable financially. You have to protect your financial interests by terminating not just the marriage but all joint financial obligations.

If you have credit cards that are jointly owned, the accounts must be paid off and closed, and each party should obtain credit in his or her own name. This is essential so that neither spouse is responsible for the other's bills. Even though the divorce decree says your ex-husband is supposed to pay the credit cards, sometimes he doesn't, and the credit card companies come after you. I take this kind of call all the time.

If the credit card accounts are not closed, you can be hurt in two big ways. One, even though you may have paid all your bills and maintained a great credit rating, your credit can be ruined and you can get knocked out of the credit market. That's trouble if you want to buy a home or a car.

Second, though you may not realize it, you are financially responsible for the credit card debt, even if your former spouse gets the merchandise. That's because a credit card agreement, like any joint credit agreement, is legally superior to the divorce decree. The contractual obligation continues regardless of what the divorce decree says. If you pay off and close those accounts, you have nothing to worry about. Otherwise, you have a time bomb waiting to explode, sometimes months or years later.

Your only recourse if your former spouse runs up debts and then reneges on the obligations is to call your divorce lawyer and file an action based on the divorce decree. But that doesn't change the fact that you owe the money to the credit grantor.

Another important asset to think about is your house. It doesn't matter if you sign over your rights to the house to the other partner. The obligation on the mortgage is where you're at risk.

**72** 💰 Before reaching a final agreement on the divorce, you need to know whether the person keeping the house can qualify for a new mortgage alone. If he or she cannot, the house should be sold so that neither party is responsible. If both of you remain on the loan, the one who leaves the house has no advantages and lots of disadvantages. You really have a problem if you can't sell the house.

If you're both listed on a car loan, the same problems can occur as with a house or credit cards. But there is a complication. If it's a five-year loan, and you're early or midway through the loan, the vehicle usually is worth less than the amount owed. If that's the case, you will need some additional money to refinance the loan or sell the car and pay off the existing loan.

Another item not to ignore in the process of divorce is each spouse's retirement plan, and if there are any, stock options. There could be more money at stake in those things than everything else the couple has.

Lawyers hate when I say this, but I believe strongly that couples should try divorce mediation, rather than immediately getting separate lawyers, going into enemy camps, and duking it out. Divorce has such a tremendous emotional toll on the individuals involved, and the legal process, being adversarial, only increases the hurt, distrust, and anger. Some municipalities now require that mediation be used in all civil cases, including divorce, before the parties may appear in court.

If children are involved and the parents fight about the divorce, they both have something to lose as the process marches on. I know of one couple that wound up in a shoving match at a shopping center after the father made off with the couple's two-year-old son in front of their young daughter. That's a tragedy for the whole family.

Another couple I know of tried mediation and now share joint custody of their five-year-old daughter. She spends four days each week at Mom's house and three days at Dad's house and everyone gets along very well. The parents live close to each other and in the same school district. Forget money for a minute and consider your relationship with your children and your children's future well-being. Mediation becomes a great tool to try for a divorce without as much hostility.

However, divorce mediation is not the entire answer. A mediator merely tries to get the two parties together and to reach an agreement they believe is fair. But before a mediation agreement is final, each party should have it reviewed by an attorney who specializes in family practice law. In the end, you need a lawyer's expertise to point out elements of a proposed mediation agreement that may be unwise or unfair to you. If you skip this step, and I know of at least one person who did, you could get burned.

Child support is a major financial issue of divorce. It's almost a cliche now that the noncustodial parent doesn't pay child support. Lots of parents do pay it. But collecting child support, either because of underpayment or nonpayment, has become a major national problem. Generally it's the mother trying to collect child support from the father.

Many states have child-support recovery offices, but as a group they are abysmal failures, mostly because the case loads are so enormous. They can be good sources of information, however. They can tell you, for example, that the law allows you to collect back child support even after a child turns 18, and that you can go back to court during the child's lifetime and request an increase in support payments. But actually collecting the money can be next to impossible if the parent truly doesn't want to pay.

The difficulty in collecting child support has spawned a booming industry: child-support collection agencies. Some are traditional collection agencies that have gone into this as a sideline. Others do nothing but collect overdue child support. For a mother who's dealing with a father who has never paid or has not paid for months or years, this could be an answer. But beware of collection agencies that ask you for money up-front before they'll start collection efforts. Don't pay. Also, if a collection agency wants more than one-third of the total due, look elsewhere.

Finally, there's the problem of what to do about income taxes. One spouse generally accepts responsibility in the divorce decree for income taxes that may result from audits of prior year's tax returns. If your spouse is involved in a business, you may want to indemnify yourself in the decree from tax responsibilities of the business. But the IRS doesn't recognize such division of responsibility and may go after either spouse if more taxes are owed.

If the tax return hasn't been filed for the year prior to the divorce, you have the option of filing jointly or separately. You pay a higher rate if you file separately, but you should consider it because it can protect you from your spouse's tax liabilities for that year. After the divorce, of course, you are single and file separately.

$ **73**

## TIPS ON DIVORCE

⦿ You have to protect your financial interests in a divorce by terminating not just the marriage but all joint financial obligations. That includes credit card accounts, mortgages, and jointly held loans. Refinance the loans or sell the house or car.

⦿ If joint accounts are not closed, you are legally responsible if your ex-spouse doesn't pay, no matter what the divorce decree says. Your credit can be ruined and you can get knocked out of the credit market.

- Make sure to consider each spouse's retirement accounts and stock options, if there are any.

- Consider divorce mediation, a less adversarial process than using lawyers, in which a mediator tries to get the two parties together to reach a fair agreement. But be sure to have any mediation agreement reviewed by a lawyer.

- If your ex-spouse is months or more behind in child-support payments, consider using a collection agency. Don't pay anything up-front and don't pay more than one-third the amount due in collection agency fees.

## CONTACT

Academy of Family Mediators
800-292-4236
www.igc.apc.org/afm/

# WILLS

It's very important to have a will, but it's amazing how many people of all income levels don't have one. I think it's because people prefer to avoid the reality that they're going to die someday.

The greatest favor you can do for your survivors is to stipulate, in your will, what you want to happen to your assets.

When you die without a will, most states write a will for you. In a legislated will, a state will distribute your assets to your family based on its own formula. The thought of your money going to a relative you can't stand should be motivation enough for you to do a will. If not, think of the person to whom you would like to give most or all of your assets. They might not get

the money because you haven't designated it in a will.

I remember one case involving a utility executive who had divorced and remarried, then died without writing a will. He left an estate worth $700,000. Because he had no will, the state divided the money equally among his two children and his second wife, about $225,000 each after expenses. He might have wanted it split some other way, but without a will, it was impossible to follow his wishes.

There's another case that illustrates the importance of having a will. A husband and wife with two small children were killed in a car accident, leaving insurance payments and other property worth $2 to $3 million. Because the couple had a will, a trust was set up to manage the inheritance, and custody of the children was decided according to the parents' wishes. Had there been no will, the state would have appointed a guardian for each child and also would have decided who would handle the child's money. Court permission would have been needed for many financial decisions, a cumbersome process that would have produced legal expenses of several thousand dollars per year for perhaps 15 years.

It's simpler than you think to create a will. For a will to be legal in most states, you have to be at least 18 years old and of sound mind. The will must be written, signed by you, and witnessed by two people who won't receive anything from your estate. That is the end of the mystery of a will. That's all you have to do.

If you want to have a will done by a lawyer, that's fine. Lawyers' fees for doing a will vary widely, depending on the complications of your estate and how much the particular lawyer charges per hour.

For most people with uncomplicated family situations, you can create a will with a computer program called WillMaker, which is the granddaddy of such programs. It's gotten more and more clear and easy to use over the years. You can order it online at www.nolo.com, or go to a computer store. Don't use a will program if you have a blended family, a situation in which you expect people to fight over

money, or assets of more than $1 million. If any of those situations apply to you, see a lawyer who specializes in wills, estates, and trusts.

Years ago when my personal and financial situations were less complicated, I used WillMaker to do my will, then had it reviewed by an attorney, who said it was perfect. My lawyer did not suggest one change in the will I drew up using the computer program.

You should do whatever is comfortable for you, either drawing up your own will or using a program, or having a lawyer do it. But if you start doing your own will with a computer program and you reach a point where there's a question you don't understand or a procedure that does not make sense to you, or language that isn't clear, stop right there and go to a lawyer. If you have substantial assets or if there are children involved, it can be disastrous to agree to things in language you don't understand, or make decisions in your will that you haven't fully thought out. Those are the two big variables that you really have to be sure about.

The amount of money exempt from estate tax is going up each year, and will reach $1 million by 2006. So if you have a great deal of assets, especially more than $1 million in assets, it is critical, in order to avoid very high estate taxes, to plan your estate with a lawyer who specializes in wills, estates, and trusts. Fewer than 2 percent of the population have that problem.

**76**  ⑤

The state processes your will after you die, and your assets are distributed through a procedure called probate. Probate usually is quick and routine, especially if the assets are less than $1 million. But in some states, probate can be inefficient, expensive, or corrupt; it can take months or years, and legal costs can seriously erode the value of the estate.

Some assets pass directly to a spouse or child if they are jointly owned. With a house, the deed must list owners as "joint tenants with right of survivorship." If you merely list two people as co-owners, the deceased's 50 percent share of the house will pass to his or her heirs as specified by the will. It works the same way with a car.

For a bank account, generally joint ownership is all you need for the co-owner to have immediate access and ownership after the other dies. For stocks or mutual fund accounts, include "joint ownership with right of survivorship" on the papers. With life insurance, it doesn't even matter what's specified in your will, because the insurance contract is a superior document. The payment automatically goes to the designated beneficiary.

There are lots of unscrupulous folks out there trying to convince you that a will is terrible and a living trust is a godsend. A living trust is a method of avoiding probate and having your assets pass immediately to your designee outside of the probate process. A living trust is appropriate only in very rare circumstances, such as when someone owns property in several states and wants to avoid multistate probate. For example, you might own a home in Michigan and a retirement home in Florida.

Or, a living trust can be used if a person is in failing health and wants to turn over effective control while he or she is still able to do so. There generally is no tax advantage to a living trust, because the same inheritance taxes apply. If you do have a specialized situation that calls for a living trust, have a lawyer prepare it because it's a very complicated document. The cost will be many times more than a will. Less than 1 percent of the public needs a living trust.

There's another document you may have heard referred to as a living will. It's a form you fill out that lets hospitals know, when you are critically ill, whether they should use extraordinary means to keep you alive. The Supreme Court has ruled that hospitals must accept these written medical care instructions.

You should complete a living will so your family won't have to agonize over what should happen to you. Ask your doctor or hospital for a living will. Even better, get a durable power of attorney, which appoints an advocate, usually a family member, to see that your wishes are carried out. For information on how to do a living will, go to my Web site, www.clarkhoward.com, or check with the American Association of Retired Persons (www.aarp.org).

### TIPS ON WILLS

- It's simpler than you think to create a will. For a will to be legal in most states, you have to be at least 18 years old and of sound mind. The will must be written, signed by you, and witnessed by two people who won't receive anything from your estate.

- You can draw up your own will, using a computer program, or have a lawyer do it.

- Don't do a will yourself if you have a blended family, if people are likely to fight over money, or if you have a great deal of assets, especially more than $1 million.

- A living trust is an alternative to a will in which your assets pass immediately to your designee when you die. But it's complicated and expensive, and few people need it.

### INTERNET

www.nolo.com (WillMaker program)
www.freeadvice.com
www.lawguru.com
www.findlaw.com
www.uslaw.com
www.abanet.org (American Bar Association)

# FUNERALS

Another thing people avoid thinking about is the arrangements for a funeral. Most of us die keeping those thoughts to ourselves and leave our grieving loved ones to decide if there will be a funeral or a memorial service, a burial or cremation. At their weakest moments, when they are often overcome by sadness or guilt, they have to make some very difficult and personal decisions.

I've been on the funeral home sales tour and it's an awful experience. The funeral director, usually someone who is very pleasant and low-key, often starts by taking you through the casket area. The caskets are arranged from the most expensive, in the front and very well displayed, to the less expensive, which are in the far end of the room gathering dust. In many funeral homes,

**78**  💰  the least expensive caskets aren't even on display.

You're in an environment in which you're encouraged, gently but persuasively, to spend more money than you would have anticipated, at a time when you're most vulnerable. You have absolutely no ability to comparison shop at this point, because you've already designated the funeral home and had the body transported there. So you are their captive in negotiations over costs and services.

Do yourself and your family a favor by making those decisions yourself ahead of time. The most effective way to hold down the costs of these arrangements, and to improve the chances that your wishes will be carried out, is to join the Memorial Society in your area. You pay a one-time fee to join and can list your wishes and get negotiated prices for caskets and burial or other services. You set the budget and pick what you want. When you die, your family goes to the funeral home you designated and they pull the file specifying your arrangements and preset costs. The funeral homes are willing to give great prices to the Memorial Society in exchange for the high volume of business generated by their relationship.

I don't recommend that people prepay for a funeral or a cemetery plot. We've become such a transient population that it's foolish to prepay for funeral arrangements in a particular city. Circumstances could change and you might move to a different city. Not only that, but what happens if the funeral home goes out of business? Your money could go down the tubes.

But even worse, there have been scandals across the country in which you may have prepurchased a plot, and they have failed to maintain the cemetery well. What looked like a beautiful place at the time you arranged to buy a plot now looks like an overgrown weed patch.

Buying a plot could be a mistake for another reason. More and more people who might have opted to be buried after they die are now choosing cremation instead. Even though it's much cheaper, people aren't choosing it because of cost, but because it's the alternative they prefer.

It's much better to join the Memorial Society, because the prices are set, but are not paid until you die.

 **TIPS ON FUNERALS**

◉ Most people die without making funeral arrangements, forcing their grieving family to make tough decisions and overpay on funeral costs. Join your local Memorial Society and make those decisions yourself, ahead of time.

● Don't prepay for a funeral or cemetery plot. You could move to another city or the funeral home could go out of business.

## CONTACT

Funeral and Memorial Societies of America/Funeral Consumers Alliance
(For a directory of memorial societies in your area)
802-482-3437
www.funerals.org/famsa

 **79**

# REAL ESTATE

**The cost** of housing usually is the largest number in the family budget. Knowing the right way to buy housing can make a big difference in your life, whether your goal is having a great home, accumulating wealth, or a combination of the two.

In this section, I'll show you how to make smart choices in buying, renting, and selling real estate, so that you can live where you want, or get what you want out of your housing dollar.

GETTING READY TO BUY

BUYING A NEW HOUSE

HOME WARRANTIES

BUYING A USED HOUSE

REMODELING

SELLING YOUR HOUSE

MOVING

HOME SECURITY SYSTEMS

REFINANCING

MORTGAGE SERVICING

BEING A LANDLORD

BEING A TENANT

# 82 🏠 GETTING READY TO BUY

Before you rush out and start looking at houses you might want to buy, do a few things to prepare.

First, get copies of your credit reports from all three major credit reporting agencies: Equifax, Trans Union, and Experian. You should do this six months before you go house shopping. That way, if there's an error or another problem that could keep you from getting a mortgage, you'll have time to straighten it out. It's devastating to find a home you want and then get turned down for the loan.

Next, go and prequalify for a mortgage, so you'll know how much house you can buy. People tend to waste a lot of time, and a lot of a real estate agent's time, looking for a home above the price they should be shopping.

You can prequalify with any bank or credit union. Or, if you currently own a home, you can talk to the company that holds your current mortgage, and prequalify for a loan on your new home. Or, you can prequalify online. There are a number of great Web sites for this. I especially like www.iown.com. You can get instant quotes for exactly the kind of loan you want, for a purchase or refinance.

The amount you qualify for should be the maximum loan amount you accept. You may qualify for a $175,000 loan, but decide that the payment on a $160,000 loan would fit more comfort-ably into your budget. The qualifying amount may be what the lender thinks you can afford under ideal circum-stances. I recommend you trim that by 10 percent, so you build a financial cushion into your life.

If you choose to shop for homes with a real estate agent, there's some-thing you need to know. Rules vary by state, but often the agent who takes you around to look for homes actually is not "your" agent, although he or she may be very friendly and helpful. In many cases, the agent represents the home seller. It's similar to the way a salesper-son at a department store represents the retailer. The sales agent is required by law to tell the seller about anything you say. So if you offer $120,000 for a house, but let it slip to the real estate agent that you can afford to pay $130,000, the agent has to disclose that to the seller. The agent also will pass on information about you, such as your income, that may weaken your negotiat-ing status. It's doubtful, too, that a real estate agent will show you any "For Sale by Owner" houses, because an agent receives no commission on such a sale.

Most home sales today involve two sales agents. One is the listing agent, who is hired by the seller to market and sell his or her house. The other is the selling agent, the person who shows you different houses for sale. Because agents split commissions, the selling agent may try to get you to buy a house he or she has been directly hired to sell. In that case, the sale involves only one agent.

Real estate agents can represent the seller, the buyer, or both. To find out who your agent represents, ask them. They are required to tell you. If you're moving from one state to another, the applicable laws are those of the state to which you are moving.

I recommend that you find an agent who works for you. He or she will prevent home sellers from learning personal facts about you and allow you to see any home in which you're interested. A buyer's agent will help you decide how much to offer and negotiate on your behalf. Buyer's agents are paid in the same way as an agent who works for the seller. They receive a percentage of the sales price. Because of that, a buyer's agent does get more if the house sells for a higher price. But buyer's agents tell me it's worth far more to them to negotiate the lowest price possible for the buyer — and get referrals from a satisfied buyer — than to get a

nominally higher commission from a higher sales price. You can find a buyer's agent at most real estate companies, or ask friends for referrals.

When you're giving a real estate agent a price range for your house shopping, it's a good idea to quote less than you're willing to spend. If you tell an agent you're looking for a $120,000 house, the agent inevitably will use that figure as a floor, not a ceiling, and will show you houses priced at $120,000, $125,000, and $130,000.

If you're moving to a new area of the country, rent before you buy. You might not be sure at first which part of your new city you prefer, and if you change your mind six months or a year later and want to move to another neighborhood or city, you won't face the hefty costs of selling another house.

Congress changed the tax law in 1997, eliminating the need for you to reinvest the proceeds of a home sale into a new home. So there's no pressure to run around a new city with a real estate agent and hurriedly buy a house.

**83**

## TIPS ON GETTING READY TO BUY

⦿ Get a copy of your credit reports six months before you start home shopping.

⦿ Prequalify for a mortgage before you start looking at houses, so you'll know what you can buy.

⦿ Choose a buyer's agent to represent you in the purchase.

## 84 ⌂ BUYING A NEW HOUSE

Buying a house is a cornerstone of what many people want to accomplish as adults. In addition to being a place to live, a home can be a symbol of financial success, as well as a major investment. But making this major purchase is also a complex process with plenty of potential for costly mistakes.

Buying a home can be a very good investment, but like most investments it carries risk. That's a good thing to remember in an era when many people think home prices can do nothing but go up. Although some parts of the country have seen massive increases in value in the last few years, there's nothing that says that will continue, and there always is the possibility that in individual markets, values will decline.

If you're buying in a red-hot market, you should plan on making a long-term purchase. People who bought homes during California's boom years in the late 1980s, then had to sell after the price bubble burst, took huge financial losses. But homeowners who waited for prices to climb back were OK.

My home city of Atlanta is in a price bubble as I write this. A house I sold in 1991 for $150,000 sold recently for $385,000, and the sellers were asking for only $375,000. They had five contract offers during the first weekend. But who knows if these values will hold.

If you're buying a house strictly for financial reasons, look at each house you're considering just as you would evaluate a purchase of stocks or bonds.

To buy a house as an investment, it's best to look for one with "people problems," generally a used house that is selling for below the fair market value because of special circumstances such as a divorce, a death, a relocation, or a foreclosure. That's a wise purchase because you are likely to be able to increase its value.

You get a true bargain on a people-problem house only if you've done your homework first. Figure out the condition of the house and — by researching other homes for sale — its normal market price. Often a house with people problems has been neglected for a while, so you may be facing extensive repairs that would negate any bargain price. You can prevent unforeseen expense by making a purchase offer contingent upon an inspection of the house. Even if the inspection reveals problems, it might be worthwhile to make the purchase.

More often, people want to buy a house as a place to live. They want something that they like and can afford, and they don't want to make any mistakes. One of the most important guidelines I can give is don't buy one of the first houses in a subdivision. It's too risky, primarily because the developer could go bust and be unable to complete the subdivision. Early buyers can end up in a home surrounded by scarred and abandoned land. Even worse, these houses could be surrounded by partially built homes. There's also the danger that amenities promised by the developer, such as a pool or tennis courts, might not be built. If the developer fails, those promises disappear.

I think it's wise for new home buyers to find out a little about the builder of a house they're considering. When you buy a car, you look for a model made by a manufacturer with a reputation for quality. But few people think to ask about the builder of a house. If you're interested in a house, ask what other homes the builder has done. Then ask the owners how they like their houses. Most homeowners will be happy to tell you whether their house was well built or whether the builder did a shabby job.

Another way to ensure your home is well-built is to hire an inspector. The quality of government inspectors varies from city to city, and you can't count on these inspectors. For an off-the-shelf new house that a builder has recently completed, an inspector you hire could discover shortcuts in materials used or necessary work that wasn't done. If that happens, a builder could be forced to make repairs. Make your purchase offer contingent on the house passing inspection.

For a house you're having custom-built, hire an inspector to check it at key stages in its construction. For example, when the framing or wiring is completed,

the inspector will check to see it was done properly. An inspector will tell you at which stages the house should be checked. Before you agree to the contract with the builder, insert language allowing you to have the house inspected during construction. It's a lot easier to fix mistakes along the way than after the house is finished.

You can locate a certified inspector through the American Society of Home Inspectors. It's not a good idea to use an inspector recommended by a real estate agent, because such an inspector might feel torn by loyalties to you and the agent, who is a source of business referrals.

Some people buy a house that's under construction and have it custom-finished with features such as whirlpool tubs, skylights, or premium-grade carpet.

Whether you're having a house custom-built or custom-finished, there's a fair chance the work won't be done by your scheduled closing date. If you go through with the closing, you give up your leverage and run the risk the job never will be completed. If you decide to close with items unresolved, give a letter outlining these items to the closing attorney and the real estate agent or agents involved in the sale. That will prevent anybody from later getting amnesia about these issues. Get assurance from the real estate agent to help see that the work is completed.

When you're negotiating a contract for the purchase of a house, especially

85

one that has not been completed yet, the contract should be reviewed by a real estate attorney. It's wise to spend some money up-front to prevent problems that could be expensive and hard to resolve. A real estate attorney also will review the closing documents. You should require in your purchase contract that the closing documents be made available to you at least two days prior to closing for review by your attorney. Real estate closings are incredibly confusing. You have no idea what documents are being put in front of you — the language is so unfamiliar and the forms are so complex — and it's easy to make an expensive mistake. The lender and seller both will have representatives at the closing. That's why you have your lawyer check everything.

Before you buy a house, try your commute to work during rush hour. When you make a long drive from a house to your workplace on a weekend, you don't get a true idea of the travel time. It's also important to learn about the area surrounding a potential new house. You should know what potential there is for new roads or new development. Is there a chance your backyard someday will look out on a new shopping center? Are there any vacant lots that might be the site of undesirable government or commercial projects? Make sure your real estate agent discloses any easements there may be for a property you're considering. An easement allows a power company or a city to run a power line or sewer line across your property. I know of someone who found out on the day of closing that there was a sewer easement running right under the house, making it possible the house could be torn down at any time. That scrapped the whole deal.

Look for potential problems such as high-voltage power lines that run near the property. There's no clear opinion as to whether high-voltage power lines are dangerous to human health, but being adjacent to power lines has become less desirable and therefore made houses harder to sell.

It's also a good idea to look at a property while it's raining, to see how water flows across it. Look for signs of poor drainage and danger of flooding. It helps, if you can, to look in the basement of a home during or just after a rainfall.

Drainage problems are quite common these days and can be very costly. One of my callers bought a $121,000 house in a very nice neighborhood, then discovered that during a rainfall, water cascaded across his patio like a river. He spent $1,300 to install an underground drain, but the system still backed up during heavy rains. A civil engineer told him it would cost another $2,000 to design a plan to solve the problem. State laws provide minimal protection for homeowners in these cases, sometimes requiring the builder or developer to make repairs. The best solution is to examine a new house while it's raining before you buy it.

Over the years, a lot of homeowners have had problems with building materials that turned out to be defective, including polybutylene water pipes, artificial stucco, and fake wood siding. People who shop for a house often interpret high quality as being a lot of extra features, like a big whirlpool tub, a great sunroom, or a lot of crown molding. But while those things are nice to have, it's more important to see if the house is well made. Most of the problems I've seen come from builders who've cut corners by using cheaper materials, as a way of trying to give people more house for their money. But you could face thousands of dollars in repairs if you buy a house with synthetic stucco siding, which in a lot of cases has trapped moisture in the walls and caused them to rot. Polybutylene pipe was easier and cheaper to install, but wound up leaking and had to be replaced. Artificial wood siding looked good, but didn't last, and homeowners had to spend tens of thousands of dollars to put a new exterior on their home. Go with time-tested materials in the house you're buying. Brick and vinyl siding work. Copper and PVC plumbing work. You want a house that's fundamentally sound, in construction and materials, even if it doesn't have the latest, greatest design features.

As part of your mortgage loan, you'll be required to purchase a title insurance policy, the kind that protects the lender in the event your ownership of the property is ever challenged. I recommend a very low-cost addition — owner's title insurance. It protects you if anyone ever claims you are not the legal owner of the property. Owner's title insurance can cost as little as $100 if you buy it at the time you buy the house. Ask the closing attorney for a quote. If the quote seems high, see if you can negotiate down the fee.

There was a title case a few years ago in which residents of an entire community almost lost their homes. A woman claimed she was part-owner of a tract of land that later was divided to form a subdivision. She sued the homeowners in the community for a partial share of the land. The woman eventually agreed to a settlement, but the homeowners spent several thousand dollars in legal fees to defend their property rights. Owner's title insurance not only protects you from loss, but the title company must defend you if your ownership is ever challenged.

 **87**

## TIPS ON BUYING A NEW HOUSE

- If you're buying a house strictly for financial reasons, look at each house you're considering as you would evaluate a purchase of stocks or bonds.

- To buy a house as an investment, look for one that is selling for below the fair market value because of special circumstances, such as a divorce, a relocation, or a foreclosure.

- Don't buy one of the first houses in a subdivision. The developer may go bust and be unable to complete the development.

- Check out the reputation of the builder by talking with people who live in some of the builder's houses.

- Make any offer on a home contingent on its passing an inspection. The purchase also should be contingent on your ability to get financing at or below a set interest rate.

- Hire a real estate attorney to review the closing papers and, if you're buying a house still under construction, to draft or review the purchase contract.

- Before you buy a house, try your commute to work during rush hour.

- Learn about the area surrounding a potential purchase, including the potential for new roads or new development.

- Look at a property while it's raining to see how water flows across it. Look for signs of poor drainage and danger of flooding.

- Buy a house that's fundamentally sound, in construction and materials, even if it doesn't have the latest, greatest design features.

- Get an owner's title insurance policy that covers you, not the lender, if your ownership is successfully challenged.

## CONTACT

American Society of Home Inspectors
800-743-2744
www.ashi.com

# HOME WARRANTIES

A home warranty is not a substitute for choosing a responsible builder or for having a home inspected. But a warranty can provide assistance and is a good selling tool when it's time to move. It's a confidence builder for the buyer.

A home warranty that comes with a new house offers a minimal amount of protection in the first two years and even less protection for three to 10 years after you purchase the house. Pay close attention to how your warranty works. Usually your builder is fully responsible in the first year, and the warranty company is responsible in the second year.

The home warranty company generally will be responsible for problems in the second year only if you've followed its procedures correctly. Let's say you have a plumbing problem in the first year and you've asked the builder to fix it, but you never notified the warranty company. By not notifying the warranty company, you may have waived your rights to getting help. So it's important to notify both the builder and the warranty company as soon as a problem develops and at the address and in the manner they require. They may require notice by certified mail, or you may prefer to send it by certified mail so you have proof it was sent. You also gain leverage by contacting the warranty company, as officials there usually tell the builder to fix the problem.

If, during the first year of warranty protection, you notify both the builder and the warranty company, and the builder attempts a repair but is unsuccessful, immediately send another letter. Document. Document. Document.

The other kind of warranty concerns a used home. I bought a home a few years ago that came with a third-party warranty designed to assure me that the basic systems of the home were working. I never had to claim against the warranty and I let it expire after one year. For around $400, I could have renewed it each year. This kind of warranty is really like extended warranties on appliances, which cost too much and rarely pay claims. Mainly what it covers is heating, air conditioning, and other major systems of the home.

Termites are another concern for buyers in many parts of the country. In some states, the seller is required by law or by the mortgage lender to have the house inspected for possible termite damage. Even if it is not required, if termites or other wood-destroying insects are a problem in your region, you should ask that an inspection be performed.

Within the first 90 days of ownership, you should interview and select a pest control company, so that you can protect the property against any future infestation. Check with the Department of Agriculture, entomology division, or the structural pest control board in your state to find out its policy. Or call the National Pest Control Network to locate the appropriate agency in your area. These agencies often will conduct an inspection for you if you suspect a pest-control company has given your house an inadequate termite control treatment.

There are two principal types of termite-protection policies provided by pest-control companies. Under a retreatment policy, the company simply promises to come back and retreat the property. There's no real risk to the termite company for its failure to spot termites. Your best bet is a repair guarantee, under which the termite company

**89**

**90**

is responsible for repairing any damage caused by termites. With a repair guarantee, the termite company is your partner in making sure your house is well treated because the company is at financial risk if it doesn't do a good job locating infestations and treating them.

A comprehensive, initial termite treatment, including a repair guarantee, can cost several hundred dollars. And pest control companies often won't provide a repair guarantee unless their company has done the treatment. After that, expect to pay for annual, follow-up termite inspections, with retreatment if needed. A good way to find a company is to ask a real estate agent.

Owners of some stucco homes have had special problems with termites. Building codes in most states required that the stucco reach to the ground. But it's been discovered that termites can easily enter the home when synthetic stucco — the kind most people have — reaches into the ground. Termite companies may refuse to renew your coverage until you create a six- or eight-inch clearance between the stucco and the ground, or they may require you to pay a much higher annual premium for termite protection. Do yourself a favor and pay for the renovations needed to create the clearance.

## TIPS ON HOME WARRANTIES

- A home warranty that comes with a new house offers a fair amount of protection in the first two years and minimal basic protection for three to 10 years after you purchase the house.

- Pay close attention to how your warranty works. Usually your builder is fully responsible in the first year, and the warranty company is responsible in the second year.

- It's important to notify both the builder and the warranty company as soon as a problem develops and at the address and in the manner they require.

- With a used home, a warranty is for one year and is renewable annually for an unlimited period. It covers heating, air conditioning, and other major systems of the home.

- It's important in many parts of the country to hire a termite prevention company to protect against termite infestation.

- The best coverage is a termite repair guarantee, under which the termite company is responsible for repairing any damage caused by termites.

National Pest Control Network
Washington, DC, 1-800-858-7378
http://ace.orst.edu/info/nptn

# BUYING A USED HOUSE  91

Just as with buying a used car, you often get a better value buying a used house. That's because part of the cost of a new house is the cost of new construction. As construction costs increase, new houses become more expensive.

An important advantage of a used home — and I prefer the term "used" to "resale" or "existing" home — is that the house, because it's located in an established neighborhood, has found its true value in the marketplace. With new construction, particularly in a new neighborhood or a new subdivision, you never have a real solid feel for a house's value.

Of course, buying a used house means taking on an added risk of breakdowns and repair costs. I've bought houses built during the Depression and just after World War II, and in both cases I bought trouble. But there are two different concerns here. It's a bad idea to buy a house that has major structural problems, such as with the roof or foundation. But there's nothing wrong with buying a house that has irritations.

I bought a house in 1983 from a seller who had already moved to another state. It was built in 1937 and needed so many repairs that my late father referred to the house as "The Howard Hovel." He couldn't imagine his son living in such squalor. It smelled terrible and had the worst paint job I have ever seen — deep dark reds, ugly greens, and rooms with absolutely bizarre color trims. The floor in the bathroom was sinking. The front steps were all beat up. The driveway had completely collapsed. It was overgrown with weeds and not usable, except by a four-wheel-drive vehicle. Nobody was going to go anywhere near this thing.

I had an inspector come out and carefully go over this place, and he found no structural problems. So I brought in contractors and got estimates of the cost to bring the place up to speed. It cost $17,000, but the house was so cheap that even with repairs included, I still bought it for less than its market value. The key with this sort of work is to avoid moving walls or expanding rooms, because otherwise it can cost $17,000 just to renovate a bathroom. It's far cheaper to accept the layout the way it is and change cosmetic weaknesses.

I turned "The Howard Hovel" into a fine house and a good buy with renovations that were mostly cosmetic. I ripped out all the carpet, which completely eliminated the foul odor, and had the hardwood floors underneath stripped and restained. A good paint job and some attractive wallpaper took care of all those weird colors, and some new sheetrock made peeling ceilings look great. I had a great time showing people the house and then bringing out my before-and-after pictures.

In fact, because the house came with a vacant lot next door, it turned out to be the most profitable real estate transaction I've ever made. The lot was considered worthless by everyone because a giant storm sewer ran through the middle of it. A few years after I bought the house, I hired an engineering company to determine if it would be possible to move the storm sewer and build a new house on the lot. It worked. I relocated the storm system for $8,800 and ended up with a lot that was worth more than $100,000. It just never occurred to anybody that you could do that.

Look for hidden values and undervalued property. This house turned out to be a grand slam home run because I got both in the same purchase. Just be careful not to fall in love with a house

you're considering. To get the best deal in any negotiation, you have to be willing to walk away.

Use good judgment to pick a used house. If you see potential, a place that can look good with some cosmetic changes, you may have something that will work. But if you would have to pay for expensive renovations to be happy, it's not going to be a good purchase.

It is critical when looking at used houses to make a purchase offer contingent on an inspection. That's the only way to get a good feel for possible repair expenses.

And, as I discuss in the section on new homes, be wary of homes with building materials that have turned out to be defective, including polybutylene water pipes, artificial stucco, and fake wood siding. If you choose a home with these materials, factor in the potentially high additional costs that could result from making repairs.

One unexpected expense that can pop up when you're buying a used home is the cost of removing a dead tree. It's not something you think about when you're looking at a house, but the cost of removing a tree, or several trees, can be substantial. To protect yourself, ask the seller if there are any dead trees on the property. If there are, ask him to remove the trees as a condition of the sale. Also, look around the grounds yourself to see if you can find any problem trees. A dead, leafless tree can be pretty easy to spot in spring or summer, but it may blend into the background in fall or winter.

When you buy a used house, it's important to put at least $50 a month into a repair fund. In an old home, you never know what can break — pipes, the heating and air conditioning system, or an appliance.

As you probably can tell, my bias is toward buying used houses in established neighborhoods. If you buy wisely, you can get a good home in an attractive neighborhood and not be overrun by the myriad problems of a booming new area.

If you buy a new house in a new subdivision in a growing section of town, there are so many factors beyond your control. You have no way to know if the rest of the houses in the subdivision are going to be of the quality and character of your home. The next street over could be developed with houses a third less expensive than yours, which ultimately reduces the value of your home. Or, a new shopping center could be built behind your house.

I get a lot of complaints from owners of new houses about drainage problems. In the typical case, there's no problem for the first year or two of ownership. But that changes after more houses are built and more trees are cut

down. Suddenly, every time it rains, the yard is flooded.

In an established neighborhood, you know the schools aren't overcrowded. You don't have to worry about so many new homes being built that your children will have to attend classes in a portable trailer. An abundance of new construction can also cause your house to lose value. Let's say you buy a new house in a new subdivision and two years later, you're forced to relocate. Because the subdivision is growing, there are brand-new houses all around your house. That's trouble, because buyers usually prefer a brand-new house to a house that's two years old.

 93

I also prefer the sense of character in an older neighborhood that comes with lots of big trees. Often when you go into a new neighborhood, the only trees you'll see are stick trees. Because of the methods of construction, there may be just a few small trees left between houses.

One advantage to buying a new house is that most tend to have large and attractive bathrooms and kitchens, which people have come to desire over the years. That's a sacrifice I've made by buying older houses.

 TIPS ON BUYING A USED HOUSE

⦿ You often get a better value buying a used home, because rising construction costs make new houses more expensive.

- A used home often is located in an established neighborhood and has found its true value in the marketplace. With new construction, particularly in a new subdivision, you never have a solid feel for a house's value.

- Buying a used house means taking on an added risk of breakdowns and repair costs. Just make sure the purchase is contingent on an inspection, and don't buy a house with major structural problems.

- When you buy a used house, it's important to put at least $50 a month into a repair fund. You never know what can break.

- If you buy wisely, you can get a good home in an attractive neighborhood and not be overrun by the myriad problems of a booming new area. With a new house, there's a danger of crowded schools, poor drainage, and an abundance of new construction that can make it hard for you to resell your house.

# REMODELING

With the huge bloc of baby boomers now mostly in their thirties and forties, America is in a remodeling boom. A lot of homeowners would rather add onto or fix up a house than move into a more expensive house in a new neighborhood.

You have to be very, very careful picking somebody to remodel your home. Do not hire people who drop fliers off in your mailbox, or who ring your doorbell and tell you your roof or gutters need fixing. Phony remodelers are one of the oldest scams around, typically preying on older people. Almost always, they take the homeowner's money and disappear.

Your house is the most valuable investment you have. Do some legwork first, before you hire someone. Believe me, that will be far easier than dealing with the problems you'll have if you hire an incompetent or crooked contractor. For a minor renovation job, take recommendations for a remodeler from friends and neighbors.

For a major renovation job, which I consider anything above $5,000, you need to be much more scientific about the hiring process. Get recommendations from the National Association of the Remodeling Industry or the Remodelors Council of the National Association of Home Builders.

If you're interested in a remodeler, check their references. Ask for a list of the last 10 homes they've worked on, a description of what they did, the dates they started those jobs, the dates the jobs were completed, and how to contact each owner. The dates are important because it will allow you to see gaps in work. Perhaps they couldn't find any work for several months or perhaps they blew a job and got sued. You'll also get a feel for how many jobs a contractor takes on at one time.

Ask what kind of insurance each contractor carries. For example, do they carry workers compensation insurance and their own liability insurance policy? Some experts might tell you not to hire anybody who doesn't have proper insurance. That's the book answer. But you're going to have some difficulty finding people who have kept their insurance current. If you pick someone who has no insurance, make sure you have enough liability coverage in your homeowner's policy in case the contractor or an employee gets hurt on your property. Be prepared to be sued if any worker gets hurt in or around your house.

As I write this, the remodeling market is so red-hot that remodelers are much less willing to come out and look at your home, much less write a bid on the job. A radio colleague of mine made appointments with seven contractors, and only three showed up. Of those, only one wrote a bid. They're just that busy. But that could change quickly if the economy slows down, as it eventually will.

There's been a big shift in remodeling away from the traditional method to a concept called design-build. Traditionally, you would decide to redo your kitchen, tell the remodelers what you wanted, and they would

bid on the job. Now you choose the company you want to do the work, and you work together to choose the design. The cost emerges from that. The problem with design-build is the consumer never really has a good feel for how expensive a job will be until after they've selected a contractor. You may wind up with a proposed project you can't afford. It's also a lot harder to price shop. Make it clear when you select a remodeler that you're not sure if you can afford to do the job. I'd rather you lose a $500 deposit than tackle a job you can't afford.

Once you decide which contractor is going to do the work, the next task is drawing up a contract. Most contractors will present you with a standard builders supply house contract. Don't sign this under any circumstances. Instead, consider using a contract from the American Institute of Architects (AIA). The AIA has dozens of sample contracts that have stood the test of time. If it's a renovation costing more than $10,000, have the contract reviewed by a lawyer prior to signing it.

In most states, you'll need to obtain lien releases as part of the renovation process. A lien release or waiver is a document the contractor can give you that you will ask materials suppliers and subcontractors who work on your site to sign. In most states, subcontractors and suppliers can place a lien on your home if the contractor doesn't pay them, even if you've paid the contractor in full. So you could be forced to pay

95

twice. It's like buying a television at an appliance store and then months later being asked to pay the television manufacturer for the TV, because the company wasn't paid by the store.

With a lien waiver, subcontractors and suppliers give up their right to come after you for payment. If you're buying a house or refinancing one, you can ask the general contractor to sign an affidavit swearing he has paid the subcontractors. But you should also get lien waivers from the subcontractors.

I have heard so many sad stories about people who have been financially ruined because they didn't get lien waivers from electricians, plumbers, and other subcontractors. And as more people remodel their homes to provide space for aging parents or teenagers, more will be ripped off.

I had a neighbor who put an addition on his home and did a major renovation of his kitchen, and wound up losing an additional $70,000 because of a contractor who didn't pay his subcontractors. He asked me what to do and I had to tell him it was too late, because the contractor had skipped town with his money.

Never agree to any remodeling contract that calls for a large payment up-front. If the contractor is short of cash and says he or she needs money to buy materials for the job, you should buy the materials. Go with the contractor to make the purchases. So many people have given a contractor a large sum up-front and have never seen that contractor again.

Devise with the contractor a reasonable timeline and pay schedule, under which the contractor is paid as work is completed. Don't frontload the money to the point that the contractor has most of the money while just a portion of the work has been completed. My feeling is you shouldn't pay anything up-front. For a small job, you might pay half the money halfway through the job, 40 percent of the money at completion, and the final 10 percent once you're satisfied everything has been done correctly and nothing further must be done. For bigger jobs, pay 10 percent of the cost after each 10 percent of the job is done, with a 10 percent holdback at the end to protect against problems that crop up. You and the contractor should decide in advance how to determine when the 10 percent levels are met.

All this may sound petty, but if you're having remodeling work done, it matters. If you set out the schedule for payment ahead of time, you keep problems from occurring while the work is going on. You don't want to be in a financial dispute with your contractor in the middle of the project, no matter who thinks the other is being unfair. That doesn't create a spirit of cooperation and communication.

It's possible you could suffer if the job isn't completed on time. For example, if you're renting a place while your house is undergoing renovation, you would have to pay extra rent if the job takes too long. If that's the case, the contract should include penalties against the contractor for failing to complete the job on time. If you have to pay an additional $250 a week to live in another house or apartment, the penalty for late completion of the job should be at least $250 a week.

Besides losing your money by foolishly paying up-front, the worst thing that can happen in a remodeling case is getting incompetent work. If you've been damaged in this way, you have a tough road to walk. You're going to have to bring someone else in to finish or redo the job, and many times it will cost more to redo it than it would have cost to do it correctly the first time. Then you have to go to court to try to get your money back from the contractor who botched the job. If the contractor has no assets, there's nothing to go after. If you can't prove your case or if you win but can't collect, you don't get

anything back. It's tough.

Then there's the distress you endure. When a home renovation gets messed up, people take it very personally and it upsets them and disrupts their lives. There's so much excitement about adding a room or fixing up a kitchen, and when things don't go right, there's an emotional crash.

One more caution about remodeling. Be very wary of contractors who not only brag about their workmanship but also say they can arrange for financing. Home-improvement loans or second-mortgage loans arranged by the contractor tend to be extremely costly, with interest rates usually far above market rates. If you need to borrow money to renovate, repair, or add to your home, go to your bank or credit union and stay away from contractor-supplied referrals.

**97**

## TIPS ON REMODELING

- Be very, very careful picking somebody to remodel your home. Do not hire people who drop fliers off in your mailbox, or who ring your doorbell and tell you your roof or gutters need fixing.

- For a minor renovation job, take recommendations for a remodeler from friends and neighbors. For a major renovation job, anything above $5,000, get recommendations from the National Association of the Remodeling Industry or the Remodelors Council of the National Association of Home Builders.

- Ask candidates for the last 10 homes they've worked on, a description of what they did, the dates they started those jobs, the dates the jobs were completed, and how to contact each owner.

- Ask what kind of insurance each contractor carries. Protect yourself by hiring people who have a current certificate of insurance or by making sure you have enough liability coverage in your homeowner's policy in case someone who's uninsured is hurt on your property.

◉ Don't sign a standard builders supply house contract for a remodeling job. Instead, consider using a contract from the American Institute of Architects (AIA).

◉ Get subcontractors to waive their right to place a lien on your home if they aren't paid by the contractor.

◉ Never agree to any contract that calls for a large payment up-front. Devise with the contractor a reasonable timeline and pay schedule, under which the contractor is paid as work is completed. In the contract, include penalties against the contractor for failing to complete the job on time.

## CONTACT

The Remodelors Council of the National Association of Home Builders
800-368-5242 ext. 216
www.nahb.com

American Institute of Architects
(For a remodeling contract, ask for the standard form of agreement between owner and contractor: A101, A111, or A201)
800-365-2724
www.aia.org

National Association of the Remodeling Industry
703-575-1100
www.nari.org

## INTERNET

www.nrca.net (National Roofing Contractors Association)

# SELLING YOUR HOUSE

While many parts of the country have seen large increases in real estate values in recent years, other regions have seen values stay the same or decline.

People who have not seen the increases are in a difficult fix when they try to sell their home, because their house, minus the real estate commission, might actually be worth less than what they paid for it. That's led to a mass migration of people to FSBOs, or "For Sale by Owner." They try to market and sell their home themselves to avoid the commission, so they can sell without losing any money.

There are a number of Web sites that allow you to list your home for sale, but it's tough to determine whether anybody actually visits these sites. Before you list, contact some of the people who have listings on the site and ask them if they're getting any response. As yet, there's no dominant site that sellers and buyers use. Beware especially of those sites that want you to pay a lot of money to list your home.

While the Internet has yet to be a major force in helping people sell their homes, it is enormously helpful in determining the fair market value of the houses in a neighborhood. It gives sellers access to the kind of information that used to be available only to real estate agents. You can visit the Web sites of the various real estate companies in your area and see the listing prices of nearby homes. That's important for FSBO sellers, who often don't know how to price their house correctly.

Still, a FSBO is not a panacea. Many people find it very hard to sell their own home, primarily because they have no training or experience in selling. They may be offended when buyers criticize the house. Owners who sell their own houses also have to be incredibly patient, because they have to deal with unqualified buyers and with people who make appointments to see the house but don't show up.

When you sell your own home, always specify on the sign that brokers or agents are welcome. That way you will protect yourself from "steering," in which agents avoid your street and don't show buyers your home because you're not paying commission. If you indicate that brokers or agents are welcome, you're agreeing to split the commission with a selling agent who brings you a buyer. Generally you should offer 3.5 percent. Don't get greedy. If that 3.5 percent brings you a willing buyer at a reasonable price, that's a smart decision on your part. You've still saved 3.5 percent.

The hardest part of selling by owner is negotiating the selling price. There's a tendency among people who don't do this often to play their cards badly and let the buyer know too much. You may end up costing yourself more money than if you'd had an experienced hand at the wheel helping with the negotiating. If you want to try a by-owner sale anyway, set a reasonable time limit. If you're going to give a real estate agent a three-month listing on a home, give yourself three months to try to sell it. If you find you're miserable doing it, then stop and go hire a real estate agent.

Be aware that when you are trying to sell your house FSBO, you will be approached by a lot of agents trying to get that listing. Some agents will be greedy and will try anything to get you to give them the listing. Others will be helpful to you, giving you advice and information, with the thought that later, if you're not successful in selling the house yourself, you'll select them to be the listing agent on your property. I call that enlightened self-interest; it is in both parties' best interest.

Interview a number of real estate agents before you hire one to sell your home. Ride around the neighborhood first and see which names keep popping up on lawn signs. When you see the same agent's name several times within your area, you know that agent is "farming" your area. You want to deal with a farmer. They know the agents who traffic that area, they know the true value of your home, and, if they have multiple listings, they probably have good strategies for selling homes in your area. If you still know how to get in touch with former neighbors, call them and ask their experiences with the listing agent they had on their home.

When you interview an agent, ask for a written sales plan of how the agent would market your home, with specifics. Limit the listing time with that agent to three months. Agents will always present you with a six-month contract, but my attitude is that this gives them all the rights and privileges and you all the responsibilities. If an agent balks at doing a three-month list-

ing because of the expenses they have, then reach an agreement with them that you can back out of the listing after 90 days in return for paying a fee to them. If you're miserable with that agent, it's worth paying the fee.

Real estate commissions by law are negotiable. However, in many real estate markets, there is de facto price setting where, by tradition or design, commissions in that area are set. It may be known as a 7 percent market or a 6 percent market or a 5 percent market. You can try to negotiate a commission, but you'll probably have to live with the de facto fixed commission in that marketplace.

Give serious consideration to any offer for your house, and never be insulted by it. Always make a counteroffer. So often when I've sought to purchase a house, agents have told me the seller would be insulted by my offer. I've always told them to pass along my offer. This is a negotiating situation, and you as the potential buyer should not make a ridiculously low offer. However, you shouldn't make an offer that's too high; then you narrow the range within which you and the seller can negotiate. Make a reasonable offer but one that is a little on the low side.

As the seller, you must first price your house reasonably, not far above the market, and be willing to enter into a good give-and-take with the buyer. Let's say you have a house listed at $135,000 and the potential buyer comes back with an offer at $110,000, and you're angry they've offered so little money. You know in your heart and mind that your house is worth more than that. Put your anger aside and come back with a counteroffer with which you'll be happy. If you and the buyer can't reach agreement, fine. At least go through the process of offer, counter, offer, counter. The first buyer is very important. It may sound trite, but it's generally true that the first offer you receive on a house will be the best offer. I've bought two houses in which the sellers accepted less than they earlier rejected.

If you think your house is worth $139,000, you should probably price it $146,000, or about 5 percent above what you'd like to get. But if you list it at $160,000, you may be so high that you don't get any offers at all.

A real estate agent will help you price your house by checking the selling price of other homes in your neighborhood. You should also check the Internet sites of real estate companies in your area for homes of similar style and location to yours. Remember that real estate agents face a constant battle to get a listing for a home. Sometimes we make the mistake of choosing one agent over another because one gives a higher estimate of the selling price. That's speculation. More important is the person's sales plan for your house.

When you're asked about your

house, tell the truth. If you're asked about the condition of your roof and you don't know what it is, don't say it's in great shape. Say you don't know. If you're asked about the air conditioning and you had to have it fixed last summer, say it. Don't lie. Generally you'll be asked to fill out a seller's disclosure statement. These forms are required by law in only a few states, so it's your choice. But I recommend that you do it. I think disclosing the condition of the house creates a sense of trust that helps make the sale. You won't be able to deceive them anyway, because most buyers will have the house inspected and the inspection may disclose things you've tried to hide. You're better off being honest and telling the buyer up-front about problems. If the buyer finds out about a defect just before closing, it could kill the sale or force you to lower the price or pay for repairs.

If you were selling your car, you would probably clean and wax it, vacuum the interior, and fix any minor flaws, like a broken tail light. The same holds true for your house. You want it to be clean, bright, uncluttered, and uncrowded. Areas of the home need to be well lit. If you furnish your house to the max, get rid of some of the furniture. Closets need to be clean. If you have both winter and summer wardrobes in your closets and they're stuffed, take out the opposite-season clothes and store them. People are buying a fantasy and they

101

 don't want it ruined by a crowded closet. They're also looking to see if their furniture and possessions will fit, so you need to make the house seem like it's at less than capacity when people walk in.

Some sellers are having their own inspections done to check out the house before they sell it. If you don't want to go that far, go through the house yourself and make sure things work. Check the heating and air conditioning system and fix minor problems such as loose doorknobs or railings. Clean, paint, patch, or replace anything that isn't up to speed, and pay special attention to the kitchen and bathrooms.

Buyers also want a house to seem fresh and inviting. Having fresh flowers in the house and decorating the front walkway is a good idea. Some agents recommend putting a saucepan on the stove with some cinnamon or potpourri to put a fresh scent in the air. Sometimes little things can give people the feeling of warmth they want to have when they buy a home.

## Clark says TIPS ON SELLING YOUR HOUSE

⊛ Many people try but often find it very hard to sell their own home. They may not price the house correctly and may be offended when buyers criticize the home.

⊛ When you sell your own home, always specify on the sign that brokers or agents are welcome. That way you will protect yourself from "steering," in which agents avoid your street and don't show buyers your home because you're not paying commission.

⊛ Interview a number of real estate agents before you hire one to sell your home. It's good to deal with someone who sells a lot of houses in your neighborhood.

⊛ When you interview an agent, ask for a detailed, written sales plan of how the agent would market your home. Limit the listing time with that agent to three months, or negotiate a fee you can pay to get out of the listing after three months.

⊛ Listen to every offer for your house and always make a counteroffer.

⊛ Prepare your house for sale. It should be clean, bright, uncluttered, and uncrowded.

## INTERNET

www.homegain.com (Information on home sales in your neighborhood)

# MOVING

Whether you buy a house or rent an apartment, changing residences means packing up your possessions and moving.

For some people, moving means renting a truck, getting some friends together to help, and ordering a few pizzas and some beer as a reward. But as we get older and acquire more furniture, books, and other things, and as our backs get weaker, we're more likely to turn to professional help for a big move.

Unfortunately, the abuses occurring now in state-to-state moves are the worst that anybody has ever seen. The federal government, which used to watch over interstate moves, has abandoned that role. State authorities have no role in moves that cross state lines. So you have to be very careful.

Some movers do a poor job or charge too much, but there now are a number of movers who are outright thieves. They take names similar to those of well-known national movers. You call them and a well-dressed person will come and give you an estimate that inevitably will be much lower than what anybody else offers. They load all your stuff in their truck and simply steal it. You never see any of it again. They do this only for interstate moves, because the distance and time frame allows the trail to get cold before the victim can look for their belongings.

To protect yourself from thieves,

check to make sure any mover you're considering is a member of the movers' trade association, the American Moving and Storage Association (www.moving.org).

If your move is related to a corporate relocation or transfer, even if the company isn't paying for the move, find out who it uses as its preferred moving company. If you use the preferred mover, you'll generally get a more reliable move and the mover will work harder to satisfy you. The mover wants to maintain a good relationship with the company, so it will want you to be happy.

It is critically important to get a binding estimate of the cost of your move. If you don't, it could cost you hundreds or thousands of dollars. Let's say you call three movers and you get estimates of $995, $1,300, and $1,600, but none is a binding estimate. You choose the mover who gave you the $995 quote. When they complete the move, the crew leader hands you a bill for $4,000. Under the law, the company can charge you anything it wants and you have to pay. If you request and receive a binding estimate of $995, that's all you would have to pay. Unfortunately, some states prohibit binding estimates.

We had an unbelievable call from someone who had moved to central Florida, and the mover raised the price on the move from $1,500 to $50,000.

**104**

The mover wouldn't give her possessions to her unless she paid, and there was nothing she could do under the law. It's legal because Congress in its wisdom chose to give up regulation of interstate moving. A new unit of the U.S. Department of Transportation is supposed to take over this oversight. We'll see what happens.

It's a good idea to buy insurance from the mover and choose replacement coverage that would pay to replace an item that was broken in the move. *Consumer Reports* once found that 46 percent of people who move incur damage, and 11 percent have damage of more than $1,000. It's a real concern. Also, check with your own homeowners insurance company and see what coverage you may have from it. Ask your insurer what happens if the mover fails to honor the policy you buy from the mover.

When the mover drops off your furniture at your new residence, don't sign the release form until you've examined your furniture piece by piece. Use a flashlight if your house isn't well-lit yet. Sit in each chair and bounce on your sofa to make sure all the legs are still solid. I know this sounds silly and I know it sounds like the last thing you want to do on the day you're moving to a new place, but actually it gets your adrenaline flowing to bounce on your furniture, so do it. Check the exterior of cartons for signs of damage and open boxes marked fragile. It's much easier to document a claim while the moving

people are still there, before you sign to receive your possessions. You can ask for a damage claim form or make a note on the acceptance that some merchandise was damaged.

Many people prefer to do their own packing when they move. And a *Consumer Reports* survey once showed that you're less likely to have items damaged when you pack them yourself. But before you choose a moving company, get a clear understanding from that mover of what happens if something is broken that you've packed yourself. Most movers will accept and insure delivery of boxes you pack yourself, but make sure you do it right. If something breaks, you'll have to show it to the company, along with the packing materials, to prove you did a good job.

The best way to protect crystal, china, and any other extremely valuable and delicate possessions is to move them yourself in your own car, if you're driving. You're going to handle those items more carefully than a mover will.

There's also a risk, when you're moving, that your stuff will arrive late, possibly very late. I talked to a woman who moved from the East Coast to California, and her possessions didn't arrive for three months. It probably would have taken longer than three months if my staff hadn't intervened.

The way to protect yourself is to require the mover — in the contract — to pay a penalty if he doesn't deliver your belongings on or before a specific date. The penalty should relate directly to the costs you would incur if the mover is late. So if you would have to spend $75 a day to stay in a hotel waiting for your bed to arrive, the mover should have to pay that for each day he's late.

Unless you add to the contract a specific penalty for late delivery, all you have to rely on is the mover's estimate of when they'll deliver your belongings. If they don't get around to it for two, three, or four months, you're out of luck.

If you want to risk your back and move your household yourself, be careful about what you buy for the move. One of the big profit centers for truck rental companies is renting and selling the accessories that go along with moving. You pay a convenience charge when you buy or rent those items from the truck rental company. You'll generally do better renting the truck from them and getting your packing materials somewhere else. Some people like to get moving boxes for free from a supermarket or discount store. If you want to do that, you'll have to get there before they're crushed for recycling.

Try to get a written confirmation ahead of time on the price per day for the rental truck, the cost-per-mile if there is one, and any additional charges that may apply. On the day of rental, examine the contract carefully to make sure the prices and information match up with your written confirmation. Although I've heard allegations in the past about truck renters who will suddenly change the rates when you show up — because it's moving day and you

don't have other options — I don't believe that's the normal method of operation for movers. I think that more often, it's a matter of misunderstanding or a simple mistake on the part of the truck renter. That's why having a written confirmation is an important protection.

You can save some money by moving during the middle of a month or in mid-week, rather than at the end of the month or on a weekend. Moving companies now use special software that allows them to price their trucks based on demand. So rental trucks will cost more on the last day of the month and on the weekends, when people traditionally move, and much less on weekdays and other dates during the month. You might pay $80 a day for the last weekend of the month, but just $45 for a mid-month, mid-week day. It works for all sizes of trucks at most moving companies. If your schedule allows, consider it.

Major movers also will negotiate with you on price. My brother-in-law got a quote for $4,400 for an interstate move, but got the price knocked down when he said his company would pay no more than $3,000. At first, the moving company representative said he couldn't do it for $3,000. But then he called back and agreed on the $3,000 price.

If you're not thrilled about hiring a mover but don't want to do it yourself, consider renting a truck and doing the driving, but hiring someone to pack and load and unload your belongings.

If you're moving to a new city, you can get some great help on the Web at

105

**106**

www.homefair.com. It has information on schools and the cost of living in most cities. And if you enter the date of your move, it will create a dated checklist of things you should do several weeks before moving day.

## TIPS ON MOVING

- Check to make sure the mover you pick is a member of the American Moving and Storage Association, and not a fake mover out to steal your belongings.

- Get a binding estimate in advance from the mover specifying the cost of your move.

- Buy replacement-value insurance on your possessions, in case something breaks during the move.

- When the mover drops off your furniture at your new residence, do not sign the release form until you've examined your furniture piece by piece.

- Before you choose a moving company, get a clear understanding from the mover what happens if something is broken that you've packed yourself.

- In your contract, require the mover to pay a penalty if he doesn't deliver your belongings on or before a specific date.

- The best way to protect crystal, china, and any other extremely valuable and delicate possessions is to move them yourself in your own car.

- If you want to risk your back and move yourself, be careful about what packing materials you buy for the move. You'll generally do better renting the truck from the rental company and buying your boxes and other materials somewhere else.

- To save money on truck rentals, move during mid-month or during the week.

## INTERNET

www.moving.org (American Moving and Storage Association)
www.homefair.com (To get information on your new city, including salaries and schools. You can also create a checklist of things to do before moving day.)
www.virtualrelocation.com (Relocation tools and information)
www.moversresource.com (Moving information)

# HOME SECURITY SYSTEMS

Many people buy a home security system after suffering a break-in or seeing a crime story on the news. So they're not in the best state of mind to buy a burglar alarm. That makes them easy prey for aggressive salespeople.

Regardless of the reason you might want a burglar alarm, it's important to divorce yourself emotionally from the decision so you can shop wisely. The first thing to do is make a drawing of your home, or a checklist, and figure out how many doors and windows you need to protect.

Next, call your insurance agent and ask what discounts are available on your homeowners insurance and what requirements a security system must meet for you to qualify. Generally you'll have to get a system that's monitored by an outside service, not just a noisemaker alarm that is intended to frighten the burglar into fleeing. There may be other requirements for you to get the insurance discount.

Always get smoke and fire monitoring as part of the system. People get a security system in their home because they fear an intruder, but the bigger danger is the potential for fire. Usually it costs just a little more to get fire protection.

After you complete your list and talk to your agent, call burglar alarm companies for tentative quotes. Don't consider any company that won't give

you a quote on the telephone and instead wants to send a salesperson to your home to give you an estimate. That's a strategy they use to close a deal. They know if the salesperson is in your home, the odds are greater that you'll agree to buy an alarm from their company, regardless of whether it's the best buy. So get at least six quotes and then decide who may come to your house.

Many companies will offer supposedly fantastic lease deals, but I don't advise you to lease a burglar alarm. If you need the security of an alarm system, you're going to want it for the long term and not for the length of a short lease. A burglar alarm can also be a confidence builder for a buyer when it's time to sell your house.

The next trap to watch out for is the monthly monitoring cost. Some companies will quote a very low price on the equipment and its installation and then have an extremely high monthly monitoring fee. Paying $17.95 a month for monitoring instead of $22.95 may not seem like much, but it will save you $120 over two years. That's why it's very important to find a good price for monitoring and often less important how much you pay for the security system itself. For a truer comparison of quotes, figure the total cost of the system and monitoring for two or three years.

It's become common for companies

107

**108**

to try to get you to sign a five-year deal for monitoring service. They may low-ball the initial cost of the system, then make it up with an incredibly expensive, long-term monitoring deal. Don't sign any contract for monitoring that's longer than one year. Or make sure you have an escape clause that will allow you to terminate the agreement. Forget the cost. If a company's doing a lousy job, you're handcuffed to it and that may put your life in danger. A security company should prove itself to you month after month, and you should want to remain with them because they're good, not because they've forced you to do so.

The company I use guarantees a monthly monitoring charge of $16 as long as I maintain the service. And the owner has made a lot of money by providing good service at a very fair price.

Sometimes the price quote you get over the phone disappears when a salesperson comes to your house. If that happens, don't give in. Try the next bidder or call around for more quotes. I've seen some terrible abuses in the sale of home security systems, mostly from companies trying to justify an unusually high price by claiming their system is far superior to others. Some of my callers have paid as much as $4,000 for a security system that should have cost well below $1,000. By getting multiple quotes and comparison shopping, you'll get an accurate reading of a fair price.

Technology changes. The burglar alarm systems I bought 10 years ago are much less sophisticated than the one I put in three years ago. But I don't buy state-of-the-art technology. I buy current technology. That's a very important distinction. The latest, greatest gadget may be unproven and usually is overpriced. With current technology, competition has reduced the price and time has allowed the system to prove its reliability.

There's no specific technology you need to buy. You'll want monitoring, smoke and fire detection, some form of perimeter security to protect the entrances to your house, and some form of motion sensor. Actually, the motion sensor is usually a heat-sensing device so the alarm isn't set off by some object falling in your home.

The latest technological improvement in security systems is the use of increasingly inexpensive digital cameras. When the alarm in your house goes off, the monitoring service can actually look to see if there is a real trigger, or if the alarm is a false one. Local police departments have been inundated with so many false alarms that burglar alarm calls have become their lowest priority. In a few cities, police will not respond until the presence of an intruder has been confirmed by digital camera, or the alarm company itself has dispatched its own patrol car to the scene to verify the break-in.

For privacy reasons, you can restrict the use of digital cameras to the more public areas of your home.

## TIPS ON HOME SECURITY SYSTEMS

- Even if you've recently had a break-in, try to stay calm when you buy a burglar alarm so you can shop wisely.

- The first thing to do is make a drawing of your home, or a checklist, and figure out how many doors and windows you need to protect.

- Call your insurance agent and ask what discounts are available on your homeowners insurance and what requirements a security system must meet for you to qualify.

- Always get monitoring for smoke and fire as part of the system.

 **109**

- After you complete your list and talk to your agent, call burglar alarm companies for tentative quotes. Don't consider any company that won't give you a quote on the telephone. I also don't advise you to lease a burglar alarm.

- Watch out for the monthly monitoring cost. Some companies will quote a very low price on the equipment and its installation and then have an extremely high monthly monitoring fee.

- Don't sign a monitoring contract for more than one year.

# REFINANCING

When mortgage interest rates fall, homeowners start to think about refinancing. Very simply, refinancing means taking out a new mortgage with a lower interest rate to pay off your existing mortgage. Through refinancing, homeowners can often cut their monthly payments, shorten their loan term, or combine a home equity loan and a mortgage into one lower payment.

Because it can be expensive to refinance, you can wind up paying more than you'll save. Let's say it would cost $3,000 to refinance and you plan to sell your house in three years. That means you'd have to lower your monthly payments by at least $84 to make refinancing worthwhile. Just figure the savings per month at the lower interest rate, multiply by the number of months you expect to stay in the house, and compare the savings to the cost of refinancing.

On the other hand, the savings from refinancing can be substantial. The monthly payment on a $120,000 loan at 9 percent interest is $966, while

**110**

the same loan at 7.5 percent costs $839 a month. Experts long had recommended that you refinance if current mortgage rates are 2 percentage points lower than your mortgage and you plan to stay in the house a while. So if you have a 9 percent mortgage and the current rate is 7 percent, you would be wise to refinance.

But an innovation in refinancing has changed the rules completely. If you're not sure you're going to be in your house long enough to recoup the costs of refinancing, you can choose a low- or no-cost refinance, and start saving money right away. With a typical low-cost refinance, you'll get an interest rate 5/8 of a point higher than the market rate for a traditional refinance. So if the market rate for a 30-year loan is 7 percent, the rate for a low-cost refinance will be 7.625 percent. If you have an 8.25 percent or 8.5 percent mortgage, it's a no-brainer. You'll save from the first monthly check you write.

The Web site that I like best for mortgage loans is www.iown.com. You fill in your state, the amount you're borrowing and whether it's for a new home or a refinance, and it gives you current rates. You can tell it to give you only loans with no closing costs, and it will show you loans from different lenders that require minimal out-of-pocket costs. Some people prefer loans with no closing costs. Others prefer loans with no discount points (a discount point is 1 percent of the loan amount) or loan origination fees (0/0),

also called "at-par" quotes. Online, it's very easy to compare apples to apples.

Most big-city newspapers list mortgage rates in the Sunday paper, but they're confusing and of little use. You can't figure out who has the best deal, because each lender lists a different combination of fees and points.

You can shop online just to compare rates, or you can actually apply for a loan. It's up to you. At the very least, it's a great source for information, and you can take the online quote to a local lender and see if it will match the online offer. The Internet gives you the ability to comparison shop for a mortgage for the first time.

Refinancing in the traditional manner can be worthwhile if you plan on staying in the house for a long time, or if the new mortgage has a shorter loan term. Let's say you have a 30-year mortgage at 8.5 percent and you can go to a 15-year mortgage at 7 percent. That 1.5-point difference may be enough to justify the cost of a refinance if you plan on staying in the home for several years.

If you're really sure you're going to be in a house for a number of years, you can get a lower loan rate by taking a loan with a discount point or two. If you borrow $100,000 with two discount points, you'll pay a $2,000 fee at closing. If the lower loan rate allows you to make back that $2,000 fee in 36 months or less, that strategy is worth considering.

Before you decide to refinance, think about how long you want to remain in the house and what length loan you want. If you have a 30-year mortgage with 26 years left, you do yourself a disservice refinancing into a new 30-year mortgage, because you're adding four years to the amount of time you'll be in debt. Approximately half of all people who refinance choose a shorter term for their new loan, and that's usually a smart decision.

Refinancing may make sense even if you don't plan to stay in the house a very long time. If you have a fixed-rate mortgage that has a moderate or high interest rate, it could be worthwhile to refinance if you could cut your monthly payments sharply by refinancing into an adjustable rate mortgage.

Be careful with an adjustable rate mortgage Studies have shown that ARMs almost always are a better deal than fixed-rate mortgages, but you trade peace of mind for savings when you take an ARM. I've purchased homes in recent years knowing intellectually I would have been better off with an ARM, but I couldn't jump that psychological hurdle. I went for the sure thing and picked a fixed-rate mortgage, because fixed-rate mortgages were the lowest they had been in decades. But the sure thing and that peace of mind cost me money.

The danger with an ARM is the possibility that the interest rate can rise, often as much as 6 points over the lifetime of the loan. If it does, your monthly payment can soar. A fixed rate doesn't change, even in a period of high inflation and high interest rates. A good compromise is to get an ARM with a conversion feature, which gives you the right to convert to a fixed rate during the loan for a modest fee — usually less than $500.

If you have an FHA loan, you may be eligible for a "streamline" refinance, which is a no-cost refinance that gets you a slightly above-market rate of interest. Streamlines are good only if you don't change the amount left to be paid. Unfortunately, a number of groups are ripping people off on streamlines and significantly increasing the loan balance. The victims don't realize until after they've signed the loan documents that their loan balance has gone up significantly, even as their interest rate and monthly payments drop. Beware of direct-mail solicitations offering a no-cost streamline refinance on your FHA loan.

Another mortgage option that's become increasingly popular is the 5/1 or 7/1 hybrid mortgages. In these loans, you get the fixed rate for five or seven years at a lower rate than a 30-year fixed-rate mortgage, and then it becomes a one-year adjustable rate loan. Most people who get these loans do so because they expect to move within five or seven years, sell the house, and pay off the mortgage. Even if you're not planning to move, a 5/1 or 7/1 is a good choice if rates are higher than they have been recently. You get a lower rate with the 5/1 or 7/1 mortgage, and if mortgage rates fall, refinance into

111

**112**  a fixed-rate loan. It's worth the gamble if you can get a rate that's 0.75 points lower than the current fixed rate.

There are now endless variations in loans, from 10-year fixed mortgages to 3/1 fixed/adjustable combinations. I bought my current house with a 3/1 mortgage, because I thought interest rates were relatively high when I bought it, yet I didn't want to be faced with a two-point increase from an ARM in just a year. When rates dropped in the next year, I refinanced.

It's very important with a refinance to insist on a good-faith estimate of the costs up-front, before you give the lender a penny. If you don't, you shift all the power to the lender and take unnecessary chances. You may find that a refinance doesn't make sense for you. If you find out too late, you could lose any money you've paid toward the refinancing costs. Another protection you have is the option of locking in the interest rate you're offered. That protects you in case rates rise after you've agreed to refinance.

Before you refinance, get a copy of your credit report to see if there's anything on it that could foul up a refinance. You don't want to lay out the money if a credit problem is going to keep you from refinancing. Get all documentation ready for the lender immediately. You need to document your employment, income, debt, and assets. When you provide the proper documentation, give the lender a dated, signed memo showing that you have given them the needed information. Make sure to keep a copy. This is to protect you later if the lender is slow to close the loan and causes you to miss a good interest rate. Lenders often can wiggle out of a commitment they don't like because the consumer was sloppy about handing over the required documentation.

### *Clark says* TIPS ON REFINANCING

⊙ Refinancing means taking out a new mortgage with a lower interest rate to pay off your existing mortgage.

⊙ With the advent of low- and no-cost refinancing, it's no longer as important to see if you're going to stay in the house long enough to pay back the refinancing costs.

⊙ In a traditional refinance, insist on a good-faith estimate of the costs up-front, before you give the lender a penny.

⊙ Before you refinance, check your credit report for anything that could foul up a refinance. You don't want to lay out the money if a credit problem is going to keep you from refinancing.

## CONTACT

Mortgage Bankers Association of America
202-557-2700
www.mbaa.org

## INTERNET

www.quicken.com/mortgage (Quicken mortgage information)
www.countrywide.com (Countrywide Mortgage: online mortgage application)

 113

# MORTGAGE SERVICING

When you first get a mortgage, you might think you'll be doing business with the same lender for 30 years. But that's rarely the case. Mortgage lenders often sell your loan to investors as soon as the ink is dry, take a fee for originating the loan, and use the money they get from selling the loan to make another loan. A single mortgage might be owned by a dozen companies during its lifetime.

A lender has to disclose to you what percentage of its loans are sold and what percentage are kept in the lender's own portfolio. If the lender sells nearly 100 percent of its loans, you know you're dealing with a loan retailer.

Investors and lenders use mortgage servicing companies to handle the everyday business of collecting your payments, keeping track of your loan balance, and letting you know if you're late with a payment. So in addition to having several owners over its life, a loan also might be handled by several different servicing bureaus. Then there are all the bank mergers and new computer systems. All this creates a large potential for mistakes, such as unapplied payments or errors in calculating your balance.

The most important thing I can tell you about your mortgage is to keep a copy of every check you ever write for your loan. I know that sounds like overkill, but if you have a loan for five or 10 years and there's a dispute about whether a particular payment was made, your best defense is to be able to produce the canceled check. Even if you pay on a mortgage for 30 years, you write only 360 checks. That doesn't take up much room.

I also recommend very strongly that you get an amortization schedule

**114**

for your loan. That's a list of how much you owe that shows how much of each payment is applied to principal and how much to interest. You can run one at Web sites such as hsh.com and easily keep track of your loan payments and balance. I had a call recently from a woman whose loan had been sold four times, and it was a mess.

All mortgage servicers must have an 800 number you can call for customer service. I've had quite a bit of experience calling these numbers, and I find it quite distressing how long I'm left on hold before I reach a human being. When you do reach a person, make sure you get his or her full name and write it down. You'll find a page in the Workbook chapter of this book to help you document mortgage and other consumer problems. If a promise is made to you by a lender and the promise isn't kept, you'll have someone you can call back and hold accountable.

If you find yourself in a dispute with a lender about a payment or another issue, don't send correspondence to the same address you send your payment. In most cases, that will be a separate bill-processing center, and clerks there will throw your letter away. Find out from the mortgage servicer where you should send correspondence. Start by sending your letters with a regular postage stamp. But if the lender ignores the letters, start sending them by certified mail.

In many states, you can also get help by contacting the local Mortgage

Bankers Association office. This trade association has a strong interest in seeing that your complaints are dealt with properly, because if they aren't, the state or federal governments may decide to regulate mortgage lending activities. In some states, the Mortgage Bankers Association will refer you to a state government office for help.

The biggest dispute in mortgage lending is escrow practices. Escrow is the process whereby your lender collects a monthly fee from you to cover the cost of taxes and insurance on the property. The lender needs this protection, because if you were to let your homeowners insurance lapse and your home burned to the ground, the lender would lose its collateral on the loan. The same thing would happen if you failed to pay your property taxes and lost your house. While the lender has a legitimate need for escrow, many lenders have proven themselves to be extremely greedy by overcollecting escrow. In most states, lenders are not required to pay interest on escrow, creating an incentive to overcollect.

Lenders are allowed to keep in reserve an amount equal to one-sixth your annual escrow needs. Let's say your annual bill for taxes and insurance is $1,200. The lender would be able to collect $1,200 annually, plus a $200 reserve. Many lenders play fast and loose with the numbers and collect far more money each year. I believe the most effective way to solve the abuses of escrow would be to require that lenders pay interest on these accounts. If your lender ignores your requests for an accounting of how escrow totals have been determined, tell them you're going to contact your congressman. Lending institutions fear congressional action more than anything else.

To give you an idea of how complex things can get, let me tell you about a loan I originated many years ago with a small mortgage lender in Ohio. The loan servicing was handled by SunTrust Banks. The loan was sold repeatedly and moved around through a series of transactions and bank mergers and got all fouled up. After paying SunTrust every month for years, I decided to do a refinance with a bank on another property. The whole process came to a halt because, to my horror, a company known as Society Mortgage was showing me in default on my credit report. They said I hadn't made a payment in five months. I had never even heard of Society Mortgage, and I certainly didn't know they owned the loan.

It took four weeks to get this straightened out. Eventually I got an apology from Society Mortgage acknowledging that the company had been in error when it reported my loan in default. Even more maddening was the fact that Society Mortgage wasn't supposed to report my loan at all, because it was not the loan servicer. Only SunTrust Banks should have reported the loan to the credit bureau. My credit report showed the same loan with both lenders and different balances.

One of the smartest things someone can do with a mortgage is to prepay on the loan. That's a lot simpler than it sounds. All you need to do is contact your lender and ask for its prepayment procedure. Generally on your payment coupons there'll be a box for prepayment. Just fill out the box and increase the amount of your check by whatever amount you choose. Some people prefer to write a second check and write on it "prepayment of principal." Once a year, check the loan balance sent to you by the lender to make sure the payments have been applied properly. Instead of throwing several hundred dollars at your mortgage one month and nothing another month, I recommend prepaying your principal by a set amount each month. Try to pay $50 or $100 extra each month, or whatever you can afford.

It's remarkable what impact you can have on your mortgage by making prepayments. For example, if you have a 30-year, $120,000 loan at 8 percent interest, adding $50 a month to your $881 payment would cut five years off the length of the loan and save you nearly $42,000 in interest over the life of the loan. Prepaying by $100 per month would cut nearly nine years off the loan and reduce the total interest paid by more than $67,000.

There are a number of Web sites with mortgage calculators that will show you how much you can save by prepaying your mortgage each month. Just plug in your loan balance, interest

115

**116**

rate, and an amount you can afford to prepay, and it will show you the savings. One of my favorites is hsh.com. Its mortgage calculators are very easy to use.

Be aware of a terrible deal that you'll be offered in the mail by your mortgage lender. The typical plan costs $300 to $500. You pay half your regular mortgage payment every two weeks, which for the full year would amount to 26 half-payments, the equivalent of 13 regular monthly payments. These organizations forward a regular payment to the bank at the end of each month, then add a 13th payment at the end of the year. Since you can do this yourself, there's no reason to pay a big fee to your mortgage company. Just take your mortgage payment, divide it by 12, and add that amount to your regular payment each month. You'll be making one additional monthly payment each year. If you do that early in a loan, it will cut seven to eight years off the length of a 30-year loan. They charge $300 to $500 for administering a prepayment system you can do better by yourself.

Although the pitch comes from your mortgage company, the company typically turns the operation of the plan over to a third party, and that's a problem. What happens if the company you're paying doesn't forward the payment to your lender, or doesn't pay on time? You could lose your money or suffer penalties. Finally, they're holding your money during the year and earn-

ing interest. If you prepay, those dollars should benefit you immediately, not up to a year later.

Some financial planners believe it's foolish to prepay on a loan, that you're better off putting the money in the stock market or some other investment. But most of us will spend the money rather than invest it. Prepayment of principal is a very clever method of forced savings and truly an investment in your future, because you reduce the length of your loan and the amount of money you pay on it.

Some people are trimming the length of their mortgage at the start, rather than after the fact. A few are doing 15-year mortgages. For many of us, that's not practical. If you can't swing a 15-year mortgage, look at a 20-year loan. While a 15-year loan may represent a significantly higher monthly payment than a 30-year loan, a 20-year loan represents only a marginally higher payment per month, and it dramatically decreases the amount of money you would pay over the life of the loan. For example, a 30-year, $120,000 loan at 7.5 percent carries a monthly payment of $839. You get a lower interest rate for a shorter term, so you could borrow the same amount on a 15-year loan at 7 percent, with a monthly payment of $1,078. That $239 difference may be too much for many people to try the 15-year loan. But a 20-year loan on the same amount, at 7 percent, would be $930 a month, just $91 more than for the 30-year loan. By choosing a 20-year term instead of a 30-year term on this loan, you'd pay $103,286 in total interest instead of $182,061. A 15- or 20-year term lets you pay off the loan quicker, with a lower rate of interest and a lower total cost.

## PRIVATE MORTGAGE INSURANCE

Another way you can save money on your mortgage is to get rid of private mortgage insurance, which you had to pay if you bought your home with a down payment of less than 20 percent. If you have a conventional loan (not FHA or VA), you were required to buy PMI, which protects the lender against the higher risk that you will default on your loan. PMI is very expensive, adding an average of $150 a month to your mortgage payment.

You can avoid paying PMI if you can come up with a 10 percent down payment. You take a first mortgage for 80 percent of the amount you're borrowing, pay 10 percent down, and cover the other 10 percent in a second mortgage. Even though the second mortgage carries a higher interest rate, the amount of money is small, and you end up paying significantly less per month with the two mortgages than if you had to pay PMI. And the interest on the second mortgage is tax deductible. PMI premiums are not.

Let's say you're buying a $150,000 house, and you borrow $135,000 at 8

percent. Including principal and interest and mortgage insurance, you might pay $1,048 a month. But if you take out a $120,000 first mortgage at 8 percent and a $15,000 second mortgage at 10 percent, you can avoid paying private mortgage insurance. Your total principal and interest payments for the two mortgages would be $1,012. So you save $36 a month by avoiding PMI, more after taxes.

If you take out a new mortgage now, you're covered by a new federal law that requires your lender to remove private mortgage insurance automatically once you've paid off 22 percent of your loan balance. With a traditional 30-year loan, that happens about year 15. Many lenders are honoring the law on existing loans, but they aren't required to do so.

The other way to dump PMI is to ask the lender. Many will agree to drop PMI when the value of your home increases, or you have paid enough on your loan that your equity in the house exceeds 20 percent (the amount you owe is less than 80 percent of your home's market value). When you believe you have enough equity, contact your lender and ask what their procedure is for getting rid of PMI. Normally, the lender will require you to pay for an appraisal of your home's value, and that you send your request to them with the appraisal. Getting rid of PMI can save you a lot of money, but don't get an appraisal unless you're confident you will be able to get rid of PMI.

117

**118**

If you have an FHA loan, you have something similar to PMI called MIP, Mortgage Insurance Premium. It's a federal program under which borrowers who make their mortgage payments effectively subsidize those who do not. If you have an FHA loan, you must pay MIP for the life of the loan, regardless of how much equity you have. If rates justify it, you could get rid of MIP by refinancing.

### TIPS ON MORTGAGE SERVICING

- Mortgages typically have many different owners over the years and many different servicing bureaus, so it's not difficult for a mixup to occur over your loan balance. To protect yourself, keep a copy of every check you ever write for your loan.

- If you call a mortgage servicing bureau about your loan, make sure you get the full name of the person with whom you speak.

- If you find yourself in a dispute with a lender about a payment or another issue, don't send correspondence to the same address you send your payment.

- Keep an eye on how much money your bank collects to cover your annual property taxes and insurance. Lenders are allowed to collect your annual escrow needs plus one-sixth this figure, but many overcollect.

- One of the smartest things someone can do with a mortgage is to prepay on the loan. All you need to do is contact your lender and ask for its prepayment procedure. Then, once a year, check the loan balance the lender sends you to make sure the additional payments have been applied properly.

- Fee-based plans that charge $300 to $500 for administering a prepayment system are a bad idea; you can do it better and cheaper by yourself.

- If you reach 20 percent equity in your home, you can save a substantial amount of money by asking your lender to drop private mortgage insurance.

### INTERNET

www.quicken.com/mortgage/(Quicken mortgage information)
www.countrywide.com (Countrywide Mortgage: online mortgage application)
www.mortgage.com
www.e-loan.com
www.iown.com
www.hsh.com

# BEING A LANDLORD

Many people end up being a landlord because they have a condominium or a house they can't sell. Because they go into renting property reluctantly, it's easy for them to get frustrated.

If you rent property, manage it as a business. First, set a rent that's fair for your market, not one that's based on your mortgage payment. People aren't going to rent your house or condo for $950 a month if they could rent something similar for $850, even if $950 or $1,000 is your mortgage payment. By the same token, if your mortgage payment is $600 and the market rent is $850, don't set your rent too low.

As prospective tenants come through your property, require those who are interested to fill out an application. Get a standard financial application from an office supply store or bookstore. If you have friends at an apartment complex, ask if you can see one of theirs. You need to check a potential tenant's historical record. Does the person move constantly? Are there gaps in employment? You're entering into a financial partnership with your tenant, and you need to know if he or she will honor an obligation to you. Ask potential tenants to provide a copy of their credit report, so you can see if they've behaved responsibly in their other financial relationships. If someone has a lot of debt or a recent bankruptcy, you may prefer a different tenant.

Choosing the wrong tenant can be a big mistake. I know of one case in which a landlord was left with a huge bill because a tenant failed to report a water leak. Under the lease, it was the tenant's responsibility to pay the water bill. But the tenant moved out without paying the bill and without telling the landlord about the water leak. The damage to the property was significant, but the leak also increased water usage. The water bill itself cost the landlord more than $1,000.

If a prospective tenant passes your screening test, set a realistic security deposit, but don't make it exactly the same as a month's rent. Make it a little higher or a little lower, so the tenant doesn't interpret it as in lieu of the last month's rent on a lease. Get a standard lease and then include any special protections that are particularly important to you.

For landlords with just one or two properties, I strongly recommend you include a repair clause that makes the tenant responsible for the first $50 cost of any repair. Tenants who used to live in apartment complexes are conditioned to calling the management office to fix any problem. That's expensive for you because unlike those complexes, you don't have a maintenance person on staff. You have to hire a contractor to do the work. Many little problems

119

**120**

could be fixed by the tenant with a $3 part from a hardware store, but might cost you $100 to have someone come in to make the repair. If you have a repair clause, you may have to charge a little less in rent. But reducing the hassle and irritation for you makes that worth it. I've done this with a condo I rent out, and it virtually stopped maintenance calls from my tenants. When they know they're paying the first $50, they don't bother me.

Another thing you should do is discount rent for early payment. You give somebody a discount, say $25 or $50, if the rent is paid prior to the first of the month. This is very important for landlords who are new to the business, since most tend to be very slack about collecting overdue rent. The penalties and the process for eviction are such a pain that you're much better off giving the tenant an incentive to get the money in early. I give tenants a $50 discount for paying prior to the first of the month. If they pay after the fifth of the month, not only do they lose the discount, but they have to pay a $50 late penalty. I started doing this a few years ago and it changed everything. I used to get rent checks on the 10th or 12th of the month. Now they always pay. No more problems.

Do a move-in inspection and move-out inspection of the property to protect yourself in case you have to keep part or all of the security deposit to cover damage. Be clear up-front what condition you expect the unit to be in when the tenant moves out.

If your tenants do not pay the rent, be prepared to evict them. Don't accept excuses. Don't be softhearted, because you're being walked on if you allow them to occupy a rental unit for free. To evict tenants in most states, you have to send them a letter demanding they pay the rent or turn over the premises. If they don't do either, you can't just go in and set their stuff out on the street. You must go to the county courthouse and begin an eviction action, and the clerk of the court will help you. The tenants will be served with an eviction notice and normally will have five to seven days to answer. If they answer and give a reason why they're not paying, a hearing before a judge will give each party a chance to explain their side. In most cases, the tenants never answer, so the court authorizes the eviction. Then the county marshal or sheriff will go to the property with you, or with people you hire, permit you to enter the premises, and put the tenants' possessions on the street.

If you are speedy about an eviction, you can have it done within 30 days. Some landlords let tenants slide for months. Others start eviction proceedings by the fifth of the month if they don't have the money. Do what you are comfortable with. If you've requested the money twice and don't have it by the middle of the month, I recommend you start the eviction process.

If you're relocating far away from your property, don't try to manage it by remote control. If you do, you're asking for trouble. Instead, ask a friend or relative to handle the rental of the property, in return for some compensation. Don't ask for it as a favor.

Professional management is another option for people who are relocating out of state or who don't want to be landlords. Many real estate companies have divisions that will manage a property for you. The typical fee for a rental management firm is half the first month's rent and a 10 percent commission each month. So the fee for an $800 condo would be $400 up-front and $80 a month. That's well worth it if you're in Chicago and the house is in St. Louis. Rates may vary in your community.

Examine closely the agreement with the rental management company to see if you're protected if the company fails to do a good job collecting rent or securing tenants. And keep an eye on the quality of tenants the management company chooses. The company may not be as careful as you would be.

 **121**

### TIPS ON BEING A LANDLORD

⊙ If you rent property, manage it as if it were a business. Set a rent that's fair for your market, not one that's based on your mortgage payment.

⊙ Require prospective tenants to fill out an application, and ask them to supply a copy of their credit report.

⊙ Make the security deposit a little higher or lower, but not the same as, a month's rent.

⊙ For landlords with just one or two properties, include a repair clause that makes the tenant responsible for the first $50 cost of any repair. To do this, you may have to charge a little less in rent.

⊙ Provide a $25 or $50 discount for early rent payment.

⊙ Do a move-in inspection and move-out inspection of the property to protect yourself in case you have to keep part or all of the security deposit to cover damage.

⊙ If your tenants do not pay the rent, be prepared to evict them.

⊙ If you're relocating far away from your property, ask a friend or relative to handle the rental, in return for some compensation, or consider professional management.

## CONTACT

The clerk of the court in your county

# 122 🏠 BEING A TENANT

The biggest mistake people make when hunting for an apartment is not asking enough questions. Before you write a check for an application fee or a deposit, get the specifics on the basics, including the length of the lease, the amount of rent, and the amount of deposit. If you have a pet, find out about the pet deposit. If you have any special needs, make sure they are met before you hand over any money or make any agreement to rent the apartment.

A lot of apartments now are adding separate charges for water, telephone, and cable television service, in addition to the monthly rent. Water used to be routinely included in the rent, and renters bought cable and telephone service from the local providers. But many landlords are making tenants buy these services from them, sometimes at higher prices. It's an extra revenue stream for the apartment complex.

Cable service from your apartment complex may be more expensive or offer fewer choices, and the worst complaints I'm hearing now about cable are from people using apartment-managed systems. But Congress has given apartment renters the right to have satellite dishes, so you have that option if the apartment has a clear view of the southern sky.

Some landlords are offering telephone service, and this service actually may be a better deal than you would get from the traditional local phone company. It's possible the landlord may offer high-speed connections to the Internet, which may not be available to residents of the surrounding neighborhood.

Unfortunately, I'm hearing horror stories from renters about massive bills for water service. Landlords may install individual water meters at each apartment, or they may take their total water bill and divide it by the number of apartments. But there's no limit under the law to what they may charge. One caller told me he had a monthly water bill of more than $250. There's no way someone in a one- or two-bedroom apartment could use that much water. So it's just price gouging.

You have to be careful what your lease says about water service. If water isn't billed separately when you move in and your lease doesn't say that water is included, management could switch to individual unit billing at any time and bill you whatever they want. Here's what you should do to protect yourself: If the lease is silent on water service, add a line to it saying water is included; if the lease breaks water out as a separate charge, make sure it specifies that water is to be billed at the prevailing rate in the community.

Never sign an apartment lease on the spot. Take it home with you and read it. If you don't understand something, put question marks next to the item and get an explanation.

But don't pay an application fee or deposit before you take the contract home to review it. In most states, if you pay a deposit or application fee and decide not to rent the apartment, you forfeit the money you've paid. The feeling is the landlord may have taken an apartment off the market while you're considering it. If you do pay a deposit so that you don't lose the apartment you want, just be aware that you probably won't get your deposit back if you change your mind.

Always add a clause to an apartment lease giving you the right to terminate the contract before its normal expiration if your circumstances change. You should have the right to terminate early, by paying a fee of perhaps one month's rent, because of a job transfer or if you decide to relocate to another city. In return for a greater fee, perhaps two months' rent, your lease should permit you to terminate for any reason.

It's important to have early termination rights to avoid a potentially huge penalty. In most states, if you leave an apartment before the end of the lease, you remain responsible for the rent for as many months as it takes the landlord to re-rent the property. If you're three months into a one-year lease, you could be on the hook for nine months' worth of rent. You need this protection even if your intent is to stay the full year, because circumstances change and you should be prepared.

Most states have their own rules for people who occupy an apartment without a lease. Usually, the state has the equivalent of its own lease that governs these "tenant-at-will" cases. Generally under these rules, you can terminate at any time by giving the landlord 30 days' written notice. The landlord can raise the rent at any time, or demand the premises back, by giving you 30 or 60 days' written notice.

Many leases renew automatically unless you notify the landlord that you are leaving. Let's say you sign a year's lease that ends March 31. In many cases, you'll have to notify the landlord in writing by March 1, or pay rent for April. Sometimes the lease will renew for another 12 months.

In most cases, your landlord will conduct a move-in inspection before you move into an apartment. Make sure to be present for it, and note everything you can find wrong with the apartment. Whatever you don't note will be held against you at the time you move out.

At the end of the lease, there will be a move-out inspection. Be present for that as well, so you can dispute anything the landlord says that isn't valid. This is vital in order for you to get back your security deposit. In fairness, the landlord may notice something you didn't. Maybe the bathroom isn't terribly clean and the landlord wants to bring in a cleaning crew. If you're present at the inspection, you can offer to clean it.

Before you sign, ask what condition

123

the landlord expects the apartment to be in when you move out. That should be pretty revealing. If he hems and haws, you might have trouble getting back your security deposit. Some landlords, due to cash-flow problems, look for any excuse to keep your security deposit. Others use it only for a legitimate purpose.

If a landlord doesn't give you back a security deposit, you have specific rights, which vary by state, to go after him. In many states, you have the right to sue for two or three times the amount of the security deposit. Act quickly. If you don't have the deposit within 30 days of when you move out, send the landlord a letter demanding your security deposit. If you don't receive it within 10 more days, sue the landlord in small claims court. Usually in these cases, the landlord will dispute the condition of the unit. If you have any reason to suspect the landlord is going to try to cheat you on the security deposit, take pictures that prove the apartment is in good condition. A roll of film costs just a few dollars. You don't even have to get the film developed if you get the security deposit back. If you want to prove you shot the pictures after you moved out, rather than when you moved in, photograph the front page of the local newspaper early on the roll of film.

Some people like the idea of renting a condominium or a house, rather than a unit at an apartment complex, because they prefer a true residential neighborhood to a transient one. The drawback to renting from a nonprofessional owner is that management tends to be haphazard and inattentive. Maintenance requests go unanswered more often with a nonprofessional landlord. The biggest risk is the possibility the property owner will be foreclosed upon for nonpayment of the mortgage. In many states, if that happens, you can be evicted on very short notice. Another danger with a private owner, condominium, or house is not being able to live there year after year. A private owner could sell it and not renew your lease. An apartment complex is always going to be there.

Safety is an important issue for many renters. If you're considering a particular apartment complex, ask the apartment management company what security measures they have on site and if there have been any incidents of break-ins or violent crimes. In many states, they must tell you. It's also good to visit the property on a Saturday or Sunday afternoon, tell people who live there that you're thinking of moving in, and ask them if they feel safe living there. Ask them also if their car or apartment has ever been broken into, or if they've heard of any violent crimes or break-ins in the complex.

Noisy neighbors are another common headache. If a neighbor is making your life miserable, try a friendly talk with him. If the neighbor doesn't respond, go to your apartment manager for help. If she doesn't do anything to solve the problem, call the police each time the noise level rises and have the neighbor cited for disturbing the peace. You have a right to live in peace and quiet.

On the other hand, people need to have some tolerance of normal noise levels. One of my callers moved into an apartment with her family and quickly learned that the people living beneath her thought her children were too noisy, even though she didn't think so. The neighbors kept complaining to management and banging on the ceiling with a broom handle, even though the noise wasn't out of the ordinary. The apartment complex eventually asked her to move to a different apartment in the complex. Because she had a lease, she didn't have to move. I recommended that she move only if she wanted to, and only if the apartment complex paid all her moving expenses, including the fees to reconnect the telephone and utilities.

Perhaps the most common complaint I hear from renters is slow or inadequate response on maintenance requests. I strongly recommend that you show some faith in your landlord. But as soon as your landlord fails to serve you, start documenting every maintenance request. If the landlord ignores your written requests, write "Request No. 2" and "Request No. 3" on subsequent letters, to reaffirm that you're having a continuing problem. If the landlord still ignores your requests, you may have to take the more drastic step of paying for the repair yourself and deducting it from your next month's rent. Do this only when the breakdown makes the apartment unlivable, such as for a burst pipe or a non-working stove, refrigerator, or major appliance. Keep the repair receipt and enclose a copy of it with the rent check.

Your explicit rights to repair and deduct vary by state, but there's an implicit right for you to have a livable dwelling.

**125**

Let's say your water heater explodes, and your landlord won't do anything about it. Hit the landlord with a written notice and let him know that, if it's not replaced within 24 hours, you will use the right of repair-and-deduct. One thing you cannot do is completely withhold rent because you don't like something. That will get you evicted.

Some landlords can be extremely gracious in major repair situations. A friend of mine had a case a few years ago in which an upstairs neighbor inadvertently set off the sprinkler system, saturating his living room ceiling with water and causing the sheetrock to cave in. The apartment complex agreed to put him and his family in a hotel for four days while repairs were made, and they returned to find a bottle of champagne waiting in the apartment.

My friend's possessions weren't damaged, because there was enough time to cover the furniture with a tarpaulin. But that's a risk too many renters ignore. The landlord is almost never responsible for damage to your possessions, even from a

**126**

burst pipe, unless you can prove gross negligence, which isn't easy. You thus need renter's insurance to protect against theft and damage. It's not that expensive, about $15 a month, and it will keep you from being wiped out. A few years ago, a friend of a friend lost all her possessions in a fire and had no insurance. She lived above a store, and when the store caught fire, her apartment and all her possessions were destroyed. Losing photos and irreplaceable items was a given, but she was left with no clothes, except what she was wearing, and no furniture. It was terribly sad and unnecessary.

Your landlord should provide you with smoke detectors, although they are not required in many states. If the landlord doesn't, buy them yourself. Most now come with 10-year lithium batteries, eliminating the need to replace the battery every year. Most deaths in fires occur when the smoke detector doesn't work, often because the battery was dead. With a 10-year battery, there's far less chance that will happen. In a multi-unit dwelling, there's a greater chance of fire than in a house, and smoke detectors are even more critical.

As I discuss in the chapter on credit problems, your mortgage or rent is the first and most important bill for you to pay, because eviction is a real danger. The eviction process is pretty standard in most states, although specific details vary. Some cities even have their own landlord/tenant laws. If you fear you may be evicted, check with the clerk of the court in your county to find out how the

process works specifically in your area.

In most states, a notice will be delivered to you or tacked onto your door informing you of the eviction proceeding. You'll have a short time, approximately five to seven days, to pay the rent or explain why you should be allowed to remain. If you don't pay and don't respond, you'll have little chance to stay in the apartment or house. But even if you do appear in court, don't expect the judge to be very sympathetic to a sad story. Landlords are not charities, and you have no right to live somewhere if you don't pay the rent.

Normally it takes about 30 days from the day the landlord begins the eviction action until the sheriff puts you out of the residence. If you know you're going to be evicted, try to make some arrangements to move your possessions, either to a friend's house or into storage. A small, self-storage rental unit will give you a place to keep your things until you find a place to live. If your stuff is put out on the street, it could be stolen or ruined by foul weather.

Some people rent storage units just to have a place to keep all their extra stuff. The number of storage units around the country has exploded. If you rent a unit, it's important to understand the rights you have and those you don't. Sometimes these units are in poor neighborhoods or low-lying areas, and your possessions can be ruined in so many ways. I spoke with a fellow whose storage facility was invaded by rats, which literally ate his possessions — including clothing and furniture.

If you rent a storage unit, make sure you purchase insurance to protect your property from theft, flooding, or other damage. Check with the agent for your homeowners or renters' insurance policy to see if your policy includes coverage for a storage unit, or buy coverage from the storage facility.

Don't fall behind on rent to a storage facility, or you could very quickly lose rights to your property. If you move often, you may not remember to tell the facility your forwarding address. Then, if you don't get the bill, you may forget you haven't paid it. Next thing you know, your unit is being rented by someone else and your stuff is gone.

 **127**

## TIPS ON BEING A TENANT

- Before you write a check for an application fee or a deposit on an apartment, ask about the length of the lease, the amount of rent, and the amount of deposit.

- Make sure the lease specifies that water service is included, or that it is billed at the prevailing rate in the community.

- Never sign an apartment lease on the spot. Take it home with you and read it. If you don't understand something, put question marks next to the item and get an explanation.

- If you pay a deposit or an application fee for an apartment and decide not to rent the apartment, you probably will lose the money.

- Always add a clause to an apartment lease giving you the right to terminate the contract before its normal expiration if your circumstances change.

- Many leases renew automatically unless you notify the landlord that you are leaving.

- Make sure to be present for the move-in inspection, and note everything you can find wrong with the apartment. Be present for the move-out inspection, too.

- If a landlord doesn't give you back a security deposit, you have the right to sue in small claims court.

- Renting from a private owner is fine, but be aware of the danger of not being able to renew your lease, or of the owner being foreclosed upon.

- If your landlord fails to respond to maintenance requests, send written requests. If a landlord doesn't respond to a breakdown that makes the apartment unlivable, consider paying for the repair yourself and deducting the amount from your next month's rent.

**128** 🏠

● If you know you're going to be evicted, try to make some arrangements to move your possessions, either to a friend's house or into storage.

## CONTACT

The clerk of the court in your county

# INSURANCE

**Insurance is** one of life's obligations. None of us wants to have insurance for anything, but we buy it because it's necessary. Because of our reluctance to deal with insurance, we tend to buy it hurriedly. We buy too little of some insurance and too much of other kinds. This chapter is designed to guide you painlessly through the things you need to know about insurance.

One piece of advice applies to all your insurance problems. Most states have a consumer help line in the insurance department to provide assistance. These folks are overwhelmed with calls, so get the name of the person you speak with and follow up with her so you're not forgotten. They're busy, but with a little effort they can get results. When dealing with an insurance claim of any kind, keep every letter and document, every phone call and promise that the insurer makes.

LIFE INSURANCE

DISABILITY INSURANCE

HEALTH INSURANCE

CAR INSURANCE

HOMEOWNERS INSURANCE

# 130 ⊚ LIFE INSURANCE

Few people like the idea of buying or even thinking about life insurance. But many of us need to have life insurance to protect our loved ones from financial chaos in the event we die unexpectedly.

Consider your own situation to see if life insurance makes sense for you, how much you need, and which type of life insurance would be best.

If your family would be unable to make the mortgage payments without your income, you need life insurance. But if you're single or married with no children, you might not. Some married people without children don't buy life insurance, believing their spouse could make due without their income. That's really a personal family decision.

I've seen a lot of formulas to determine how much life insurance to buy, but none supplies a definitive answer. My rule of thumb is to buy insurance equal to 10 times your annual salary, before taxes. So if you make $30,000 a year, get $300,000 of life insurance, to replace your income for 10 years. If both spouses work, both should have life insurance to replace their own income. If either works at home, consider insurance to cover the cost of child care if the homemaker dies. Don't buy insurance on your children. A three-year-old doesn't earn a salary, so there's no need to replace his income.

Insurance agents sometimes talk about life insurance as a one-size-fits-all

investment. In their eyes, it's a way to invest and save for the future, pay for retirement, pay for a child's college education, beat the tax man, and by the way, help your survivors financially in the event of your death. You should focus on the purpose of life insurance, which is to provide for your family if you die.

Insurance products have become incredibly complex. That complexity makes them hard for consumers to understand and leads to abuses. I had a call from someone who had been sold a policy 15 years earlier called a "vanishing-premium variable universal life policy." That's pretty complicated just to say. Buyers were supposed to pay premiums for a number of years, and then the policy would magically pay for itself. It didn't work, and it's been a big scandal, with consumers losing billions of dollars. While many insurers have settled the claims involving vanishing-premium policies, most policy holders saw their money vanish instead of the premiums. The settlements were for pennies on the dollar.

The best way to buy life insurance is to get back to basics, with term life insurance. Term life is the type of life insurance that provides a payment only if you die. It's like automobile insurance in that you buy it year to year and if you stop paying, the coverage stops.

Term life is very affordable. In fact,

because of greater competition, it's as inexpensive now as it has ever been. And the Internet has made it easier than ever before to compare costs from company to company. For example, a 35-year-old nonsmoking woman could get $250,000 worth of term life for about $170 a year. The same $250,000 death benefit on a complicated whole or universal life policy would cost several thousand dollars a year.

Insurance agents don't like to talk about term life because there's very little profit in it for the agent. Agents like to sell universal life and variable universal life. Variable universal life is a product that packages mutual funds and life insurance as one. Sales people claim you get a tax benefit if you buy both together. The problem is, there are massive sales commissions and ongoing costs included that may more than wipe out any tax advantage. For most consumers, it's a bad deal.

Whole life, which used to be the most popular insurance product, builds a cash value and serves as a savings vehicle. Part of each premium payment you make is set aside and accumulates value, and eventually, it can amount to a sizable sum. But whole life premiums are high and the policies also contain high commissions.

A 25-year-old man who doesn't smoke could buy $250,000 worth of term life insurance for about $180 a year. A whole life policy with the same death benefit would cost $2,000 a year. But after 15 years, the whole life policy would build a significant cash value — probably more than he'd have if he paid $200 a year for term life and invested the $1,800-a-year difference in the premiums.

If you can afford the premiums and can dedicate yourself to making the payments for at least 15 years — no small feat — whole life is a better deal. Most of us don't fit either of those circumstances and are far better off with term life insurance.

If you decide to get term life insurance, the best way to buy is by calling an independent shopping service, or shopping with one on the Internet. There are an increasing number of Web sites, including www.quotesmith.com, that allow you to get a quote instantly. You type in your age, sex, and state, how much insurance you want to buy and whether you smoke. You get a long list of companies with the premiums.

You will have to pass a medical exam, and if you smoke or have health problems, you'll have to pay a higher rate. But you'll still get a far better deal by shopping.

I recommend you buy level-term coverage, which simply means the premium is guaranteed to stay the same for the number of years you choose, say 10, 20, or 30 years. Buy coverage based on how long you expect to work. So if you're 55, buy 10-year level term. If you're 35, buy 30-year level term. There's so much competition now in insurance that you can get a very good price and know what

131

**132** ☯ you'll be paying well into the future.

I don't recommend buying the cheapest policy, but the least expensive one with a financially stable company. Choose a company that is rated at least A+ or A++ by the A. M. Best Co., which means they are top-rated for financial stability and strength, or rated AAA by Moody's Investor Service, Standard and Poor's, or Duff & Phelps. The death benefit is of little use if the insurance company goes out of business first. The company I bought from charged 30 percent more than the cheapest company.

This was a touchy family issue, because my brother sells life insurance, and he was very upset with me that I would buy my insurance on the Internet, instead of through him. But he was shocked that he could not match the rate I got.

If you don't have Internet access, ask a friend for help, or pick up any issue of *Money* magazine or *Smart Money*, and check the ads for insurance quotation services. Although most have 800-numbers, it's much easier to get quotes on the Web.

If you don't use an online service to get a life insurance quote, make at least one call to USAA Life Insurance. USAA Life is a financially strong company and offers exceptional pricing on both term and whole life insurance. Normally, you have to be a member of the military, a military retiree, or a dependent to do business with USAA, but not for the purchase of life insurance.

Most people who buy life insurance still do so through an insurance agent, because people generally won't buy life insurance, even if they know they need it, because it forces them to deal with the possibility that they are going to die. Agents earn their commissions by getting you to do what you need to do, but wouldn't otherwise. If you chose to deal with an agent, remember that the financial strength of the company the agent represents should be your first priority. Then, look for an agent who talks more about your goals rather than trying to figure out how much money you have available each month to put into an insurance policy.

If an agent tries to sell you an insurance product you don't understand, don't buy it. Insurance agents have a number of increasingly complicated products they can offer you. If what you want is to insure your life and someone presents you with a policy that has seven different riders and 12 different payout formulas, none of which you understand, that's a policy you don't want.

If the agent starts making promises about what a policy will do — that a policy can pay for itself after 15 years or cut your taxes in half — make them put it in writing. I've never had a consumer say they can produce paperwork showing something the agent promised.

If you buy a whole life or variable universal life policy and become disillusioned with it, don't cancel it and convert to term insurance or you'll lose a lot of money. These policies include massive commissions in the first few years. So once you're already in, if the company is financially strong and you can afford to pay the premiums, keep the policy in place. If you need additional insurance for your family, supplement the whole life or variable universal life with a term policy.

People who've been taken in vanishing-premium life sales pitches will have to continue paying and hope for some compensation as a result of legal action against the insurer. Usually you get a much more generous offer if you're still a customer.

Older readers have to weigh a few different factors. Many times they buy insurance through age 65, then drop coverage. If that's your situation, it's okay to buy term life insurance. But if your survivors would need replacement income in addition to what they would inherit, shop for insurance based on a need that goes into your 70s

or beyond. In many cases, that would mean buying whole life, rather than term, while in your 50s. The cost of $200,000 worth of term life coverage for a 50-year-old nonsmoker would be quite high, at least $340 a year for a man, $300 a year for a woman. At age 70, the annual cost would be more than $2,300 annually for a man, $1,200 annually for a woman. In those cases, it might make sense, at age 50, to buy a whole life policy for $5,000 to $7,000. The whole life policies would build cash value and the premiums would never increase.

Whichever insurance you prefer, avoid buying more than one policy for any person. Every insurance policy you buy has fees hidden in it. So two $50,000 policies would cost more than one $100,000 policy. Some of the worst abuses I've seen concern poor people who've ended up with a dozen or more small life insurance policies when they could have bought one large policy for the same amount of money.

133

### TIPS ON LIFE INSURANCE

⦿ Consider your own situation to see if life insurance makes sense for you, how much you need, and which type of life insurance would be best. If your family would be unable to make the mortgage payments without your income, you need life insurance.

⦿ Life insurance is meant to replace your income. My rule of thumb is to buy an amount equal to 10 times your annual salary.

⦿ If both spouses work, both should have life insurance to replace their own income. Don't buy insurance on your children.

## 134 ◉

- Term life insurance provides a payment only if you die. Other policies, such as whole life or universal life, include investment components.

- If you decide to get term life insurance, the best way to buy is by using an independent shopping service to get quotes, on the Internet or by phone.

- Don't cancel a whole or universal life policy. Once you've purchased it, it's best to keep it.

- Avoid buying more than one policy for any person. Every insurance policy you buy has fees hidden in it. So two $50,000 policies would cost more than one $100,000 policy.

### INTERNET

www.quotesmith.com
www.ambest.com (Insurance company ratings)
www.masterquote.com (Insurance quotes)

# DISABILITY INSURANCE

Your odds of being disabled are far greater than your odds of dying during your working years, yet few people buy disability insurance. People have an aversion to the idea they might become disabled, so they don't protect themselves financially.

Imagine the powerlessness you would feel as the breadwinner for your family if you were disabled, could not work, and had no source of income. Your family wouldn't have any money to live. With disability insurance, you're buying a financial safety net for your family.

The cost of disability insurance is affected dramatically by some of the purchase decisions you make. Disability insurance that kicks in after 30 days or 60 days costs a lot more than coverage that takes effect six months after you are disabled. I recommend six months. That holds down the premium and still gives you good coverage. It's wise to have enough savings so that you can survive for six months if you lose your job or in case of any other emergency. If you don't have enough savings to cover a six-month loss of income, consider a disability policy that pays benefits after 90 days.

At the other end, people sometimes

buy disability coverage that stays in effect for too short a period. Don't get a policy that will pay for only three or five years. Get a policy that covers you through age 65.

The next question is how much coverage to buy. I recommend you get an amount equal to 60 percent of your gross pay. That will give you about what you take home after taxes.

Look very closely in these policies at the definition of a disability. Because the Social Security Administration has such a strict definition of a disability, it pays benefits on just a third of its claims. If your policy has the same definition, you could lose twice. Social Security might determine that you're not disabled under their guidelines, and your insurer will make the same determination. Look for a policy that uses this definition: "The insured is

totally disabled when he (or she) is unable to perform the principal duties of his (or her) occupation."

The Social Security Administration pays Americans up to $1,300 a month if it accepts their claim of total disability. Private insurers offer disability policies that pay $2,000 a month in benefits, tax-free, for a cost of about $670 a year (with benefits taking effect after 90 days). It costs more if you're older or have a high-risk job, or if cost-of-living adjustments are built into the benefits.

I don't recommend buying either life or disability insurance through your employer. The coverage may cost more, and it won't go with you if you change jobs. Worse, if you develop a health condition that makes you unable to buy these types of insurance, you will have squandered the opportunity you had to buy them while you were healthy.

**135**

## TIPS ON DISABILITY INSURANCE

- Your odds of being disabled are far greater than your odds of dying during your working years, so disability insurance is more important than life insurance.

- It's best to get a disability policy that begins making payments three or six months after you are disabled and continues until retirement.

- Buy coverage equal to 60 percent of your current pay before taxes.

- Get a policy that uses a more liberal definition of disability than the one used by the Social Security Administration.

# 136 ⊛ HEALTH INSURANCE

I try to get it right as often as I can, but I'm not at all ashamed to say when I'm wrong, and I was all wrong on managed health care. I believed strongly in the concept of managed care, especially during the 1993 debate in Washington about adopting a government-run health system. I was totally opposed to that, and very much in favor of a private marketplace solution. I thought that if you had a system of managing care that included direct incentives to control cost, that we would end up with a good compromise. Boy, was I wrong.

The health-care system in this country is set up backwards. Most people get their health insurance through their employers. So the employer, whose greatest concern is driving costs down, is the insurance customer, not the patient. The managed care plans care more about making the employers happy than they care about the patients. So we have a system that patients don't trust and doctors hate.

I believe the system needs to be completely reworked, so that the patient is in control of the process, starting with buying insurance. Employees want to be able to choose the health care they want. I should be able to choose a health-care plan that has limited benefits, one that offers everything, or something in between. It would be just like anything else we buy. We decide what level of customer service we want, what

quality of merchandise we want, and how much we're willing to pay.

I'd love to see health insurance go to a system like there is for Medicare supplemental coverage. There might be 10 standard health plans that insurers would sell to individuals. Employers could subsidize it, but the employees would be the customer. Each plan would be sold individually, just as with home or auto insurance. Individuals can buy health insurance on their own today. But insurers allow only the healthiest people to have these plans, or they charge others exorbitant rates. Under my system, premiums would be based on a large community of people, just as in today's group health insurance. New York state already has community rating. So instead of premiums for a small group being based on their loss ratio, they're based on the loss ratio for the entire state or region.

I'm convinced this is where we're going to end up, because there's too much resistance in this country to a socialized medicine system. And based on what's happened in Canada, I wouldn't be in favor of that anyway. Canada has a shortage of services, so even people with critical illnesses such as cancer face long delays before they can receive treatment.

The system we have now is broken, with 44 million people uninsured, and it is the most expensive system in the world. And the pain people are suffering is very real. I took a call from somebody in Missouri who has an illness that developed while he was employed. The employer was acquired, the employee lost his job and was on COBRA, which provides a temporary extension of health insurance after you lose your job. He's about to lose that coverage, and because his illness now is a preexisting condition, he won't be able to purchase coverage anywhere at any price. At a minimum, it's a death sentence for this family's finances, and if they can't afford medical care, it could be an actual death sentence.

Jobs are so portable today. People no longer work at the same company for a lifetime, and far fewer people work for large employers. So why should health insurance be sold under the idea that we're going to stay with one big employer until we're eligible for Medicare? There is some portability of health insurance under the law now, but it's a joke. It's almost impossible to make the provisions work for you.

That's where we're going. But while we're getting there, you still have to make choices based on the system we have. The best thing you can do is be as knowledgeable as you can about what choices you have. When we have open enrollment at my company, a month-long period in which people can change their coverage, a lot of people ask me which plan they should choose. I want you to sit down and read the boring choices, and understand what

trade-offs you're being offered.

If you have a choice of health-care plans, it likely will be either a traditional plan, a health maintenance organization (HMO), or a preferred provider organization (PPO).

The traditional plan is rapidly disappearing. That's the kind in which you choose your doctor, and the insurer pays their share of the cost of a visit, usually 80 percent, after you reach a yearly deductible. But it isn't a true 80 percent. The insurer pays 80 percent of what they say is a reasonable charge. You wind up paying closer to 50 percent of the cost, which can be substantial. Costs for "fee-for-service" plans have grown so much that few employers still provide them.

That's pushed us into managed care, which includes both the HMO and PPO. In the HMO, there's a closed system of doctors and medical facilities. You may receive treatment only from the HMO's doctors at their facilities. But in return for that rather severe limitation, you get a great financial deal. Your out-of-pocket cost is minimal. When my wife gave birth recently, our cost for the hospital stay was zero. Not one cent.

So the HMO offers the starkest of choices. You give up a great deal of freedom and mobility in selecting your medical care providers. But you have virtually no financial risk.

The real movement in the country has been not to HMOs but to other managed-care choices, such as the preferred provider organization. PPOs

137

**138** 🔊  don't force you to go to a closed system of doctors, as do HMOs. Instead, they provide incentives to choose specific doctors and facilities, and disincentives for you to choose others. For example, you might have a $15 co-pay to visit a PPO doctor, with no deductible, and get a 90 percent reimbursement for other costs. If you go outside the plan to a non-PPO doctor, you might have a $250 annual deductible, and get an 80 percent reimbursement for your costs after you meet the deductible.

The biggest complaint I get about PPOs is you have to be absolutely certain before you go to a medical practice that the individual physician you see is on the plan. If the doctor says you have to go to the hospital, you have to make sure the hospital is on your plan. If you need surgery, unless it's emergency surgery, you have to make sure that the attending physicians and anesthesiologists are on your plan. If you don't, you could be exposed to enormous out-of-pocket costs.

We had a case in which my caller thought she had done all her homework before undergoing a hysterectomy, but wound up responsible for a $3,500 bill, instead of the $200 she thought she would pay. Her doctor was in her medical plan, but the hospital the doctor recommended was not. You almost need to complete a checklist to avoid financial disaster.

These are the consequences when we aren't the customer, and the provider doesn't have any financial incentive to make sure we are happy. The result is the customer is forced to decide between quality of care and financial safety. When you're sick and in pain, you want relief and it's even more difficult to make the right choices. That's the reality of the marketplace.

The biggest problem with HMOs has been what to do if you're sick and don't believe you're receiving proper care. Until better consumer protections are enacted, the first thing I recommend is to complain and complain loudly to the state insurance department in your state. Most states regulate HMOs. Second, send a letter directly to the medical director of your HMO, both by regular and certified mail. If you're not well enough to do it, have a family member send the letter for you. State your condition, why you believe you're not receiving proper treatment, and what you want the HMO to do. If necessary, go to see a specialist outside the HMO, pay for his or her opinion, and attach that information to the complaint you file with your insurance department and the medical director of the HMO. In addition to that, go through the appeal process at the HMO. But if you're really sick, go directly to the medical director first. The HMO may hope that you die or get better before your appeal is heard.

Many Americans are having trouble getting health-care coverage, or are worried that they can't afford the cost. If you aren't insured but are in very good health, get quotes on Medical Savings

Account plans. An MSA is a combination plan that includes a health insurance policy with a very high deductible and a tax-advantaged savings account, the MSA. The policy protects you if you have a catastrophic illness or injury, but because the deductible is usually $2,500 yearly, it's useless for minor medical expenses. But it also has a very low premium. The money you don't pay in ultra-high premiums goes into the savings account, free of income tax. When you have medical expenses, you draw money from the MSA account until you meet the deductible.

Good health is important because you need some time to build up the amount of money in your MSA before you are faced with medical bills. If you need surgery 30 days after you open an MSA, you'll bear the cost of the first $2,500 in bills.

Essentially, an MSA gives you a tax break to self-insure your health, and over time, for most people, an MSA will work out well. In the short-term, MSAs are a smart financial risk mostly for people who could not afford having coverage otherwise, or for people who have a good deal of money in savings that they could draw from if they had an unexpected illness or accident.

MSAs are a great choice if you rarely get sick, because you roll over the money in the savings account from year to year, and eventually you get it, tax free. They are also a good choice if you're under age 30, and are active and in good health. People under 30 generally call on the health insurance system only for a major illness or accident, so they're great candidates for MSAs, or any other catastrophic health-care policy.

You can get more information on MSAs at http://www.blueshieldca.com/options/msa/msa.html

Many employers offer a benefit called a cafeteria plan or a flexible spending plan, which you can use to help pay medical or child-care costs. They work a little like a medical savings account in that you ask your employer to take a specified amount of money out of each paycheck, and you use that money to pay for deductibles, co-payments, and other medical costs that aren't paid by the company health plan. The advantage is you can pay those costs out of gross dollars, not net. Since $200 off your gross pay often will equal $120 to $140 of your net pay, you get a substantial discount.

However, you can't tell your employer to take out more or less money during the year, and you lose any money that's left in the account at the end of the year. So if you have $1,000 taken out and draw only $600 from the account, you lose $400. That's the reason I don't favor using flexible spending accounts for medical care, unless there are known expenses like a prescription medicine you must have that isn't covered by insurance. If you don't budget well, you could lose. For child care, you'll know the cost in advance, so putting money into a "dependent care account" is a great idea.

**139**

**140** 

In some markets around the country, individuals or small groups can join an HMO. I strongly advise this to people who are looking for minimal out-of-pocket costs when they face an illness. If that's you, contact the HMOs in your area, and see if they accept individuals. You'll have to pass medical screening, which generally means you cannot smoke and cannot have any serious medical history.

Another option is to call the agent who handles your homeowners or auto insurance and ask for a referral to a health insurance broker, who can advise you on what options are available for an individual in your part of the country.

## TIPS ON HEALTH INSURANCE

- Employer-paid plans may offer a traditional fee-for-service plan, a health maintenance organization, or a preferred provider organization. Choose the one you find least objectionable.

- HMOs protect you from financial risk, but you have no freedom to choose your own doctor, and many patients have complained about access to quality care.

- PPOs give you a choice of doctors in or outside the plan, and use a carrot-and-stick approach to encourage you to choose plan doctors.

- If you're not getting the care you expect from an HMO, send a letter to the medical director, by certified and regular mail, go through the HMO's appeal process, and consider paying for a second opinion from a doctor outside the HMO.

- In a PPO, make sure every doctor you see and hospital you go to are in the plan.

- If you don't have coverage and are healthy, consider a medical savings account, which combines a catastrophic insurance plan with a tax-advantaged savings account.

## INTERNET

http://www.blueshieldca.com/options/msa/msa.html (MSAs)

# CAR INSURANCE

The most important thing to know about auto insurance is that you should carry it. It's been estimated that a third of all motorists in America don't have any auto insurance, even though carrying it is required by law in most states.

People who don't carry insurance usually fail to do so because of the cost. Premiums are high and many can't, or won't, pay. But not carrying insurance is a false savings. If you have no insurance and are involved in an accident, you could end up with no car and no money.

If you have a car loan and you don't get insurance, the lender has the right to force-place insurance and may not tell you what they've done until the end of your loan. That means the lender buys insurance for your car, at a cost of five or six times what you would normally pay. It's a giant profit center for the lenders and a rude surprise for many borrowers. I heard of one case in which the borrower thought he'd made his last car payment when a bank officer told him he still owed $2,600, plus interest, for not carrying insurance.

Because so many people have no insurance, or too little insurance, you should make sure to purchase uninsured motorist protection as part of your car insurance policy. For $20 to $100 a year, uninsured motorist coverage protects you against expenses that could come up if you have a collision with an uninsured driver. My wife had

such an accident, and we ended up having to claim against our insurance.

There are several types of auto insurance, and you should think about how much of each you need. Collision coverage takes care of damage to your car from an accident that is at least partially your fault. Normally you'll be responsible for a deductible of $250 or $500, and your insurer pays the rest. You should maintain collision coverage in almost all circumstances.

If you have an older car that's worth very little, it may not make sense to carry collision coverage. The other exception is for people with substantial assets, who may prefer to self-insure an older car worth $6,000 or less. I had a car that was six years old and a borderline case of maintaining collision coverage. I was paying $262 a year for collision. If the car had been totaled in an accident, I would have received about $2,700 from my insurance company. It really wasn't worthwhile to keep the coverage.

In general, if your annual premiums for collision and comprehensive coverage exceed 10 percent of the value of your car, consider dropping them.

One way to limit the cost of collision coverage is to carry a higher deductible. If you can afford to pay the first $500 in damage, you can save $50 to $100 a year by carrying a $500 deductible instead of a $250 deductible. Over five to 10 years, that's a substantial savings. Plus, you

**141**

**142** ◎ don't want to make a lot of small claims because insurers tend to count against you the number of claims, and you could be canceled if you make too many claims. But don't carry a high deductible if you can't afford to pay that amount if you have an accident.

Comprehensive coverage takes care of noncollision calamities, such as damage from a break-in, theft of the car, windshield cracking, or damage from natural disasters such as flood or hurricane. Use the same rules of thumb for deductibles as you would for collision coverage.

Liability is the most important component of auto insurance and the one to which people pay the least amount of attention. This is the type of insurance many states require you to carry, because it pays for damage to property and physical injury from an accident that is your fault. Most people try to save money by buying the absolute minimum liability coverage, often $15,000 per person up to a maximum of $30,000 per accident. That's okay if you don't own anything. But if you have personal assets, you need to protect them against the threat of personal-injury lawsuits. If you injure somebody in an accident, that person's medical bills will exceed the minimum liability coverage very quickly. I recommend you carry coverage of $300,000 per accident, which sometimes has a limit of $100,000 per person. Better to have too much liability coverage than too little. It won't cost you much more.

If you are very wealthy, get an umbrella policy. It shields you from liability in almost every phase of your life. Umbrella coverage, which is sold in amounts of $1 million, $2 million, and above, supplements your auto and homeowners liability coverage. You can buy umbrella coverage around the country for $100 to $350 a year, not a big cost because the potential risk of a catastrophic liability claim against you is very small.

Uninsured motorist protection is especially helpful because so many drivers have too little liability coverage.

The last decision to make about insurance is a medical coverage rider, which is available in some states. I'm opposed to such riders, because they often duplicate your own health insurance. If you don't have health insurance, consider getting it rather than adding medical coverage to your automobile insurance. Agents will try to sell this by saying it will protect a passenger in your car. But here's my answer to that: If it's a friend, they'll claim against their health insurance; if it isn't a friend, they'll sue you against your liability. You're covered in either case.

There are two important considerations in picking an auto insurer. One is the premium cost. The other is the quality of service. On the issue of premium, first decide what coverages you want in the three major areas: collision, comprehensive, and liability. Then it's a fairly easy matter to call insurers and get quotes. The quotes vary tremendously from company to company, so don't take the first offer.

There's an even larger difference in customer service from the best insurers to the worst. Ask friends, relatives, and co-workers whom they use and how they've handled claims. Another good source is *Consumer Reports* magazine (www.consumerreports.com), which occasionally surveys customers to determine service quality. In the Cars chapter of this book, the section on auto accidents lists the top insurers as rated by *Consumer Reports*.

*Consumer Reports* also offers to shop for you to find the lowest-cost auto insurance in your state, for a small fee. This service is offered in more than half the states around the country and is saving people a ton of money. The difference between insurers is incredible, and shopping can save you hundreds of dollars a year. In fact, one insurer sometimes will charge up to six times more than another company for the same driver. And you don't get better quality coverage by paying more. For the shopping service, you pay $12 for the first car in the family, $8 for each additional car. You get detailed information for companies that will write you a policy

in your state, based either on the coverages you have now, or on the coverage levels *Consumer Reports* recommends.

Occasionally I'll get a call from someone complaining that *Consumer Reports*' service was inaccurate, but that's often because someone forgot a speeding ticket they have. If *Consumer Reports* does make an error, they'll refund the fee.

As I write this, shopping for car insurance on the Internet is still in its infancy, but comparison shopping for insurance will become a lot easier as it grows. Before long, you'll be able to type in your age, the vehicles you have, and a description of your driving record, and get instant quotes from multiple companies.

 **143**

If you get a better quote from another insurer, you'll have to decide whether or not to switch. If you've had claims in the past and you were thrilled with how you were treated, that's a reason to consider staying. But if you have no claims experience with your insurer, check *Consumer Reports*' ratings of auto insurers. If your insurer isn't ranked among the best and you can get a better price elsewhere, particularly one with a better customer satisfaction rating, I'd fire them and switch.

 **TIPS ON CAR INSURANCE**

⦿ Buy uninsured motorist coverage to protect yourself against uninsured or under insured drivers.

⦿ If you have a car loan and don't carry insurance, the lender may buy insurance for you at five or six times what you would normally pay.

**144** ❧

- Collision coverage takes care of damage to your car from an accident that is all or partially your fault. Normally you'll be responsible for a deductible of $250 or $500, and your insurer pays the rest.

- Comprehensive coverage takes care of noncollision calamities, such as damage from a break-in, theft, or windshield cracking.

- Liability is the most important component of auto insurance and the one to which people pay the least amount of attention. It pays for damage to property and physical injury from an accident that is your fault.

- Medical coverage riders, available in some states, often duplicate your own health insurance. If you don't have health insurance, consider getting it rather than adding medical coverage to your automobile insurance.

---

# HOMEOWNERS INSURANCE

Shop for homeowners insurance the same way you buy other kinds of insurance. Figure out what limits you want and what value you need to insure, then call several insurers for quotes. Sometimes you'll get a better deal if you buy your homeowners and auto insurance from the same company. If you're happy with your auto insurer, get a quote from your agent and ask about a multiline discount.

Make sure you get a quote for insurance that would pay to replace your belongings, rather than pay you based on their depreciated value. There's a big difference. If your television is stolen, replacement coverage would allow you to buy another, instead of giving you half of what you paid for it three years ago.

I recommend that you get a homeowners policy with a high deductible. The premiums are cheaper, and it will prevent you from making small claims. I'm getting deluged with calls from people whose insurers have canceled their coverage, even after they've been with the company for many years, because they've recently had a couple of small claims. This has become far worse in the last few years. Insurers are notoriously inefficient, and it's hugely expensive for them to process the paperwork for a claim and pay an adjuster. So they now grade you on the number of claims you make, rather than simply the amount of money you might cost them in a claim.

Never make a small claim. If you have a relatively small loss, say $750, you're far better off absorbing the loss than filing a claim. If you have a $500 deductible, the insurer would pay you $250, but you would risk losing your coverage. If your insurer cancels you for making too many claims, finding replacement coverage will be enormously expensive. Other insurers will ask you if you were canceled and why, and then will place you into a high-risk category. You can avoid that by raising your deductible to $1,000 or $2,500. My preference is $2,500, but if that's just too far for you to go, choose a $1,000 deductible.

I raised my homeowners insurance deductible to $2,500 and saved 38 percent on my coverage. If you do that, you'll save so much on premiums over the years that it will more than make up for any lost benefits on smaller claims. If someone breaks into your house and steals a couple of televisions and a VCR, it's going to kill you to have to spend $1,000 to replace the stolen items. But over the long term, you'll benefit more from having a higher deductible. If you don't believe me, check with your insurer to see how much money you would save each year by going with a higher deductible. And think how many years it's been since you've actually had to make a claim with your insurer. Multiply the savings by the number of years, and you'll get it.

If you ever do have to make a claim due to theft or fire, ask your agent what documentation you need to substantiate it. The insurer makes big money over the years from you in premium payments. You want to make sure that if you have a major claim, you will be compensated for your loss. My favorite method of documenting what you own is to use a video camera. If you don't have one, borrow one from a friend. Walk through your house, room by room, and shoot a video of your possessions. As you're taping, talk about each item, when you bought it, and if you remember, how much you paid. Make sure to get the electronics, the furniture, and anything else you consider valuable. If you have an expensive wardrobe, pan your closet and talk about how many suits or dresses you have. If you have a fire or other loss, you'll be reimbursed for each item. So you'll need to indicate that you have eight suits and 15 pairs of underwear. There are limits in some basic policies on jewelry. If you have an individual piece worth more than $2,000, or several pieces collectively worth more than $5,000, you may need to purchase additional coverage.

If you don't like the idea of using video, use a still camera and take pictures of each room and each item of value. Put the pictures in a photo album with a written description of everything, or if you're lazy like me, take a cassette recorder and make an audio description to go with the pictures. Keeping receipts of your purchases is ideal, but the number of us

145

**146** ✪ who keep receipts is minuscule.

It's helpful to make a new video or take new pictures once a year, because you may buy new things. When you're done, store the tape or photos somewhere safe — not in your house. If there's a fire, a melted tape or burned album won't do you any good.

It's also critically important to update the amount of your coverage every few years, because your house may have grown in value. If you bought a $125,000 house a few years ago and now it's worth $150,000, you may not have enough coverage to protect yourself from a catastrophic loss. Even if you have replacement value coverage to rebuild your home, you may not have enough insurance to pay current construction costs. When you've been in your home three years, check to see what builders are charging for homes like yours. Check the price per square foot for new homes in your neighborhood, and multiply by 0.8 to eliminate the cost of the land. Then multiply that figure by the square footage of your home. That's a good way to see if the coverage you have is adequate to rebuild your house if it were destroyed.

Check the coverage on your possessions, too. You may have accumulated so many things over the years that you don't have enough coverage to protect the contents. Check your coverage every five years, or when you refinance your mortgage. The additional cost in your premiums is tiny, but the risk is great. If you raise your deductible and increase your coverage at the same time, you'll pay less and be better protected.

As with auto insurance, liability coverage is an important consideration in your homeowners policy. You need to have enough liability coverage to protect your assets in case someone gets hurt on your property, or if your dog bites someone. Many policies offer minimum liability coverage of $100,000, but it costs only about $20 more for $300,000 in coverage.

## TIPS ON HOMEOWNERS INSURANCE

- ◉ Figure out what limits you want on your homeowners insurance, and what value you need to insure, then call several insurers for quotes.

- ◉ Sometimes you'll get a better deal if you buy your homeowners and auto insurance from the same company.

- ◉ Make sure you get a quote for insurance that would pay to replace your belongings, rather than pay you based on their depreciated value.

● Raise your deductible to $1,000 or $2,500. You'll pay less in premiums, but more importantly, you'll reduce the risk that your insurer will cancel your coverage because you made too many claims.

● Ask your agent what documentation you need to substantiate a claim in case of theft or fire. I think it's easiest to videotape your house and describe your possessions. Don't store the tape in your house.

● Update coverage for the value of your home and its contents every three to five years.

● Carry enough liability coverage to protect you against a lawsuit if someone gets hurt on your property.

..................................................................................................................................................................

 147

# TECHNOLOGY

**The growth** of the Internet has completely changed the way I do consumer research for my radio show, and the advice I give to listeners.

You can use the Internet to find the value of a used car, figure out how to shop for a mortgage or pay one off early, look for a job, get a price quote on life insurance, or check the value of stamps and coins in your collection. You can even post your complaints about a company on the Web. By providing an open marketplace of information, it totally changes the balance of power between seller and consumer.

Getting information from the government sure is a lot easier. Information that once took days to get now is available instantly on government Web sites.

As the Internet era continues to dawn, people are getting more and more excited about its benefits. As the ultimate in free speech, it also gives a forum for a number of unsavory characters, promoting schemes and ripoffs. Be very careful with "information" you find in cyberspace. There are a lot of very impressive Web sites that are impressive mainly in their cunning.

Another danger is from material on the Internet that can be objectionable or harmful to children. There are a variety of computer software "filters" available to help parents protect their children from adult-oriented content and violence, but I'm not sure any of them work very well yet. I think parents have to be the ultimate filter of what children view on the Internet. As the parent of an 11-year-old daughter, I know there are things there that can be dangerous to her, but until there's an effective way to screen what she sees there, it's my responsibility to monitor and control her use of the Web.

Technological change makes the need for information even greater. In this chapter, I'll help you buy a computer, get a wireless phone, choose between cable and satellite television, and tell you a little bit about long-distance calling, free e-mail, and Internet access.

## 150 🖳

BUYING A COMPUTER

E-MAIL

INTERNET SERVICE

FREE STUFF

ONLINE BILL PAYING

WIRELESS PHONES

LONG-DISTANCE CALLING

SATELLITE TV

# BUYING A COMPUTER

Before you figure out what computer to buy, think about what you're going to use it for. Most people use a computer for basic things such as word processing, surfing the Internet, and game playing. Many are using their computer to pay bills. Almost any computer will be able to handle these kinds of tasks, so the lowest-cost system you can find is fine. People want to know what speed chip they should buy. Well, my answer is buy the cheapest chip.

If you're going to use your computer for a specialized function, let the software required for that function drive your hardware purchase. So if you're doing graphic design or heavy game-playing, get a computer that meets the requirements of the specialized software. But never buy more computer than you need because of what you think you might use it for in the future. With the continuing drop in computer prices and increase in performance, it's a big mistake to spend extra money now. You can upgrade fairly inexpensively when your needs change.

One of the main factors that makes a difference in your enjoyment of the computer is its short-term memory, or RAM. Today the most common recommendation is 128 megabytes of RAM.

A good monitor also is important, because a poor one can cause eyestrain. The size isn't as important as the crispness of the display. You should take some time to look at monitors to find one that's comfortable.

If you're going to use a computer just to surf the Internet, consider a Web appliance, a device that lets you browse the Internet but is far less complicated than a computer. Web appliances, which are made by a number of manufacturers, cost up to $200. Some are being given away for free. If you want an inexpensive, easy-to-use device to surf the Web, plus inexpensive Internet service, this may be a good option.

One of the companies experimenting in this area is Richard Branson's Virgin family of companies. At www.virginconnectme.com, you can apply to receive a free Web player and Internet service for a total of $50 a year. This is typical of offers that should be available for Web-only appliances. These devices are great for people who don't want to know how computers work. You just take it out of the box and plug it in. When you hit the power button, it automatically starts dialing in to the Internet.

## WHERE TO BUY

Once you've decided what kind of computer to buy, the next decision is where to buy it. There are plenty of choices, including a traditional retailer, an online computer seller, or a local shop that builds your computer to order.

Where you buy matters only if you must have your computer constantly available in order to conduct your business, or if personally it would create a great hardship if your computer wasn't up and running. If that's you, buy only from a place that will provide 24-hour turnaround on service or replacement. Either the manufacturer or retailer would provide that guarantee, and you'll pay more for it. But if your business depends on it, it is absolutely key.

I get calls from people who use their computers for business and buy their computers at consumer electronics stores. Then the computer goes down, and the service center the stores use, or the manufacturer, have no concept that time matters. People will complain that they haven't had the computer for five weeks. There's nothing in the general consumer warranties that says you'll have the computer back in 72 hours or seven days.

If you want to buy a computer that's dirt-cheap and it is for business use, make sure your old computer is available in an emergency.

## LAPTOPS

Laptop computers have come a long way. The capabilities available in them today are up to par with what you would get in a desktop computer, with very good screen quality. But because of all the miniaturization, they're far more expensive than a desktop. They're also more expensive because of the ego issues — buyers always wanting the latest and greatest.

There are two problems with buying

💻 151

**152**  on ego. First, laptops are very suscepti-ble to theft, especially as you travel through airports or hotels with them. If you buy the most expensive laptop, you make yourself more of a target.

Go back to what you're going to use the computer for — basic things such as hooking into the company net-work, surfing the Web, reading and writing e-mail, word processing, and spreadsheets. If that's what you need, buy a base-level model laptop for between $1,000 and $1,500.

There are other factors to consider.

How much battery power do you need? How much is the laptop going to weigh? And are you going to use it for long periods at one sitting — requiring a crisper screen to avoid eyestrain? But you can address all of these things with-out spending a fortune.

Laptops all require compromise. Because everything has to be miniatur-ized, you either have to spend more money, lower the capabilities, or raise the weight. There's no perfect laptop for all qualities, including price. So be pre-pared to pare your list of wants.

## *Clark says* TIPS ON BUYING A COMPUTER

- ◉ If you're going to use a computer for basic things such as word processing and surfing the Internet, buy the lowest-cost computer you can.

- ◉ If you're going to use your computer for a specialized function, such as graphic design or heavy game-playing, let the software required for that function drive your hardware purchase.

- ◉ As far as features, get at least 128 megabytes of RAM and a crisp monitor.

- ◉ If you're interested only in surfing the Internet, consider a Web-only appliance.

- ◉ Where you buy a computer is important only if you need a quick-turnaround guarantee on repairs, and you'll pay more for that.

- ◉ If you need a laptop, get a base-level model. They're less susceptible to theft.

## INTERNET

www.virginconnectme.com

# E-MAIL

Most people set up their e-mail account with their Internet service provider, and that's a mistake. Instead, you can have an e-mail address that will never change, yet is still free. If you change Internet services, you won't have to go through a mail-forwarding process, or lose contact with people.

There are many such services. The three largest are Yahoo!(www.yahoo. com), Hotmail (www.hotmail.com) and Juno (www.juno.com). I use a Yahoo account, and wherever I go in the world, I can check my e-mail, regardless of whether my Internet service provider is available.

If you want to have an e-mail account on your own Web site, you can register your name for free or nearly free, because there's now competition in the domain-name business. My wife registered her name for free at www.namezero.com. Other sites, such as www.geocities.com, will host a Web site for you for free, and many of these sites offer very easy tools for you to build your own site.

If you operate a business, perhaps a home-based business, or you simply want to establish a nice presence for yourself, www.ohgolly.com offers a good setup for building your own Web site for free. They hope to make their money by selling you other services that would add value to your page.

🖥 153

## INTERNET

> www.yahoo.com (Free e-mail)
> www.hotmail.com (Free e-mail)
> www.juno.com (Free e-mail)
> www.namezero.com (Free domain name registration)
> www.geocities.com (Free Web site hosting)
> www.ohgolly.com (Build your own Web site for free)
> www.econgo.com (Free e-commerce site)

# INTERNET SERVICE

These days, you have to have a good reason to pay for Internet access. There are now more than 100 companies offering free Internet access, among them www.altavista.com, www.netzero.com, www.bluelight.com, and

**154** 🖥

www.juno.com. In return, you must put up with a band of advertisements on your screen. Unless you hate the ads or you need special hand-holding, there's no justification for paying for basic dial-up Internet service anymore.

If you want high-speed Internet service, either through a cable modem or digital subscriber line (DSL), I have some special recommendations. If you live in an area where either is an option, pick not based on price, but on which company you expect to provide the best service — either your phone or cable company. One of the advantages of DSL is that even if your phone company has a lousy reputation, there are outside companies that can provide DSL that may be very customer-oriented.

Be careful with either product, though, if it requires a large up-front fee or a contract. If you have to sign a contract in order to get a particular deal, don't sign one for longer than 12 months. And add a clause that gives you the right to cancel if you don't find the service to be reliable. I've received complaints from people who've signed two-year contracts with a particular company, then found the service to be down a lot. The company doesn't care, and there's nothing in the contract about service reliability.

To see if DSL is available in your area, go to www.dslreports.com. To see if cable modem service is available, go to www.cable-modem.net.

There's a third way to access high-speed Internet service, and it's a great choice if you live in an area that may never have high-speed connections from the phone or cable company, or if you don't trust either one. Both DirecTV and Dish Network offer high-speed Internet service via satellite. This service is an enhancement over the prior effort by DirecTV that involved a phone line for your outbound request and satellite for inbound service. It costs about the same as cable modem or DSL service. Unfortunately, if you're already a customer of DirecTV or Dish Network, you probably will need new hardware — a new dish and box — to use it.

## INTERNET

www.dslreports.com
www.cable-modem.net
www.altavista.com
www.netzero.com
www.bluelight.com
www.juno.com

# FREE STUFF

I love getting a great deal when I buy something, but what I like even more is getting something for free.

Thanks largely to the growth of the Internet, it's now possible to get free long-distance calls, free faxing, and free Internet access. The tradeoff is you'll have to listen to or view a few advertisements, or fill out a form that gives some information about your interests or shopping habits. But I think it's worthwhile.

A lot of companies have started using the advertiser-supported business model, which really has been around for a long time. Network television, which we sometimes call free television to distinguish it from cable TV, uses the same advertiser-supported model. Viewers watch commercials and get the programming for free. This is really just a refinement of the traditional broadcasting and print model for TV and radio brought to all different kinds of consumer and business products.

I use a service called Freeway (www.broadpoint.com) to make free long-distance calls, and I use one of the free services to access the Internet. America Online, by far the nation's largest Internet service, had to change its strategy in England because it couldn't compete with free access. So AOL, which has plenty of advertisements anyway, switched to free service. What AOL sells is ease-of-use. People pay the monthly fee because it is so consumer friendly. AOL also provides its own content, not just access to the Internet.

If free Internet service isn't enough for you, you can now get paid to surf the Net. A service called alladvantage.com pays you for the time you spend online. Alladvantage pays up to $7.50 a month, plus more if you refer friends. The tradeoff is a small window at the bottom of your screen that contains advertisements.

Alladvantage isn't an Internet service, so you still have to sign up for Internet access with someone else. But using alladvantage can either cut your monthly Internet cost or, if you combine it with free Internet access, earn you a profit for doing what you do anyway. Trading a little bit of time to get things of value for free is worth it to me.

These offers are likely to change, but the idea of advertiser support has been around for more than 100 years. Newspapers and magazines used it well before TV, radio, and the Internet came onto the scene. A newspaper would cost a lot more than 50 or 75 cents if not for the ads.

I am continuously updating the information on my Web site, www.clarkhoward.com, as new offers are introduced and others scrapped.

155

156

TIPS ON FREE STUFF

◉ Freeway (www.broadpoint.com) lets you make free long-distance calls if you agree to listen to audio commercials first.

◉ All advantage.com pays you an hourly rate to surf the Internet, if you agree to have an advertising banner on your screen.

## INTERNET

www.broadpoint.com
www.alladvantage.com
www.altavista.com
www.netzero.com
www.bluelight.com
www.juno.com

# ONLINE BILL PAYING

I've been paying my bills electronically for nearly two years, and it's been fantastic.

Depending on who you sign up with, it ranges from free to about $10 a month. Ultimately, it will be free or nearly free, because it's cheaper for the financial system to allow you to pay electronically than to pay millions of dollars to print bills, mail them to you, and have hundreds of people process the checks you send.

Until now, there's been no guarantee a bill you pay will make it to the other side. Plenty of mortgage companies and utility companies are telling customers they didn't receive a payment, and charging customers late fees and interest. There's been no way to prove that you sent your payment. But electronic bill payment changes that, providing a digital record of your payment. Plus, if you have a recurring payment that's the same every month, you can set it up to be paid automatically, and you never have to worry about forgetting to pay.

If you're going to use electronic payment, use a service that stands behind the system. I use Charles Schwab's electronic payment service, and it guarantees it will pay any late fees and handle any problems with the vendor if I make the payment date at least four days before the actual due date. So if the payment's due on the 10th, I post it to be paid on the 6th. If the vendor says they didn't get it, the service handles it.

Don't worry about paying a small monthly fee. When you figure the cost of a check, a stamp, and an envelope, it costs you about 50 cents to mail a payment. If the fee for electronic bill payment is 50 cents a transaction or less, you're even. And it's so much more convenient.

Some small organizations are still using an archaic system, where you request an electronic payment, they deduct the money from your account, print a check, and mail it to the utility company. But that's a transitional problem that will go away before long. More than half of my payments now are going all-electronic. Before long, you'll be able to make an electronic payment on the day it's due and it will be instantly credited to your account. And you'll be able to receive all your bills electronically.

# WIRELESS PHONES

 157

My oldest daughter is 11, and sometimes I imagine her trying to explain to her children when they're watching an old movie on television why there was a cord coming out of the telephone.

We still think of the traditional wired telephone as something different than a wireless telephone. But Japan now has more wireless phones than wired phones, and we'll be at that point in the United States probably by 2003.

Wireless phones started out as an exotic gadget for the wealthy or pretentious, because it was so expensive to use one. Now there are many cities in which using a wireless phone is equivalent in price to using a traditional wired phone. Some cities have wireless

flat-rate calling plans, which allow you to make an unlimited number of calls for one monthly fee. And ultimately that's going to happen everywhere with wireless, just as it did for traditional wired calling.

But picking a wireless plan is much more difficult than choosing traditional phone service. You have to decide if you want it for local calling, for long-distance, and/or to make calls while you travel around the country or even overseas. You have to decide whether you're going to use just a few minutes a month or a ton of minutes.

I'm a talkaholic and I travel a lot, so my plan allows me to talk up to 2,000 minutes a month and use it around the

**158**

country. But you may need a wireless phone only for emergencies. The best way to decide is to avoid the advertising hype and make a list that will help you concentrate on what you really need.

One Web site, www.decide.com, will help you figure out if coverage is close to what is claimed. They've made thousands of test calls in medium and large cities and will show you a true path of coverage rather than the fake one provided by the wireless phone company. Both it and www.point.com do a great job of letting you compare plans side-by-side. You plug in your list of needs, or your monthly budget, and these Web sites help you compare.

I do have a key rule. No matter whose offer looks best, if you're required to sign a contract, that's a huge strike against the plan. Pricing and plans change so quickly that it's terrible for you to be handcuffed to somebody's contract. If the deal is so good that you're willing to sign a contract, don't sign one for more than one year. In all contracts, include a 30-day right to test the service. In spite of the beautiful coverage maps you'll get from the various providers, the true coverage you get can be very ugly, with dropped calls or no service available in your normal commuting pattern.

One thing you don't need to worry about is the technology somebody's bragging about, digital vs. analog, tdma vs, cdma vs. gsm. All you want is a phone that's reliable and gives you the best package of services for your dollar.

If you do these things up-front, you'll dramatically improve the odds that you'll be happy with your service. Too many people, because they're confused, are relying on commissioned sales people or cute advertising, and they end up with something that isn't suitable. In this case, it saves you money and annoyance not to be lazy.

### TIPS ON WIRELESS PHONES

◉ Choose a wireless plan that best meets your needs. Consider how many minutes per month you'll use, whether you need long-distance service, and whether you'll be using your wireless phone a lot while traveling.

◉ Unless a plan is just incredible, don't sign a contract. If you sign a contract, don't sign for more than one year, and make sure you're allowed, in writing, 30 days to test the service.

◉ Go to www.decide.com and www.point.com to compare plans and check the coverage area.

www.decide.com
www.point.com

# LONG-DISTANCE CALLING

It's hard to believe that in 1984 the average cost of a coast-to-coast long-distance call was 69 cents a minute. Today, it's possible to make long-distance calls for free, and as you read this, I hope you're not paying more than seven cents a minute for regular monthly service.

Long-distance has become a commodity. It now costs a phone company the same amount to transmit a call from Chicago to Los Angeles as it does to send a call from one side of Chicago to the other. And because of the Internet, many companies are going to offer long-distance for free, or as a throw-in with other services.

Dialpad (www.dialpad.com) is one of the pioneers in using the Internet to make free long-distance available. You dial the number on your computer, and it rings at the other person's phone. Quality varies. Some calls are very clear. Others are not. But people tell me they absolutely adore it. You need speakers and a microphone or a headset, which you can buy yourself or from an affiliated company for about $25.

That's just one of the offers you'll

see. Many use a technology call IP, or Internet Protocol, which is a very inexpensive way of transmitting your voice around the world in data packets. That means that instead of having an entire circuit for your phone conversation, your voice and thousands of others can travel simultaneously on the same line. That's why it can be so much cheaper.

 159

But even traditional long-distance is getting super-cheap. For example, www.telephonechoice.com offers traditional "dial-1" service from your home at 4.7 cents a minute, with no monthly fee and no monthly minimum. Your calls are simply billed to your credit card.

When you're looking at long-distance plans, whether you want to look at traditional or Internet Protocol plans, I have three key "don'ts" — don't pay any monthly fee, don't pay any monthly minimum, and don't pay any minimum per call. There are a lot of offers out there on prepaid phone cards and monthly calling plans that try to lure you in with extra-cheap per-minute rates, but snare you with minimum charges of 50 cents

**160** 🖳 per call, 75 cents per call, or $1 per call. That's a terrible "gotcha."

I read somewhere that four cents a minute for regular or wireless calls is the psychological equivalent of free for many people. At four cents a minute, a half-hour phone call is just $1.20. I've been using a service called BigZoo, www.bigzoo.com, which is 3.9 cents a minute with no monthly fee and no minimums. With BigZoo, you buy a block of minutes in advance, and I buy $10 worth at a time, a little more than 250 minutes. The call quality is just like any other, and you can use it from any phone in the United States to any other phone. You dial an access code, then the number you want. I put the access number on a speed-dial button, so it's not a bother at all.

As I mentioned, I also use a service called Freeway (www.broadpoint.com) to make free long-distance calls. Each time I want to make a call, I dial Freeway's toll-free number, enter an ID number, and listen to a few ads. For each 10- to 15-second ad I listen to, I get 2 free minutes of long distance. So if I plan to talk to someone for 10 minutes, I listen to about a minute's worth of ads.

But BigZoo is so cheap that I sometimes get lazy. I made a 40-minute call recently and paid the $1.56 to make the call via BigZoo, rather than calling for free on Freeway. I could have listened to 20 ads and it would have taken me five minutes, and I would have saved $1.56. So that day when I went to lunch I

ordered something on the menu that was cheaper than what I'd normally get.

I'm getting a massive number of complaints from people who are being ripped off when they make a call from overseas back to the U.S. when they use traditional calling cards that post the charges to your monthly phone bill. I've heard charges from $7 a minute to $50 a minute. It's very, very important when you go overseas to buy a prepaid calling card that will allow you to make calls from overseas, free of any setup charge, at prices from 12 cents a minute to 55 cents a minute. That way, you take any of the surprise out of it. The best deals on prepaid cards are at the warehouse clubs, Sam's Club, Costco, and BJ's.

A lot of the hotels overseas have lost so much revenue to people using prepaid cards to call back to the U.S. that they're now blocking access numbers through the hotel phone system to any of the discount services. When I went to Switzerland in March 2000, I went to a phone booth late at night, with my teeth chattering in the cold, to make a call back to the U.S. Somebody on my staff was laughing at me, but they stopped laughing when they got a bill for $15 for a one-minute call they made from the hotel. I paid 17 cents a minute from the pay phone.

Hotels, hospitals, and other public phones in the U.S. no longer block you from using a calling card or a prepaid card, but you'll pay a fortune if you simply pick up the phone and dial 1 and your number. Use the toll-free access number for your prepaid card or your regular long-distance calling card.

Another area that's been quicksand for people is something called "casual billing rates." When you move and sign up for phone service with the local phone company, they'll ask what company you would like to handle your long-distance service. If you give them a company name, you also have to call the long-distance company and choose a calling plan. If you don't, you'll be billed as a casual billing customer and pay astronomically high rates, even if you had a discount calling plan from the same carrier at your prior address. Casual billing rates can be as much as $3 a minute.

Since I make all my calls from home using prepaid plans, I have no long distance carrier at all. That also protects me from a couple of Internet-based scams. There's one that hits your computer when you visit a certain Web page. The site turns down the volume on your computer while it's supposedly loading the page, hangs up, and dials back to a Third-World country. People are getting billed hundreds of dollars for these calls.

In another scam, a site places an icon on your screen, and then in the middle of the night, instructs your computer to dial a country such as the Ivory Coast or Madagascar. The long-distance companies are saying the call came from your house, so you have to pay for it. There's a way you can make sure this doesn't happen to you. Unless you have a need to make overseas calls, sign up with your local phone company to block international calling from your phone.

 161

## TIPS ON LONG-DISTANCE CALLING

- ◉ Consider long-distance calling services that transmit your voice inexpensively over the Internet.

- ◉ Don't pay monthly fees, don't agree to make a minimum number of calls, and don't pay a minimum charge per call.

- ◉ When you're overseas and calling back to the U.S., use a prepaid calling card.

- ◉ When you select a long-distance provider through your local phone company, call the long-distance company and select a calling plan, or you'll face high per-call rates as a "casual billing rate" customer.

## INTERNET

www.dialpad.com (Free long-distance over the Internet)
www.telephonechoice.com (Inexpensive 'dial-1' long-distance)

www.bigzoo.com (Inexpensive prepaid long-distance)
www.broadpoint.com (Free advertiser-supported long-distance)
www.fcc.gov (Complain about long-distance carriers)
www.speak4free.com (Free long-distance over the Internet)
www.phonefree.com (Free long-distance over the Internet)

# SATELLITE TV

I'm so excited at how people have taken to satellite TV. Both Dish Network and DirecTV, the two major satellite TV companies, are booming, and they are providing serious competition to cable TV for the first time.

Satellite TV gives viewers a sharper picture and clearer sound, along with more varied programming and better cost. One area in which satellite TV had a big leg up on cable TV was customer service. But unfortunately, based on what I'm hearing from listeners, the satellite TV providers are having customer-service problems because of their rapid growth.

That negative is partially outweighed by fantastic deals on equipment. One of the biggest obstacles to choosing satellite service has been the enormous up-front cost. That's now gone, as a parade of offers has made equipment and installation free or extra-cheap. Programming is significantly less expensive than that offered by cable TV.

The other thing that had been restricting demand for satellite TV was the lack of local channels. But now the satellite systems provide local channels in all major markets of the country.

If you want to be able to watch different programs in different rooms of the house, it's going to cost more. You'll need a separate receiver box for each such television, installation will cost more, and you'll pay more per month for programming. So when you pick a satellite system, think first about how many TVs in the house you want to get satellite service.

Although programming costs less with satellite TV, people often buy more of it, so a typical satellite bill might be more than a cable bill. So it's a good idea to plan before you buy. Try setting an amount you're willing to spend, then make compromises to fit within that cap. Satellite companies don't generally mention this, but you can get a discount if you pay for programming one year at a time instead of monthly.

Around the country, 99 percent of people will be able to receive satellite service. But 1 percent won't be able to position the satellite dish so it can have a clear line to the satellite in the Southern sky. If hills, trees, or other barriers may block the signal, make sure the equipment is fully refundable.

The two providers, Dish Network and DirecTV, are slightly different, and because their equipment isn't compatible, you can't start with one and switch to the other. DirecTV has put a big emphasis on sports programming, while Dish Network has emphasized movies. DirecTV is a better choice if you're worried about being able to receive the satellite signal, because its satellite is at a higher angle in the sky than Dish Network's.

 **TIPS ON SATELLITE TV**

- Satellite TV has exceptional picture and sound quality and choice of programming, and costs less than cable.

- If you want to be able to watch different programs in different rooms of the house, it will cost more.

- A small percentage of homes, about 1 percent, can't receive satellite TV service because the signal is blocked by trees, hills, or other barriers.

- There are two major providers: DirecTV emphasizes sports programming, while Dish Network emphasizes movies. Their equipment is not compatible. 💻 163

# TRAVEL

The travel business has changed more in the last few years than at any time I've ever witnessed, and the change has been brought about by the Internet. Travel already was democratized by deregulation that occurred in 1979. It used to be something people did for business, or because they were rich enough to visit exotic places. Today, most people see travel as something they can do.

I was in the travel business for six years and was fortunate to do very well in it. I ended up with a chain of travel agencies, which I sold in 1987. Since I got into the business, I've traveled constantly. I've visited every continent in the world, except for Antarctica. My visit to the Arctic Circle, the flip side, will easily suffice.

Traveling around the world is incredible fun, I've found, but it has also taught me something — the importance of saving money. Many people, I've observed in my travels, make things last; they don't have to have the latest of everything, unlike many in our consumption-oriented society. I've also seen a lot of people in poor countries who were very happy despite their lack of material things.

In this chapter I'll tell you more about how to travel for less, what hazards to avoid, how to save on hotels and car rentals, and some great places to visit.

SAVING MONEY ON TRAVEL

CAR RENTALS

HANDLING MONEY

OPPORTUNITIES AND HAZARDS

CLARK'S FAVORITE PLACES TO GO

# 166 ☀ SAVING MONEY ON TRAVEL

It's one of the ironies of travel that vacationers get the best deals, and business travelers, who travel far more often, get the worst deals. The Internet has only accelerated that trend. An airline, cruise line, or hotel can now post last-minute discounts on the Internet, and people who act quickly can get amazing savings.

There are certain travel strategies that will save you the most money when you travel. The No. 1 way to save is to be ready to buy when there's a great deal available, then figure out a reason you want to go. My wife and I were planning to take a trip to Japan, using frequent flier miles. Three weeks before we were supposed to go, there was a sale from my home city of Atlanta to Rome, Italy, for $318 round-trip. I didn't even have to think about taking advantage of that good a deal. We immediately bought a pair of tickets to Rome and cashed in the frequent flier miles, paying a $50 penalty to use the miles at a later date.

I go on incredibly cheap trips, none of which are to places I planned to go in advance. When a deal pops up, I go. I've traveled from Atlanta to San Francisco for $79 round-trip. I've been to Tucson, Arizona, for $99; Portland, Oregon, for $100; Salt Lake City, Utah, for $110, all round-trip. And many of my listeners joined me on a special from Atlanta to Honolulu, Hawaii, a journey of nearly 5,000 miles, for as

little as $182 round-trip. I paid $320 for a trip that included a free stop in San Francisco.

Now, I recognize that a lot of people don't have the travel flexibility that I do, but many of us are able to wait for a special bargain instead of planning a trip months ahead to a specific place. For the technologically savvy, finding the deals that happen along actually is pretty easy. The first step is to register at all the airlines' Web sites for weekly mailings of deals. Initially the airline Web sites offered deals only for unsold seats at the very last minute, which turned many people off. Now they list deals that can be good for immediate travel or for travel months in the future, for destinations around the world. It's very easy to register for the automatic e-mail notification. Then whenever a special pops up, you get an e-mail. The biggest aggravation is dumping them if you're not interested in reading them.

I took my staff to Zurich, Switzerland, on an Internet-only sale for $239 round-trip, when the lowest published fare was $548 round-trip. That's a pretty big difference.

The airline Web sites fall into two categories, those that are good for routine travel and those that are good for "distress" or bargain travel. Except for the bargain fares, most major airline sites will cost you more money than all other methods of booking travel. So don't use them to book, except for the special deals. The airlines use their Web sites to sell convenience, not low fares. For routine travel, you'll find much lower fares by calling a travel agent.

But you can use the Web sites of the discount airlines routinely. Southwest Airlines, for example, has become the most successful Internet enterprise in the United States, selling more than $1 billion in tickets in one recent year. The discounters, led by Southwest, have made their Web sites so easy to use to find low fares that they are selling a far larger percentage of their tickets over the Internet than are the full-fare airlines. People have figured out that the full-fare airlines are good to find schedules, but not for low fares. The discounters are serving the customer the way the customer wants to be served.

If you don't like using a travel agent because of the fees many now charge, and you do want to try to book your own flights, try using one of the general independent travel sites. In fact, try a minimum of four to book each trip. Some of the major ones are www.travelocity.com, www.expedia.com, www.onetravel.com, and www.thetrip.com. You may have others that you prefer. You have to use several because all four could show you different fares for the same trip, and usually will. These sites are inconsistent, because you won't see the depth and breadth of possibilities that you get from a travel agent. That could change over time.

The other area of travel involves price above all else, pioneered by

Priceline.com. With Priceline, you bid for seats, without being able to choose the airline, the routing, or the time of day you'll get to your destination. If you bid on one of these sites, understand that you have no control over travel times on your chosen day of departure or your return day. You could leave at 6 a.m. or midnight. So you should consider both days lost to you.

How much you bid for a ticket depends on the amount of time you have before your trip. If you're leaving in a few weeks, check with a travel agent or another Web site to find the cheapest fare available, and bid 25 percent below that price. That's the minimum additional discount you deserve for giving up all control over your travel. If you're trying to go at the last minute and you want to avoid the outrageous fares you're being quoted, make your bid equal to the airlines' best price for the same ticket with a 21-day or 14-day advance purchase. So let's say the lowest fare for your destination with an advance purchase is $300 and you have the advance time, bid $225. If you don't have the advance time, bid $300. The last-minute full fare might be $1,500, so if your bid is accepted, you'll save some 75 percent.

I've had lots of complaints about Priceline with customer-service issues, and my staff and I, when we've tried to intervene, have found Priceline's people difficult to deal with. That could be just a byproduct of growth. We've seen two major complaints: Priceline has filled

**167**

**168** ✸

the trip for the wrong dates and has been slow to correct the error, or Priceline's add-on fees and/or airline junk fees increase the price as much as 30 percent above your bid. So take that into account. Whenever you book online, always print a hard copy of your work. So if there's a dispute later with the credit card company or the Web site about the amount, you'll have proof of what you purchased and what you agreed to pay.

There are a number of reasons that extra-cheap airfares pop up so often these days. One reason is that a certain airline may be trying to send a signal to another. One day, Northwest Airlines was mad at Continental Airlines, so Northwest published extra-cheap fares out of Newark, Cleveland, and Houston. Newark, Cleveland, and Houston happen to be Continental's three main flight centers. Northwest probably was retaliating because Continental ran some fare specials out of Detroit, Minneapolis, and/or Memphis, which are Northwest's main flight centers. Sometimes we benefit from these competitive scuffles.

I share a vacation home near Salt Lake City, Utah, with several members of my family (it's not a timeshare), and I got three incredibly cheap fares in one year from Atlanta to Salt Lake City — $110 round-trip, $134 round-trip, and $172 round-trip, and all three times it was because of airlines dueling with each other. Delta has hubs in Atlanta and Salt Lake City, and the other airlines were mad at Delta for

cutting fares to their hubs.

The second-most common reason for an unusually cheap fare is that somebody just makes a mistake. There are so many hundreds of thousands of fare changes a day that sometimes somebody just enters the wrong price. The fare is still perfectly good, although it may not be available for more than a few hours or a day.

Finally, airlines run specials when seats on a particular route aren't selling well, so the carriers dump these "bottom bucket" tickets. Because of the economic turmoil in Asia in 1998, airlines were heavily discounting seats from the U.S. to cities all over Asia. Fares dropped to as low as $399 round-trip from the U.S. to Asia. The same thing happens every time there's unrest in the Middle East — airfares to Israel and Egypt drop precipitously.

My in-laws have totally changed their thinking about travel. They used to think it was too expensive, and they took most of their trips by car. But I've got them going everywhere, because I'll call them at 10 P.M. and tell them about some great special they have to try. I have them going to Anchorage, Alaska, for $205 round-trip; to Italy for $388 round-trip; and to Paris for $365 round-trip. I like people to use a travel agent to book their trips, but if you find a hot special at night, you're stuck calling the airline to buy your ticket.

A great strategy to save money on travel is to do the reverse of what everyone else does. Obviously if you go to the beach Christmas week, you will pay the highest possible prices of the year. But believe it or not, if you go from December 1 to December 15, you'll pay a fraction of the cost, even though you're still aiming for a warm-weather getaway. One of the key secrets to unlocking savings in travel is to know the calendar. Ideally, you go to a place at a time when the weather is right and the rates, because of a quirk of the calendar, are especially low. If you're willing to live with less-than-ideal conditions, you'll go during the opposite season, such as a visit to south Florida in the summer.

Europe is a perfect example, and the price gaps have gotten even larger. From November 1 through March 31, the very lowest rates are offered on airfare to Europe. On the other hand, summertime is very expensive. It would not be unusual for a summertime ticket to Europe to cost several times the winter equivalent of the same seat. In the winter of 1999–2000, European fares dropped below $200 from the Northeast United States, and below $300 for everywhere except the Far West. That's cheap.

Prices to the Caribbean work similarly, although the swings in price are not as extreme. Rates from April 15 through December 15 usually are about 30 percent below the prices from December 15 through April 15. I love going to the Caribbean or Florida during the off-season or summer. Some people worry about hurricanes, but the chances are very small, even during hurricane season, of you being in the wrong place at the wrong time. With modern forecasting technology, seldom could you be in any real danger.

You can also use the calendar to save on your hotel bill. I've taken combined vacations to San Francisco and Lake Tahoe, Nevada, and paid bargain rates at hotels in both cities. In an urban area such as San Francisco, hotel rates are lowest on weekends, when volume from business travelers is minimal. In a resort area, it's just the opposite, with the best deals available during the week. So I visit both cities during the same trip and spend the weekend in San Francisco and the rest of the week skiing in the mountains.

Off-season travel to Florida isn't as cheap as it used to be, however, because Florida has become so urbanized that a lot of Floridians are filling rooms at resorts in the offseason that might have gone empty before. Resorts that used to offer fantastic deals are now offering more modest discounts.

You can save a lot of money if you're willing to be flexible about the dates you travel and the airports you fly out of or into. Be willing to travel on a Saturday, rather than a Friday, for example. Fly into Newark Airport in New Jersey instead of LaGuardia Airport in New York, or vice versa. If you're going to Los Angeles, think about what else is nearby. There are five metro area airports, and the fares are different to all five. San Francisco has three.

If a discount airline serves the airport

**169**

you want to fly into, you're in great shape. But if they don't, you still may be in luck. A nearby airport or city may be served by a discounter, and that could make a massive difference in what you pay. If you are going to Boston, for example, you should always check fares to Providence, Rhode Island, because Providence is served by Southwest Airlines, the nation's premier low-cost carrier. If you're going to Washington, D.C., check Baltimore, another Southwest Airlines city. This same strategy applies with any of the lower-profile discount airlines as well.

A bonus for business travelers is that Southwest Airlines and its imitators do not charge higher fares to business people.

One thing that's always amused me is how desperately people want nonstop flights. So often you'll find a moderate to huge discount by taking a connecting flight. I think it's worthwhile spending two hours of your time to get a much better deal on a connecting flight.

And don't be fixated on frequent flier miles. A thousand frequent flier miles is worth about $10 in free travel. If you're going on a 2,000-mile round-trip, that's $20 in frequent flier value. If you can get a fare $30 cheaper by flying on a different airline, do it.

## HOTEL BARGAINS ONLINE

The hotel business is still in the very early phases of adapting to the Internet. They're way behind the airlines, but moving very quickly to take advantage of it. There are some independent sources that I find are good possibilities for discounts. One I like is www.room-saver.com, which is good for people who are looking for discounts on moderately priced hotels, such as Courtyard by Marriott, Red Roof Inns, and La Quinta. The discounts aren't huge, but they offer discounts on properties that usually don't offer discounts. Another is www.hoteldiscount.com. With the hotel sites, although in many cases you'll snag a great deal, make sure you check with the hotel, either directly or through their 800 number, to make sure it's a good deal. It's possible that the hotel could offer a better deal directly than through an independent booking source.

Here's another warning: so far we've had two hotel discount sites that went bust after people had paid for their rooms but before they took their trip. They ended up losing all the money they had paid for their rooms. If you're going to book with a site that requires you to pay in advance, don't book more than 60 days in advance or your money could be at risk.

Some of the hotel sites are offering discounts that they'll e-mail to you, just like the airlines will. These are almost always great bargains. Radisson and Hilton hotels have been the most innovative in offering special hotel bargains on the Internet. They have specials for specific hotels on specific dates. They might have a conference center hotel that doesn't have any major bookings for a few days, so they'll heavily discount the rooms on the Web site. I've used it and the savings are fantastic. I took my staff to Santa Fe, New Mexico, and we booked the Radisson Sante Fe for $59 a night, a wonderful deal. I've seen deals for Scottsdale, Arizona, during the peak season for $105 a night, which is nothing for that area. When I went to Norway a few years ago, I looked at the Radisson site and they had a special for Oslo that I thought was expensive until I got to Norway. Then I realized it was a great deal.

With these hotel specials, you can book the rooms yourself right online. Rooms tend to be available from one to four weeks in advance.

## TIPS ON SAVING MONEY ON TRAVEL

- Be ready to buy tickets when there's a great deal available, then figure out a reason you want to go.

- Check the Internet for special fares, but don't use it to shop for the best fare to a particular destination.

- Register with each airline to receive special deals via e-mail.

- Use independent Web sites to shop for routine travel, but check at least four, because fares vary widely.

- Do the reverse of what others travelers do: Buy airfare and hotel rooms during off-peak seasons, when rates are lower.

**171**

- Plan vacations so you can take advantage of weekend specials in urban areas and mid-week specials in resort areas.

- Be flexible about the dates you travel and the airports you fly out of or into.

- Consider taking trips that involve changing flights. They're cheaper and often don't take that much longer.

- Be flexible about the airline you use, and don't be fixated on frequent flier miles. A thousand frequent flier miles is worth only about $10 in free travel.

## INTERNET

www.travelocity.com (Booking airfares)
www.expedia.com (Booking airfares)

www.onetravel.com (Booking airfares)
www.thetrip.com (Booking airfares)
www.roomsaver.com (Hotel discounts)
www.hoteldiscount.com (Hotel discounts)
www.hotelbook.com (Hotel discounts)

# CAR RENTALS

I get more complaints about car rentals than about any other phase of travel. People don't rent cars that often, and the transaction at the car rental counter can be confusing and unpleasant.

Most upsetting is the array of choices car renters are hit with for insurance-type products. When you rent a car, you'll often get a very heavy-handed pitch for a collision damage waiver, or CDW, also known by the codes LDW or PDW. This is a ripoff fee whose sole purpose is to build profits for the car rental company. By paying it, you supposedly waive your responsibility in the event the car is damaged or destroyed in an accident. Nationwide, the fee averages $16 a day. On an annual basis, that's nearly $6,000, a lot more than you pay for total coverage on your personal automobile.

My advice is to reject collision damage waiver, which is your option, under almost all circumstances. Check with your auto insurer before you go on a trip, because many times your own policy will cover you for temporary use of a rental car.

Another way to avoid CDW is to use a credit card. Certain VISAS, MasterCards, and American Express cards provide secondary coverage when you rent a car. They pay for whatever your own automobile insurer doesn't. Diners Club provides full primary coverage for car rentals. If you rent a car more than six times a year, pay the huge annual fee for Diners Club.

If you have no collision coverage on your personal automobile, use a credit card that provides coverage or see if you can purchase a short-term rider from your insurer.

Whether you take the collision damage waiver or not, check the rental car carefully before you leave the rental lot. Quite often I'll see a dented fender or a broken taillight after looking closely at a rental car. At night, I pull the car up underneath a light to check it. If you see any damage on your rental car, have an official of the company note it on the rental contract before you leave. If you don't, you'll probably have to pay for the repair.

I had a caller whose rental company

claimed his wife had broken an outside mirror and wanted him to pay $371 for it, an outrageous price even if she had broken it. My staff called the company and got him out of that.

The second type of insurance you'll normally be offered is excess liability coverage. Again, check with your own automobile or homeowners insurance provider, because either or both may provide you with such coverage, making it unnecessary to purchase it from the car rental company. The cost is about $7 a day.

There are two other optional insurance coverages you'll see quite often on a car rental contract. Personal effects coverage, or PEC, is to cover you against theft of your possessions from the rental car. Normally your homeowners or renters insurance will cover that. Personal injury protection covers some of your medical bills if you're injured in an accident. This coverage is completely unnecessary if you already have health insurance.

Car rental rates have gone up a lot in recent years. I probably pay 50 percent more than I used to pay. For many years, car rental companies were so focused on grabbing market share from one another that nobody worried about making money. They all seemed to change their minds at the same time. In addition, the travel market has grown a lot, and that demand has helped pushed prices up. Finally, the auto manufacturers used to own the rental companies, and to help keep the factories running,

they'd provide cars for almost nothing. That isn't the case anymore.

At one time, you got the best deals on car rentals through your travel agent. But recently the rental companies have made it harder for travel agents by putting their sale deals under special fare codes. Without the code, your travel agent can't get you the special rate. If you ask your travel agent or the car rental company for their cheapest rate in Philadelphia, they might say it's $36.99 a day. If you ask for the rate for a special fare code, say "2GL," they might say $24.99. So it pays to know the code.

When I rent a car, I use a three-step strategy to find the best price. When I book my flight, I book a car, so I know I have a rental available during my trip. Just before I leave, I recheck. If bookings have turned out to be softer than the rental companies expected, I'll be able to rebook at the last minute at a lower price. If they're not lower, I'm still okay, because I have my existing reservation. There are no penalties to change or cancel a car-rental reservation. Third, I'll try various car rental Web sites and look for specials. I do that when I first book the car and when I recheck. I find consistently that I get the cheapest deals at Alamo, Budget, and Dollar.

Alamo does something every week called Out-of-the-Blue Specials, which are deals available for slow booking periods around the country. They're great deals. I saved my brother-in-law $21 a day on a car in Tucson. The cheapest deal he could find was $46 a day. I found

173

**174** ❧ him an Out-of-the-Blue deal just before his trip for $24.99. My mother flew into Phoenix and I got her a deal for $29.99. I had a Dollar deal for $21.99 that I got when I booked my ticket. In that case prices had moved up after I first booked, so I stayed with the original rate.

Another change in car rentals is most of the inexpensive rates require you to keep the car for a Saturday night. The car companies have taken a lesson from the airline industry and found out how to keep business travelers from getting the best rate.

If you're planning to go somewhere during peak season, say Florida during the winter or Europe during the summer, make sure you can find an affordable car before you buy a nonrefundable airline ticket.

A great trick to saving on a car rental is to rent the smallest car available at the cheapest rate. I always rent the smallest car, but I get a larger car for the same price 80 percent of the time. Car rental companies load their fleets with larger cars, so they rarely have the smaller car you ordered when you show up.

When you book a small car, the rental company may try to sell you up to a larger car, at a higher cost, when you get to the counter. Just remember that four out of five times you'll get the larger car without paying for it. So don't give in.

The only time I've ever received the subcompact, ironically enough, was at my wedding. And my mother-in-law is probably never going to forgive me. The wedding was very posh, and as we left the reception hall, we got into this two-door econo-box, probably the cheapest car sold in America. It just killed my wife's mom. But believe me, it virtually never happens.

Some rental companies will offer you fuel options. You can pick the car up with a full tank and drop it off with a full tank. Or pick it up full and bring it back empty. The only option to choose is taking it out full and bringing it back full. Just stop at a service station on your way back to the rental lot and fill the tank. If you forget, they'll charge you two to four times the normal retail price for gas.

Don't fool with any of the other options that require a calculator and a mathematics degree. Any of the plans that require you to bring the car back with an empty tank are dangerous. With crime so prevalent, it's not smart for you to play it cute and run out of gas trying to coast in on fumes.

If I rent on a weekend, I usually find the best rates with one of the major on-airport rental companies, such as Hertz, Avis, National, and Budget, which rely almost exclusively on business travelers. There's little business travel on weekends, and these companies have huge fleets they need to push into the marketplace, so they discount heavily.

If your rental is for weekdays, you'll usually pay a high price per day with on-airport rental companies, and find much better prices with "second-tier" companies. The largest second-tier renters are Thrifty and Alamo. There is a substantial number of third-tier renters in major markets, but the quality of service varies tremendously.

If you're renting for five days or more, a weekly rental will provide a large discount. A seven-day rental usually costs less than a three-day rental. That's because car rental companies have high costs for processing a rental.

With a short-term rental, you're paying mostly for the cost of the people needed to prepare the car for rental and accept it for return. If you begin Thursday at noon and return the car usually by the same time Monday, you're eligible for weekend rates that are up to 70 percent below weekday rates.

## TIPS ON CAR RENTALS

⦿ To get the best deal, book a car when you book your flight. Then recheck before you leave to see if there's a cheaper rate. Check car rental Web sites for bargains at both times.

⦿ When you rent a car, don't accept the insurance options the company wants you to buy. Check with your own auto insurance agent to see if you're covered under your policy, or use a credit card that offers travel insurance.

⦿ Check the rental car carefully before you leave the rental lot. If you see any damage, have an official of the company note it on the rental contract before you leave.

⦿ If you're planning to go somewhere during peak season, make sure you can find an affordable car before you buy a nonrefundable airline ticket.

**175**

⦿ Rent the smallest car available at the cheapest rate. Four out of five times, the rental company won't have the small car you ordered and will have to give you a larger car at the small-car price.

⦿ Always take the car out with a full tank of gasoline and return it with a full tank.

⦿ If you're renting for five days or more, a weekly rental will provide a large discount.

## INTERNET

www.alamo.com
www.drivebudget.com
www.dollar.com

# 176 ≋ HANDLING MONEY

Cash and traveler's checks used to be the two staples of overseas travel. But that's not true anymore. Credit cards are so common now that they're a good way to pay even in many developing countries. They're virtually all you need in the countries most of us will visit.

However, I have two warnings for you about using credit cards overseas. First, you have no chargeback rights when you leave the U.S. That makes it very important for you to keep all your charge slips and reconcile them against your credit card statement. I get several calls every summer travel season from people who made purchases overseas, then discovered that the merchant conveniently added a couple of zeros to the credit card receipt after they had left. Your only hope in that situation is being able to show the original copy of that receipt.

Second, some credit cards are now adding additional charges of up to 5 percent on overseas purchases, and not disclosing these charges. Using a credit card to buy something overseas is a great deal because you get the banker's buying rate, which is the wholesale rate of exchange, plus a 1 percent transaction fee. But it's not such a good deal if your credit card company is adding extra charges. Before you travel overseas, contact your credit card issuers and find out if they charge any nuisance fees. If one does, use another of your cards that doesn't.

The other technique, which works very well, is to use the automated teller machine card from your bank. The Web sites of VISA and MasterCard will help you determine where there are ATMs in cities and countries around the world. Once again, you should get the wholesale rate of exchange, plus whatever junk fee your bank chooses to charge you for using an ATM.

The worst problem I've had using an ATM was in Oslo, Norway. My wife and I got to the airport to find two ATMs — both broken. Travelers were in a daze about what to do, because using ATMs has become the accepted way of getting foreign currency, especially in Europe, where people often travel from country to country. So we got in our rental car and started driving to town. Lo and behold, we came to a tollbooth, but it was an automated tollbooth, and we had no money. I had to drive through the tollbooth without paying, and I still feel guilty. I've never run a tollbooth before or since. The first time I saw an ATM in Oslo, I stopped and immediately got money.

I had some trouble with an ATM in Italy also. Not only would the machine not give me my money, but it ate my card. It was 1:30 A.M. and I hadn't slept in what seemed like a couple of days. So I started banging on the machine and beep, my card popped out. But this stuff doesn't happen very often.

If you decide to exchange currency, don't just go for the posted rate of exchange at a change booth or bank. Make sure you know if there's any service fee or any minimum transaction charge. London is infamous for change places that advertise great rates of exchange on the dollar. But when you look at the fine print, the service charges are even bigger. It's a huge ripoff.

When I visit a foreign country, I get off the plane without a bit of their currency. I always find a teller machine or a money-change facility somewhere. Even at a foreign airport, where the rate of exchange offered is poor, you'll usually get a better deal than at an American bank.

### TIPS ON HANDLING MONEY

- For the best exchange rate on your money overseas, use credit cards as often as possible and get cash from automated teller machines using your bank ATM card.

- You have no chargeback rights when you use a credit card overseas, so keep your original charge slip.

- Check with your credit card issuers to see if they add fees to overseas purchases.

- If you're exchanging currency, don't just go for the posted rate of exchange at a change booth or bank. Make sure you know if there's any service fee.

≋ **177**

### INTERNET

www.visa.com
www.mastercard.com

# OPPORTUNITIES AND HAZARDS

Airlines routinely overbook flights, because of the frequency of no-shows. That creates a big opportunity for people who are flexible. Every time I show

up at a gate and I see a big crowd, I go straight to the podium and volunteer to give up my seat if they're overbooked. It works like a charm, because volunteers

**178**

are placed on the list in the order they give their names. If you're picked, ask to fly out on your airline's next flight or the next flight on any other airline, whichever is sooner. Always remember to ask when the next flight is, so you'll know if you can live with the delay. For your trouble, you usually will get a voucher for a free airline ticket, good for one year to anywhere in the continental United States. With some airlines, the voucher is good for a free flight anywhere in North America. I earn about three free tickets a year and use them during holiday periods, when airfares may be extra high or seats may be hard to find.

Sometimes an airline will be oversold and will not have enough volunteers. That triggers a game of musical chairs that leaves someone without a seat. There are very specific rules governing what you get for being involuntarily denied a seat. For details, go to the airline ticket counter and ask to see the contract of carriage.

If you're changing planes and the airline causes you to miss your connection, don't panic and don't allow it to ruin your day or your trip. If I get stranded, I'll take the free shuttle to an airport hotel and eat there, or check my bag in a locker and go jogging.

In addition to putting you on the next flight, the airline usually will compensate you if you're stranded — but don't take just any offer. If you get stranded overnight, don't accept anything less than an airline-provided hotel room, plus meal vouchers and long-distance calls to alert others where you are. For a minor delay, up to four hours, ask for a free meal and free long-distance at the airport terminal. Be nice to the gate agent, even if you don't feel like it, because they have a lot of power.

If your bags are lost, file a claim immediately with the airline baggage service desk. Don't leave the airport without filing a claim. Many airlines have extremely hostile policies about lost baggage claims. While it's still fresh in your mind, try to detail every item that was in your bag and keep a copy of the claim. Better yet, keep a list in your wallet or carry-on of what's in your checked bag.

On a domestic flight, the airlines have a maximum liability of $2,500 per passenger for lost bags. Do not put any jewelry, electronics, rare manuscripts, breakable items, cash, or prescription medicines in checked baggage. The airlines don't have to reimburse you fully for their loss, plus they invite theft. Put these items in your carry-on baggage. International rules are even more restrictive. Payments made for lost or stolen items are minimal, based on a rate of $9.07 per pound of checked baggage.

You can purchase excess valuation insurance, which costs about $1 per $100 of declared value. But I follow the simplest rule of all: I don't trust the airlines with my luggage. I have a carry-on bag with wheels and if I can't carry it on, I don't take it. That goes even for a long trip. If they have laundries here, they have laundries where I'm headed.

Hotel overbookings are another big travel hazard. Even if you have a reservation, it's possible the hotel won't have any rooms. In industry lingo, that makes you a "walk." If a hotel walks you, they should pay for a free night for you at an equivalent property, and move you back the next night. If you arrive by cab, they should transport you to the alternate hotel or pay for your cab there. The hotel also should allow you to call business associates or family, at no charge, to give them your new location.

You have a right to be happy with the hotel, even if your reservation is guaranteed prepaid. If you check into a hotel and it's dirty or dumpy — or if you feel unsafe there — go back to the desk immediately and tell the clerk the hotel is unacceptable to you and you're going to leave. It's traditional in the hotel industry to release you from your obligation if you are unhappy or afraid. You might want to call around to make sure there's another hotel room available in the area before you leave. If there's a convention in town and all the rooms are booked, you may be stuck.

Several hotel chains now offer a 100 percent satisfaction guarantee, promising that if you're not happy, you don't pay. Unfortunately I got a couple of calls from people who were not happy, and the hotel did not honor its money-back guarantee. One caller checked into a Comfort Inn with a young child, only to find the room reeked of marijuana. She went back to the desk and was told it was the only room they had. She tried to exercise her right not to pay, but the hotel made her pay. Even after my staff and I raised a ruckus with officials at the company's headquarters, they only reluctantly honored the guarantee. So be aware that the guarantee is only as good as the location and the chain. In order to protect yourself in this situation, put something in writing before you leave the hotel, and speak to the highest-level management person on-site at that time.

Another hazard of staying at a hotel is paying in cash or traveler's checks. When you check into any hotel, they take an imprint of your credit card. When you check out, you're free to pay for the hotel in any way you wish. A lot of times, people prefer not to charge the cost to their credit card, so they hand over cash. Unfortunately, I've heard of at least half a dozen cases in which a customer pays by cash, only to find later that the charge shows up on their credit card bill. Unless the customer keeps a receipt, and people rarely do, there's no proof they paid by cash and the clerk who stole their money is long gone. So the customer ends up paying twice. If you provide a credit card imprint for a hotel room or car rental, pay by credit card.

If you're shopping for a hotel or resort on the Internet, remember that photos you see online are no different from the glossy brochures you get in the mail. A hotel room or property may

179

**180** ☀

look great on your computer screen, but be worn or dirty when you get there. My wife and I stayed at a place in Kauai, Hawaii, that looked spectacular on the Internet and very ordinary when we got there. The beach was much smaller than we expected, and it was right in the middle of a construction zone.

People are more likely to be unhappy with hotels when they rely on brand name alone. There are certain brand names that don't maintain consistent quality. One hotel might be nice, but another old and in disrepair. All you need to do to know if a particular hotel is good is have your travel agent check in the *Travel Planner*, a publication that rates hotels from one to five stars. Consumers can also buy the *Mobil Travel Guide*, which does the same thing. Members of the Automobile

Association of America (AAA) should rely on the recommendations of the company's tour books. I prefer to stay at hotels that rate two stars or above in the *Mobil Travel Guide* or three diamonds or better in the AAA books. Hotels are rated in all price ranges, so it's useful for car trips as well as resort vacations.

There are certain brand names of hotels that deserve mention for the consistent quality of their product from city to city. Among them are Courtyard by Marriott, La Quinta, Fairfield Inn, and Hampton Inn.

Some hotels have affinity programs that are useful. You pay a nominal fee to join and in return get discounts and sometimes amenities packages, such as free local phone calls or free faxes. These programs are worthwhile only if you travel several times a year.

## TIPS ON OPPORTUNITIES AND HAZARDS

◉ By volunteering to give up your seat on an overbooked flight, you usually get a free ticket for travel anywhere in the continental United States.

◉ If you miss a connecting flight and are stranded, ask the airline to provide a free meal and long-distance calling. If you're stranded overnight, ask for a free hotel room, meals, and long-distance calls.

◉ If your bags are lost, file a claim at the airline's baggage service desk before you leave the airport.

◉ Be careful what you put in checked baggage. On a domestic flight, the airlines have a maximum liability of $2,500 per passenger for lost bags. On international flights, you get just $9.07 per pound of checked baggage.

◉ If a hotel sends you away despite a reservation, the hotel should pay for a free night at an equivalent property, and move you back the next night.

◉ If you check into a hotel and it's dirty or dumpy — or if you feel unsafe there — go back to the desk immediately and ask for your money back.

◉ Remember that photos you see on the Internet are no different from the glossy brochures you get in the mail. A hotel room or property that looks great on your computer screen may be worn or dirty when you get there.

◉ To check on the quality of a hotel, ask a travel agent or get the *Mobil Travel Guide*. Certain brands of hotel are consistently outstanding, including Courtyard by Marriott, La Quinta, Fairfield Inn, and Hampton Inn.

## INTERNET

www.dot.gov/airconsumer (Complaints)
www.passengerrights.com (Complaints)
www.travel.state.gov (Warnings about overseas travel)
www.unclaimed.org (Recovering unclaimed property)

# CLARK'S FAVORITE PLACES TO GO

Infrequent travelers often lose out on a great vacation by choosing the security of a travel package over the spontaneity of a less-structured vacation. In a package, everything is arranged in advance — air, hotel, and ground travel.

For people who are going to a beach resort, a package in many cases will be a better deal than buying the individual components separately. In fact, for people from the Eastern U.S. going to Cancun, Cozumel, or Jamaica, a package that includes airfare, hotel, and some other features usually will be cheaper than buying airfare alone.

But to non-resorts, such as Europe or Asia, a package usually costs more than going on your own. That's because travelers to Europe and Asia often are looking for more guidance, and there's a cost to that.

While resort packages designed for the budget traveler are cheap, I hear a lot of complaints about them, particularly trip packages to Nassau, Jamaica, or Cancun. In fact, I hear more complaints about those three places than everywhere else in the world combined. Sometimes travelers are victims of overbooking. They arrive at the destination, and the accommodations they paid for are not available. Other times it's just a

 181

general problem of poor service.

But the thing that leaves the bitter taste in people's mouths is the attitude that often surfaces when there is a problem. Nobody seems to care or does anything to resolve it. Many people who go to these places have a wonderful time and go back year after year without problems. But it's too risky to plan your vacation around the hope that everything will go perfectly.

If you haven't traveled a lot and want to get real value for your dollar, start off with trips to familiar places. If you're looking for a beach, go to a nice one in Florida. As you get more comfortable as a traveler, then maybe look to the Caribbean. There are lots of wonderful islands in the Caribbean. But be careful what you ask for; a lot of times I hear people say they want to go someplace where there's absolutely nothing to do, a place of absolute peace and tranquility. When they get there, they're bored — because there's absolutely nothing to do. Many of us require more activity than we'll find in a completely out-of-the-way spot.

Don't rely on brochures when you're thinking of the Caribbean, because every glossy brochure presents a picture that's not really accurate. Instead, buy one of the comprehensive guides to the Caribbean. My favorite is the *Caribbean Islands Handbook*. These books give you enough information to select the island that fits your lifestyle. One other thing you need to know is that when you fly to the Caribbean,

you'll have to change planes at least once, and many times twice. By the time you've been through all of that, you'll give up one day in each direction in travel time.

Of the Caribbean destinations, Aruba has become increasingly popular because it's pretty affordable and has good air transportation and decent accommodations. Grand Cayman is a great spot to go to, with beautiful beaches and great snorkeling and scuba diving. It has decent air services, although prices tend to be sky-high once you get there.

Florida has a handful of places I really like. On the Gulf Coast, I love Marco Island, Naples, Sanibel Island, Sarasota, Destin, and Pass-A-Grille. On the Atlantic side, I like Ponte Vedra Beach, Melbourne Beach, and Indian River Shores. All have nice stretches of sand and are relatively uncrowded. The main difference between the Gulf Coast and Atlantic beaches is the water tends to be very calm on the Gulf side, while the waves are moderate to rough on the Atlantic side.

First-time travelers to Europe seem to have an unnatural fear of moving around once they land, so they remain sealed in a tour bus. The tour offers the safety and security of traveling with a group and removes worries about handling money, picking a hotel, and communicating with someone who doesn't speak English. But if you lock yourself in a tour bus, you'll miss the essence of Europe.

I used to go to Europe with reckless abandon. I booked my airline ticket and my car rental in advance, and that was it. I made no hotel reservations and I usually didn't have an itinerary. When I got there, I was completely on my own. I would land, get in the car, and drive. One time I was in France and the highway was about to split in two directions. One direction was to Amsterdam and the other was to Paris. I had two kilometers to decide which way to go. At the last second, I decided to go to Amsterdam.

But I have started booking hotels ahead of time for Europe, at least for my first night. That's because using the Internet, I'm able to find out so much more about what might be available. When my wife and I went to Munich, we found our hotel online. One of the nice things about that is you can map everything. We had a car and wanted a place where there was free parking. But we also wanted to be able to walk from the hotel to downtown. The Internet offers a layer of information for trip planning that wasn't available before. Just use any search engine and type in the name of the city you want to visit. Be careful, though. As I say in the Opportunities and Hazards section, pictures of a hotel you see online may look better than the place does in reality. Treat the information as if it was a brochure.

The big advantage of going to Europe on your own is you can concentrate on visiting the smaller towns and villages, where prices are lower and people are friendlier. You can stay in small hotels and bed and breakfasts, meet local people, and enjoy local flavor. The bigger cities in Europe are so international in size and outlook that there isn't much difference between them. It makes little sense to spend three days in London, three in Paris, and three in Rome. Better to fly into Paris and spend the rest of the trip visiting the French countryside.

I realize there are some cities people desperately want to see, and Paris is one. But I find Frankfurt has no charm or redeeming value, and you should get out of it as quickly as you can. Brussels is another city to avoid. There are some great cities in Belgium, including Bruges and Ghent, but Brussels is a complete waste of time. While northern Europe is generally cleaner and things run like clockwork there, people seem to have a better time in southern Europe.

For those of you who think my unstructured form of travel is nuts but are willing to take a little more of a chance than with a fully escorted tour, there is a third choice in Europe. It's called a hosted itinerary and it allows you to take local tours when you get to a city. You have a tour representative in each town you can call for help, and your hotels are preplanned and prepaid. To me that's a good compromise for people who are willing to step out a little bit but who don't want to wing it.

If you have more money and want more planning, there's a fourth option called an FIT. Under this format, the

**183**

**184**

travel agent customizes the trip for you, planning details even down to dinner reservations at a particular restaurant.

If the whole idea of going to Europe scares you because of the language gap, make your first trip to Great Britain.

My favorite continent in the world is South America. In spite of the similarity in language, the difference from country to country in South America is greater than that between countries in Europe.

I've been to Latin America five times. I loved Chile, Argentina, and Bolivia, an odd choice because Bolivia is one of the world's poorest countries. Latin America is dramatically different from either Europe or the United States. People are unusually friendly. Lots of people resist going to South America over fear of political instability or crime, but I've never been afraid anywhere in South America, except in Brazil, and even Brazil knows it has a major crime problem. I particularly enjoyed the rural scenery of South America and the people. But the beaches were a disappointment. Even the most famous beaches of South America don't touch the quality of a Florida beach. The best travel guide to South America is the *South American*

*Handbook*. Nothing else comes close.

If you have frequent flier miles, try to use them for international travel, rather than domestic. You often can travel abroad for about the same number of frequent flier miles as you would spend flying to another American city, even though the cost of the tickets in cash would be far higher for the international trip.

Traveling to Asia on frequent flier miles is usually a better deal than Europe. Airfares to Asia are much higher than those to Europe, and you will actually receive more value for your miles. So if you're thinking of taking two trips, buy your trip to Europe and use your frequent flier miles to go for free to Asia.

Most airlines offer lower mileage requirements to Asia, Europe, and Latin America during off-peak periods. So if possible, try to schedule your international trip during the winter.

Using your frequent flier miles for domestic travel can, however, make sense in the event of an emergency. I know someone who had to travel quickly because of a family crisis, and used 60,000 frequent flier miles for a pair of tickets instead of paying $800 per ticket. That's smart.

**TIPS ON CLARK'S FAVORITE PLACES TO GO**

◉ Travel packages offer security at the expense of spontaneity. Budget travel packages, such as those to Nassau, Jamaica, or Cancun, tend to generate a lot of complaints.

◉ If you're interested in the Caribbean, buy one of the comprehensive guides to the Caribbean, such as the *Caribbean Islands Handbook*.

- The big advantage of going on your own to Europe is you can concentrate on visiting the smaller towns and villages of Europe, where prices are lower and people are friendlier.

- If you have frequent flier miles, try to use them for international travel, rather than domestic. For international travel, Asia is a better deal than Europe.

- Airlines offer lower frequent flier mileage requirements to Asia, Europe, and Latin America during off-peak periods. So if possible, try to schedule your international trip during the winter.

 185

# THE BASICS

The essence of my radio show, my Web site (www.clarkhoward.com), and this book is helping people solve problems. Many callers I talk with have been mistreated by a company or government agency and don't know what to do about it. I don't have a magic wand that forces companies to admit they're wrong and make amends, but I know what works.

In this chapter, I'll show you some simple techniques to make your voice heard. You'll be surprised at how effective they are and how easy they are to use.

When cajoling and prodding don't work, you may have to go to court. I'll tell you how to file a case in small claims court — and how to collect on your judgment if you win.

This chapter also includes some important tips to guide you in returning merchandise to retailers, choosing a dry cleaner, and signing a contract. I'll tell you when it's critical to use a credit card and what you need to know when you purchase major items such as furniture, carpeting, bedding, and jewelry.

SOLVING PROBLEMS

SMALL CLAIMS COURT

RETURNING MERCHANDISE

CHARGEBACKS

CONTRACTS

INFREQUENT PURCHASES

DRY CLEANING

FRANCHISES

MULTILEVEL MARKETING

# 188 ❦ SOLVING PROBLEMS

Part of the trick to solving consumer problems is having a strategy you can use to get results. Too often, consumers get frustrated and just go away mad, and going away mad is not a solution.

Whether it's a business that's confounding you or the government, the first strategy is to try talking to somebody at a higher level. If a higher-level official is unresponsive, go still higher in the organization. Go as high as you can, either by phone calls, letters, or visits to the organization. If a salesperson won't help you, go to the manager. If it's a chain, go up the ladder to the regional vice president or the home office. To get results, you have to get out of the normal loop and straight to the decision makers who can actually solve problems.

One of the big problems in corporate America is that those who have the most direct contact with the public are given the least amount of power to solve customer problems. I always shake my head when someone in the customer service department says there's nothing he or she can do. More and more, the companies that succeed are those that connect with the public and solve problems. When front-line employees don't have the latitude to find solutions, customers get angry and sales plunge.

If you reach nothing but dead ends on the phone, or you can't even find out who to speak with, your next strat-egy should be documenting your attempts to solve the problem. Keep a log of the phone calls you make, who you spoke with, and what was said. In the Workbook chapter of this book, you'll find worksheets to help you document the calls you make and the letters you write.

One of the most effective tactics to get a company to pay attention is to go to one of the gripe Web sites about that company. Almost any large company now has one or more Web sites set up by people who have complaints with the company. You can find them by using a search engine and searching for the company's name. The good companies have employees who review these complaints and deal with them. It's a great way to get around the traditional customer no-service bureaucracy. Just don't say anything that isn't true.

Other companies, unfortunately, go on the attack against both the gripe sites and anybody who complains on them. They sue or threaten to sue. Obviously those are the companies that have no concern for the customer, and nothing other than taking them to court will do.

E-mailing these companies used to work, but that's a tactic that does not seem effective anymore. Companies started ignoring e-mails due to overuse. If you send an e-mail, you may get a canned response that shows your e-mail hasn't been read by anyone.

That's why traditional letters are still the most powerful tool. I take dozens of calls from people who have complained repeatedly by telephone, then given up. I had one call from an apartment renter who wanted to move out after a problem with her landlord. She had tried to resolve the dispute by phone and got nowhere. But at that point she had no solid evidence that she had made any effort to find a solution. Writing letters not only gets attention, but it's a great method of documenting your efforts.

In your first letter, list whom you've spoken with about the problem, what attempts you've made to solve it, and what specific action you would like from the recipient of your letter. Give the person a specific period of time to deal with the problem. If you don't get a response by the allotted time, immediately send a second letter with a copy of the first attached. It takes very little time, but it's effective at working toward a solution.

Always keep a copy of your letters, and always, no matter what the situation, make the tone positive and friendly. Never write a nasty, angry letter. Words can hurt or help. Angry words send a powerfully negative message and may prevent you from getting any cooperation.

If you try to contact people by phone, by e-mail, by letter, and in person, and you get nowhere, you have to look for another pressure point. If a U.S. government agency is ignoring you or not serving your needs, call the constituent service office of your congressman or U.S. senator. If it's a state agency, call one of your state legislators. And if it's a city, county, or town issue, call the elected official who represents you in those governments. Your elected officials know they can gain a loyal voter by taking care of your needs. That's why you turn to them.

I know of a fellow who found out about a supposed mortgage loan default when he applied for a credit card. The Department of Veterans Affairs said this fellow had defaulted on a loan in another state. But it was a matter of mistaken identity. He had never defaulted on the loan — he had never even been to that part of the country. He wrote to the V.A. explaining that it was a mix-up, but the agency insisted he had defaulted. So he wrote to one of his U.S. senators, whose vote on federal appropriations helps decide the department's funding. The senator's office then contacted the agency on his behalf, and, not surprisingly, the matter was cleared up rather quickly.

If your problem is with a private organization and all attempts to resolve it have failed, try sending one last letter by certified mail. It's not necessary, in fact it's undesirable, to send your first couple of letters this way, because certified mail is a hostile gesture. Assume that the company has been negligent toward you, but not malevolent, and that your letter will get proper attention.

**189**

**190**

Most times, if you are persistent, you will get results.

Even if a company doesn't satisfy you, remember that you have the power to vote with your wallet. If a business treats you poorly, spend your money somewhere else. In a consumer-driven society such as ours, that's the ultimate power.

### TIPS ON SOLVING PROBLEMS

- If you're having trouble resolving a problem with a business or government, talk to a higher-level official. Go as high in the organization as you can.

- Try writing your complaint on one of the gripe Web sites for the company.

- If phone calls or complaints to the Web site don't work, write a letter detailing the problem and requesting some action to resolve it. If you don't get a response, send a second letter with a copy of the first attached. Always keep a copy of your letters and always make the tone positive and friendly.

- If a government agency is not serving your needs, call the constituent service office of your congressman, U.S. senator, or local elected official.

- If your problem is with a private organization and all attempts to resolve it have failed, try sending one last letter by certified mail. If that doesn't work, you may have to sue the business in small claims court.

## SMALL CLAIMS COURT

With the proliferation of high-profile legal cases in recent years and the growth of cable channels such as Court TV, Americans are getting a lot more familiar with the courtroom.

When phone calls, meetings, and letters have failed to resolve a dispute you have with a company or individual, small claims court is a great place to turn. The process works best when two parties have an honest disagreement. It does not work as well if your adversary deliberately set out to cheat you.

Taking a case to small claims court is fairly easy. Before you file a case, send a letter by certified mail to the other party. The letter has to cover a few basic elements, including:

● How you've been harmed.

● Why that particular person or company is responsible.

● How much money you seek and why it is justified.

Write this letter in a friendly tone, because it may be read later by a judge. You want the judge to view you as a reasonable person who tried but failed to solve a problem and has turned to the courts for help.

You sue in the county in which your adversary lives, the county in which you were injured, the county in which the business is located, or the county in which the product was manufactured. You need an exact address so the party can be served notice of the suit. If the defendant is served and doesn't show up to argue his or her side, you win by default.

Call the clerk of the court in the county in which you'll be filing your case to find out that court's procedures. Some areas have a kit or brochure to help you. You'll pay a filing fee — generally less than $100 — which you may recover if the judge rules in your favor. In most cases, you don't need a lawyer. In fact, some states prohibit lawyers in small claims court. The rules vary on other aspects of the process, such as whether you can appeal the decision.

On average, you can sue for up to $5,000 in small claims court. But in Kentucky and Rhode Island, the limit is just $1,500. In Tennessee, you can sue for up to $15,000 in small claims court, up to $25,000 in counties with more than 700,000 residents. You can see a state-by-state list of the limits, along with other information about small claims court, at www.nolo.com. Just go to the "courts and mediation" section, and select "small claims court." If there isn't enough information there, you can buy the book, *Everybody's Guide to Small Claims Court*, from Nolo Press, which runs through the process in great detail.

Once you get your trial date, it's time to prepare your case. The most important things to remember are to be well organized and bring strong documentation. The judge wants to hear a short version of your story, so carefully think through the three points you stated in your certified letter. Try to provide documentation for each area: 1) how you've been harmed; 2) why that particular person or company is responsible; and 3) how much money you seek and why it is justified.

Bring letters you've written in the past, records of phone calls you've made, and, if you can, photographs. Let's say someone put sod in your yard and the sod didn't take. Take pictures of it and bring the pictures to court. Or, if you had repairs done to your house and the repairs were done poorly, take pictures that illustrate the sloppy work.

If the judge finds in your favor, be prepared for the hard part — collecting on your judgment. If you're dealing with an honest individual or business,

191

you'll get a check right on the spot. If the other guy is going to fight tooth-and-nail not to pay you, your ability to collect the money will depend on your persistence. A judgment means you have a license to search for money or other assets. If you can't find any, the judgment is worthless.

Depending on the state, you may have the right to take money from the person's paycheck or checking account, put a lien on his or her house, or seize the person's automobiles. Mississippi even provides help in collecting on your judgment. Check with the clerk of the court to see what the rules are in your area.

It's possible that you won't be able to collect, particularly if someone is unemployed or self-employed, or if they skip town. The only way you'll ever have a chance to get your money is to try. If you're trying to locate some-one's checking account, try to remember whether or not you've ever written the person a check, or if the person has ever written a check to you. If so, you can find the person's bank name and account number either on the back of your canceled check, or, if you deposited the check written to you, on your bank's microfilm copy. If you've never exchanged checks, have a friend write the person a small check. You'll get the account information when the check clears and is returned in your friend's bank statement. With your judgment, you'll be able to garnish the person's bank account before he or she knows it.

It's easiest to garnish someone who works for a large employer or the government. The clerk of the court will be able to provide the forms and tell you how to garnish someone's wages or checking account.

Atlanta collections attorney Gary Jackson tells some great stories of the lengths he's gone to collect on a judgment. One of Gary's clients took his car to a mechanic for a major repair, then became ill and couldn't immediately come back for the car or call the mechanic. Three weeks later, after he was feeling better, the fellow came back in to settle his bill and pick up the car. But the mechanic, having neither seen nor heard from the car owner, had sold the car to pay the repair bill. Under local law, he couldn't do that without filing a lawsuit, so the car owner took the mechanic to small claims court and won a $5,000 judgment.

The mechanic refused to pay, and because the garage didn't take checks, Gary couldn't locate his checking account. He did find out through a records check that the mechanic owned a camper, so he had the sheriff seize the camper and it was auctioned off for $1,000. That didn't come close to covering the judgment, so the sheriff went back and seized some engine hoists, a cash register, and a set of golf clubs. On the third trip, the mechanic refused to let the sheriff onto the premises. Gary protested to the judge, but local law at the time allowed the mechanic to keep the sheriff off his property. Gary solved the problem by contacting his state legislator and getting a new law passed that allowed the sheriff to enter. A year later, Gary presented the judge with a copy of the new law and the judge ordered the mechanic, who was in the courtroom, to let the sheriff take anything he wanted from his garage. The mechanic immediately stood up and paid the car owner a portion of what he owed — $500. He eventually paid the full amount.

In another case, a woman went in for breast-reduction surgery, and the insurance company mistakenly sent the benefits check to her instead of the doc-

tor. She cashed it and refused to pay the bill, so the doctor sued and won a judgment. She refused to disclose information about herself and was called before the judge. She walked into court wearing a neck brace from an auto accident in which she was hit by another driver. Jackson asked the judge to force her to disclose who had hit her, then garnished both drivers and both insurance companies. Because she wouldn't pay directly, Jackson intercepted the money due her from the auto accident and collected on the judgment.

## TIPS ON SMALL CLAIMS COURT

- Small claims court works best when two parties have an honest disagreement. It doesn't work as well if your adversary deliberately set out to cheat you.

- Before you file a case, send a letter by certified mail to the other party. Write this letter in a friendly tone, because a judge eventually may read it.

- You generally sue in the county in which your adversary lives, or if it's a business, the county in which it is located. You'll pay a filing fee — generally less than $100 — that you may recover if the judge rules in your favor.

- If the judge finds in your favor, be prepared for the hard part — collecting on your judgment. A judgment means you have a license to search for money. You can garnish the person's checking account or paycheck, put a lien on the person's house, and seize cars or other assets.

 193

- If someone is unemployed or self-employed, or skips town, you may find your judgment is worthless.

## REFERENCE

*Everybody's Guide to Small Claims Court* (Nolo Press)
www.nolo.com

# 194 ❧ RETURNING MERCHANDISE

Few things inspire confidence and loyalty among customers more than a retailer's willingness to pay refunds or exchange merchandise cheerfully. If you buy something and it's the wrong size or color, or you just don't like it as much as you thought you would, it's great to know you can bring it back. It's also very disturbing if you can't.

Returns, refunds, and exchanges have been a big problem with e-commerce. Of all the issues involved with buying things on the Internet, there's nothing I've had more complaints about.

In the real world, a store can have whatever policy it wishes. If the store wants to make all sales final, it can. If it wants to provide in-store exchanges only, but no cash refunds, it can do that as well. It can even provide refunds under certain conditions, such as requiring you to return a television in its original packaging.

It's been very hard for people to deal with the mechanics of returns online. I hear complaints every single week from consumers who say the merchant is telling them "We didn't get that back," or "We have no record of that," or some variation. How can you prove you sent it back?

This goes to the core of buying online. Before you do business with an online merchant, call its customer service number and see what happens. If it's hard to find the number or address on the Web site, you shouldn't do business with them. See if you can get through easily to a human being. You want to determine if the company will be there to serve you if there's a problem after the purchase.

There are a lot of Web sites offering seemingly extraordinary prices that are selling merchandise that is refurbished, not new. You might not be aware of that until you receive the goods.

Because you can't see what you're buying online until you get it, my recommendation is to buy only from sites that give you a full right to a refund. In the real world, you can make the decision with more information. In a clothing store, you can try on a garment and decide to buy it, understanding that you can't return it later. But I do not recommend that with the online world.

I have the same advice when you shop from catalogs. Understand the company's return policy and be aware that you buy at your own risk if you don't have the right to return it for a full refund. Even then, you may have to pay shipping and handling charges to return something.

One of my favorite ways to buy things online is to buy from a merchant that also has bricks-and-mortar stores. I bought some sporting goods at an online discounter and had the merchandise delivered to me. But if I was unhappy with it for any reason, I could return it to a local store. That's a huge advantage the traditional stores have over the Internet-only merchants.

If you're going to buy from an Internet auction site, you're buying from people you don't know. We've had a number of anguished callers who've paid for things they bought at auction sites, such as eBay, and when the goods arrived, they were not what the buyers expected. When that happens, you have no recourse. If you buy at an auction site, it should be an item that's inexpensive enough that you're willing to lose your money, or pay the extra fee (1 percent to 3 percent) and use one of the escrow services available. These services hold your money, releasing it to the seller only when you receive the goods and are satisfied.

Wherever you shop, find out their policy on returns and exchanges before you buy. Be aware, too, that return policies are different from refund policies. A store may be very liberal about allowing you to bring merchandise back and exchange it for other merchandise or receive an in-store credit. But it may be inflexible about giving your money back. Many items that you purchase cannot be returned for cash, and you're simply expected to know that policy. The best example is an airline ticket, which is almost always nonrefundable.

You have to make your own deci-

sion about whether to patronize a store with a rigid refund or exchange policy. If you are willing to take your chances in return for a better price, then go in with your eyes open. If you often buy something and change your mind, then be selective in where you shop. If you're buying a gift, be fair to the recipient. You may believe it's the best gift ever, but he or she may disagree, or may already have something exactly like it. Buy gifts only from merchants that have liberal return policies.

I don't recommend buying floor samples or clearance merchandise marked "all-sales final," where the item is not packed in its original factory carton. Then you really are at risk if you've spent money and, when you get the item home, it's damaged or doesn't work.

The fastest-growing retailers in the nation all have very customer-friendly return/refund policies, and I don't think that's a coincidence. Treating customers fairly is just good business. It's a shame that some stores are so unbending with customers, and it's sadder still that those policies are adopted because of a few who abuse return privileges. Think about how harshly you're often treated when you write a check. Blame it on the very few people who write most of the bad checks.

**195**

## TIPS ON RETURNING MERCHANDISE

⦿ Before you buy online, call the merchant's customer service number and see what happens. If it's hard to find the number or address on the Web site, don't do business with them.

◉ Buy only from Web sites or catalogs that allow you to return merchandise for a full\ refund.

◉ In most states, retailers are permitted to adopt any return or exchange policy, as long as they announce the policy to customers. That includes refusing any refund or exchange.

◉ Find out the store's policy on returns and exchanges before you shop there. Be aware, too, that return policies are different from refund policies. The policy may be printed on your receipt or posted near the cash registers.

◉ You have to make your own decision about whether to patronize a store with a rigid refund or exchange policy. If you are willing to take your chances in return for a better price, then go in with your eyes open.

◉ If you're buying a gift, make sure the item can be returned for a full refund.

## INTERNET

www.iescrow.com (Internet escrow service)

# CHARGEBACKS

When you pay for something in advance, such as an airline ticket or a custom-made sofa, you're taking on some risk. What if the airline or furniture store goes out of business, as so many have over the past few years? What if you order from a catalog and the merchandise never arrives? If you prepay and you don't get the merchandise or service, you could lose your money.

If you write a check, use a debit card from VISA or MasterCard, or pay cash to a merchant who fails to deliver,

the only way to get your money back is to sue. If the merchant goes out of business, you become a claimant in bankruptcy court, where you'll wait forever and, if you're lucky, collect a few cents on the dollar for what you're owed.

There's a simple way to protect yourself from the risk of prepaying — use a major credit card. That way you offer yourself the privilege of a chargeback, a refund paid by your credit card company.

Banks, credit unions, and other credit card issuers are deluged with chargebacks and in many cases refuse to honor them. But the limited rights you have to receive a chargeback from your card issuer are bolstered by broader protections provided by VISA International and MasterCard International. Contact VISA or MasterCard if you have a chargeback denied by your bank, credit union, or other card issuer.

If you pay a deposit to order furniture and the store shuts down before you receive it, VISA or MasterCard will refund your deposit. But you must follow the right procedure. Here's the key: If you haven't received your furniture in 50 days, write to your credit card company and file a chargeback claim. Because once the 60-day window closes, so has your right to do a chargeback. Go ahead and put the item in dispute no later than 60 days from the date of the original charge. Later, if the furniture is delivered, just contact the credit card company and it will release your chargeback request.

Whether the chargeback is perma-nent or whether the amount is re-posted to your bill should be deter-mined by the facts of your case, but that depends on the fairness of your card issuer. You find out about your credit card company's loyalties when you do a chargeback. Some consider the merchant their most important customer, not the consumer.

Furniture remains the most expensive item people order and then never receive because a store closes. But we get a lot of chargeback questions concerning merchandise ordered online and then either never received or only partially shipped. The same rule applies. If you haven't received it in 50 days, start a charge-back. Once the 60-day window clos-es, you're toast.

Beware, VISA and MasterCard give you no chargeback rights on their debit cards, which look like a credit card but instead draw money from your checking account. Don't use a debit card for online purchases or any-thing you buy that you're not going to receive immediately.

 **197**

 TIPS ON CHARGEBACKS

- When you pay for something in advance, such as an airline ticket or a custom-made sofa, you're taking on some risk. If you prepay and you don't get the merchandise or service, you could lose your money.

- If you use a credit card when you prepay, you give yourself the privilege of a charg back, a refund paid by your credit card company.

**198** ⚜

- If you order something and don't receive it, file a chargeback claim before 60 days have passed. If you later receive the merchandise, tell the credit card company to drop the chargeback claim.

- You have no chargeback rights if you use a VISA or MasterCard debit card.

## CONTACT

VISA International Customer Service
800-227-6811 (Traveler's checks)
800-847-2911 (Lost or stolen credit cards)
www.visa.com

MasterCard International
800-307-7309
www.mastercard.com

# CONTRACTS

Most people don't bother to read the contracts they're asked to sign when they buy a car or rent an apartment. But you do yourself a disservice when you sign one without knowing all its contents. Ask for time to take the contract home and read it.

If the party trying to get you to sign a contract refuses to let you leave with it, or pressures you to make a decision right then, don't sign the contract and don't do business with that organization. That happens a lot in health clubs, which often try to press you into signing expensive, long-term deals.

It's important to remember that a contract is a negotiated document, not a unilateral declaration. Many stan-

dard pre-written contracts are very one-sided, with the consumer having all the responsibilities and the other side having all the rights and privileges. But you can insist on changes. If an organization says the terms and conditions of a contract aren't negotiable, think about doing business with somebody else.

If you read a contract and something sounds unfair, or you don't understand something, mark it out with a pen and put your initials by that item. Don't agree to any clause in a contract you don't understand or you don't like. Once you sign the contract, you have to live with that provision.

TIPS ON CONTRACTS

- A contract is a negotiated document, not a unilateral declaration. Always ask for time to take a contract home and read it.

- If the party trying to get you to sign a contract refuses to let you leave with it, or pressures you to make a decision right then, don't sign it and don't do business with that organization.

- If you read a contract and something sounds unfair, or you don't understand something, mark it out with a pen and put your initials by that item.

# INFREQUENT PURCHASES

It's easy to sympathize with a young couple buying a new sofa. Buying items such as furniture, jewelry, and carpet can be daunting, indeed; we buy them so infrequently that it's difficult to know how to shop. Here are some special tips.

When buying furniture, you should deal only with reputable retailers — healthy businesses with knowledgeable salespeople. You also need to think through how a piece of furniture will fit into your home. If you're considering a sofa with an unusual pattern or color, ask if you may take home a cushion for a few hours and look at it with the rest of your furniture. Many times something that looks like a perfect match in the store will look like a sore thumb in your home.

Don't ever feel you need to make a snap decision, even if an item is on sale. Furniture sales scream at you every week in the newspaper.

There are a few things you can look for to determine if a piece of furniture is well made. For wood pieces, such as a desk or dresser, the top should have a very smooth finish, ideally hand rubbed. If you see tiny bumps and craters, like the surface of an orange peel, it's a poor-quality finish. Solid wood is great, but veneer, a thin piece of wood applied to another piece of wood or particle board, is good, too. Many fancy pieces with intricate inlays in the top are veneer. What you don't want is a plastic top with a wood-grain finish that's photo-applied to particle board. It's basically plastic with a picture of wood on it.

Next, open a drawer and look at the connection between the front of the drawer and the side. You want something that's dovetailed, that is,

199

connected firmly by a series of stubby, interlocking fingers on both the front and side. In a cheap piece, the drawer fronts may be stapled or nailed to the side and eventually will pull right off. The inside of the drawer should be smooth enough that you can rub a piece of gauze on it and the gauze won't snag. Also, the drawer should be deep when measured from front to back. Sometimes manufacturers cut corners by using shorter drawers.

It's harder to judge the quality of upholstered furniture. You could place a $399 sofa next to a $1,399 sofa and not see much difference. One thing to look for is whether the patterns line up correctly. Just as the stripes on a shirt pocket should match up with the rest of the shirt, so should the patterns on furniture. It costs more to have the pattern on the back match up with the rest of the piece, because that takes more fabric. Also, it's helpful to ask the salesperson about the springs. "Eight-way hand tied" — in which the springs are tied together with twine in eight directions — is a classic way to put furniture together. Another spring design, an independent Marshall unit, is okay, too.

If you're buying furniture and taking it home with you immediately, it doesn't matter how you pay. But if you're paying a deposit or waiting for it to be delivered, pay only by credit card. It's not uncommon for furniture stores to shut down suddenly and leave stunned consumers without their furniture or their money. Some eventually get their merchandise or partial refunds, but they are the lucky ones. Many others learn an expensive but important lesson. If you pay by check, VISA or MasterCard debit card, or cash, you could lose your money. If you buy with a credit card and the furniture store fails to deliver the merchandise, you are protected by your chargeback rights.

## BEDS

I've had a number of questions in the past few years about how to buy a bed. My own solution is pretty low-tech. I go to my favorite warehouse discount store with a book or magazine and read for awhile, in different positions, to see if I'm comfortable on the bed. If I am, I buy it. If I'm not, I don't. The most recent mattress I bought, a Sealy, has been the best one I've ever owned. And I've never had a problem with a bed I've purchased in this manner.

The book answer is somewhat more complex and probably will end up being somewhat more expensive. But the experts say spending a bit more for a bed is pretty reasonable when you consider that you spend one-third of your life in bed, and that a good set of bedding should last 10 to 15 years.

It's recommended that you look primarily at mattresses and boxsprings made by one of the four major bedding manufacturers Simmons, Sealy, Serta, and Stearns & Foster. Look for a mattress that's priced in the middle of the manufacturer's product line. The most expensive mattresses will be loaded with bells and whistles you don't need. The cheapest won't be of adequate quality.

The most important characteristic a mattress should have is the proper firmness. A soft mattress won't give your body the support it needs, and you'll wake up feeling achy, like you slept in a hammock. A mattress that doesn't give at all will make you feel like you slept on the floor.

The right mattress should give enough to accommodate the contours of your body, yet provide good support. A 200-pound man will need more support than a 130-pound woman, so it's absolutely necessary to try a mattress out before you buy it. Wear comfortable clothes and see how each mattress feels. If you're married, go shopping with your spouse. Any reputable store is fine.

You'll hear a lot about mattress construction when you talk to salespeople or read product materials. The most important part of all that gibberish is the coils and the upholstery, which determine the firmness of the mattress and its ability to react to your body. A good-quality full-size mattress will have 400 to 800 separate coils. Queen- or king-size mattresses will have more coils than their full-size counterpart of the same brand and model, and twin-size mattresses will have fewer. Ask the salesperson how many coils the full-size version has, and use that figure to help evaluate quality. Don't buy a full-size mattress with fewer than 312 coils.

At least one top-of-the-line mattress has coils that are individually wrapped in a cloth pocket, which I'm told enables it to better adjust to shoulders and hips. That's great, but there are plenty of excellent mattresses with the more standard, open-coil design.

The surface layer of a mattress isn't just cosmetic. Manufacturers use materials from horsehair to high-density foam, in combination with cotton batting, to help adjust the level of firmness. But don't worry too much about the content or design of the upholstery fabric. A silk surface will cost a lot more, and you'll have it covered most of the time with sheets and blankets. Another worthless extra is a "Pillow-top," a spun Dacron filler manufacturers use to give the surface a layer of extra puffiness. They're very popular, but not worth the extra cost in my opinion, and you may need special sheets.

It's also strongly recommended that you buy a new boxspring at the same time you buy a new mattress. Some people try to save money by buying just the mattress. But experts say boxsprings wear out just like mattresses, although not as visibly. Putting a new mattress on an old boxspring may cause the new mattress to sag. Some new boxsprings have metal frames, rather than wood. That adds weight, but it may add strength as well.

Any bed frame will do, as long as it has a center support bar or enough horizontal slats to support the bed.

Retailers that sell only beds seem to close more often than other retailers, so

201

use a credit card to buy and choose a place you feel comfortable. I have a place at the beach that has a little restaurant nearby. Next to the restaurant one fall I saw a new bedding store, which opened with a splashy advertising campaign. A few months later, it was gone. There was a handwritten note in the window advising customers to contact the manufacturer if they had any problems with a bed they bought.

## CARPET

When you buy carpet, it's important to buy from a good dealer, get a good-quality carpet yarn, and make sure it is properly installed. It doesn't matter if you buy from a carpet store or a department store, just don't buy it over the phone. Generally someone who tries to sell carpet over the phone is trying to rip you off, selling cheap-quality carpet at inflated prices.

When you buy from a carpet store, make sure the showroom is neat and well kept, not a sloppy warehouse. An owner who takes care of his showroom is more likely to insist his installers do a good job in your home.

Choosing the carpet itself is relatively easy. Buy a carpet made from a premium carpet yarn, such as DuPont's Stainmaster, Monsanto's Wear-Dated, or Allied Fibers' Worry-Free. Zeftron from BASF and XPS from Hoechst Celanese Corp. are two more good yarns. It's less important which mill turns those yarns into carpet, but you should look for a finished product whose yarn has a good twist to it. If you look closely at the carpet fibers, the tips should have a sharp, pencil-point appearance. That means it's been properly twisted. Poorly made carpet will have very little twist, and the tips will have a frayed look. Quality carpet should look good for 5 to 10 years, but cheap carpet can look ugly in as little as six months.

Installation is critical to the way the carpet will look in your home. Most carpet dealers use contractors to do the installation, rather than their own employees, and most contractors are poorly trained and use sloppy procedures. Ask the dealer what kind of guarantee is offered on installation. Ninety days to one year is normal. More than one year is a plus.

For proper installation, carpet should be power-stretched into place so it is drum tight. Most installers use a knee-kicker to stretch carpet, a technique that won't achieve the right tautness. Loose carpet looks terrible and wears unevenly. When you buy, get it in writing that the carpet will be power-stretched. As for padding, the best kind is half-inch, six-pound rebond, a dense padding made from chopped, pressed foam.

If you live in the Southeastern U.S., consider taking a trip to Dalton, Georgia, northwest of Atlanta, where most of the nation's carpet is made. There are a number of outlets there that sell massive volumes of carpet. The best deal is to buy factory seconds, but there are some seconds to buy and some to avoid. Usually the best irregulars are the ones where the color doesn't match the store sample, and those pieces usually come at the beginning and the end of a production run. The piece you buy will be uniform in color — it just won't exactly match the national sample. That doesn't matter at all if you like the color.

My wife and I bought carpet in Dalton for $2.99 a yard, and it's great carpet. We went into the fancy showroom and I told the salesperson I was there to buy the cheapest carpet they have. From that point on, he was done with us. He handed us off to a junior salesperson — it was probably the guy's first day — and he took us back to the area with the cheap stuff. The quality was great, but it was the end of a manufacturing run, there was very little left, and the color didn't exactly match their sample card. That's the stuff they just want to get rid of. We liked the color and there was plenty for our needs.

Buy only from a store that unrolls the carpet you want to buy. Then, get on your hands and knees and inspect it. A good outlet will have a very well-lit area for you to check it. Don't buy carpet that's irregular because of a stitching problem. One example is a weave defect called "chicken feet."

You can figure the number of yards of carpet you'll need by dividing the square footage of your room by nine, then add 10 percent to account for waste. If you pay $15 a yard, it would cost about $460 to carpet a bedroom that measures 12 feet by 21 feet, or

about $3,300 for an entire 1,800-square-foot house. Even if you don't buy irregulars, carpet prices have declined, probably because of the influence of mass-market discounters such as Home Depot and Costco.

But make sure to get a few quotes on the amount of yards that will be needed. Telephone salespeople and other unethical installers commonly mislead customers by quoting a cheap price but overestimating the yardage. It's no bargain to pay $12.99 for 195 yards (total price: $2,533) when another dealer, charging $15.99, says you need only 150 yards (total price: $2,399) to do the job.

One company no longer in business quoted its prices in "units" that were actually equal to half a yard. A buyer who needed only 27 square yards wound up paying for 54 "units" at $12.99 a unit. In other words, she bought cheap, builders' grade carpet at the outrageous price of $25.98 a yard, paying more than $700 for cheap carpet when she could have bought good carpet for $500 or less.

Others are listing carpet prices per square foot, rather than per square yard, to make the price look cheaper. You have to multiply a square foot price by nine to get the real price. Carpet that sells for $3 a square foot is really a very expensive $27 a square yard. That's so dishonest.

Ask the installer how much carpet he's brought and make sure it's the amount you've purchased. Also check the manufacturer's name on the carpet and look at the padding. Some dealers will pull a fast one by giving you cheaper carpet or padding than what you bought, or selling you one quantity of carpet and sending the installer out with less.

## JEWELRY

I'm often asked how to buy an engagement ring. If you just go out to look for a ring, it's easy to become confused. You're looking at these things under special lighting and circumstances, and they all look great and the prices are all over the board.

So how do you decide if you're getting a fair deal? The answer is to base your purchase on the "three C's," color, clarity, and carat weight. You should look at a few first and then decide how much you are willing to spend, or on the level of color and clarity you want. The true value of a diamond is determined primarily by how clear it is and its color scale. There are standard industry ratings for both. So a diamond rated D, E, or F, which means it's virtually colorless, would cost more than one rated at the bottom of the scale, S through Z, or light yellow. Clarity ranges from F, or flawless under 10x magnification, down to I, which means particles called "inclusions" can be seen with the naked eye. The Better Business Bureau has an excellent guide to understanding the various quality grades of diamonds, gold, and other jewelry. It's on the organization's Web site at www.bbb.org.

Once you've decided what color and clarity you want, you can pick a carat weight and then easily compare, store to store. Or, if you have a budget, you can request the color and clarity you want, and ask what carat weight you can get for the amount you want to spend.

By doing this, you take a purchase that's very subjective and emotional, and make it a clear, objective one.

When you buy a diamond this way, you must receive a written appraisal not of the diamond's value, but of the color, clarity, and carat weight. You should buy only from a store that allows you 72 hours to inspect it and, if you choose, to return it for a full refund. Then, if the purchase is $2,500 or above, you can use that time to go to an independent graduate gemologist, have him or her create a map of the stone's structure, and give you a verification of color, clarity, and carat weight. If it isn't right, return it. Below $2,500, just buy on faith.

Don't ever accept somebody's appraisal of value. That doesn't mean anything.

If your diamond is very valuable, having the diamond appraised and mapped will give you added security. The map of each diamond is unique. So if you suspect after a cleaning that a jeweler may have switched diamonds, take it back to the gemologist, who will be able to tell you in minutes whether it is the same or a different diamond.

The Better Business Bureau guide also has tips about colored gemstones, such as emeralds and rubies.

## COINS AND STAMPS

I've found only two effective ways to sell collectible coins and stamps. One is to wait for a coin or stamp show to come to town. In one afternoon at a show, you can get quotes from many different dealers, and find out what seems to be fair market value on what you have.

Or, you can do the same thing online at many different sites. One is www.collectorsauction.com, but there are plenty of others.

If you're a buyer of coins, stamps, and other collectibles, unfortunately a very large percentage of what you might buy could turn out to be counterfeit. A federal raid called "Operation Bullpen" found that up to 90 percent of this stuff is fake. If you're going to spend any large amount of money, hire an expert in that field to verify the authenticity of the collectible you might buy.

## TIPS ON INFREQUENT PURCHASES

- If you're paying a deposit for furniture or waiting for it to be delivered, pay only by credit card. With your credit card chargeback rights, you are protected if the furniture doesn't arrive.

- When buying furniture, you should deal only with reputable retailers — healthy businesses with knowledgeable salespeople.

- If you're considering a sofa with an unusual pattern or color, ask to take home a cushion and look at it with the rest of your furniture.

- Wood furniture should have a very smooth finish. With upholstered furniture, make sure the patterns line up.

205

- Try out a bed before you buy it, even if you shop as I do at warehouse discount stores.

- Experts recommend that you look primarily at mattresses and boxsprings made by one of the four major bedding manufacturers: Simmons, Sealy, Serta, and Stearns & Foster.

- It is important to buy a mattress with the proper firmness. A decent full-size mattress needs to have at least 312 coils to provide good support.

- When you buy carpet, it's important to buy from a good dealer, to get a good-quality carpet yarn, and to make sure it is properly installed.

- Buy a carpet made from a premium carpet yarn, such as DuPont's Stainmaster, Monsanto's Wear-Dated, or Allied Fibers' Worry-Free.

- When you buy, get it in writing that the carpet will be power-stretched for proper installation.

- It doesn't matter if you buy from a carpet store or a department store, just don't buy over the phone.

- Buy jewelry only from a store that allows you 72 hours to inspect it and, if you choose, to return it for a full refund.

## INTERNET

Better Business Bureau
www.bbb.org (Online guide to jewelry purchases)

Coins and Stamps:
www.collectorsauction.com
www.stampsonline.com
www.money.org (American Numismatic Association)

# DRY CLEANING

As much as I love a bargain, I have to tell you that price is not the most important factor in every consumer decision. It's more important to choose a dry cleaner that will do a good job of cleaning your clothes and will be fair to you if problems ever develop.

Get this clear before you bring your first garments in to be cleaned. Tell the dry cleaner you don't ever expect to have a problem, but you're curious what the cleaner will do if a piece of clothing is lost or damaged, because you've heard so many horror stories. The answer will help you decide if you should take your clothes to this particular dry cleaner.

If there's a change in ownership, talk to the new owner and see what his or her attitude is about service. If you don't like what you hear, you may want to switch cleaners. It's a good idea to get to know the owner or manager in any case. If a problem ever develops, it's easier to resolve if you already know someone in charge. If the only person you ever speak with is a clerk, you may have trouble getting satisfaction.

Just as with a doctor, lawyer, or accountant, one of the best ways to find a dry cleaner is to ask friends and neighbors whom they use and whether they're happy with the service.

It's also a good idea to choose a cleaner who is a member of the International Fabricare Institute (IFI). If you ever have a problem with an IFI cleaner, you can have an evaluation done of that item by the IFI testing laboratory in Silver Spring, Maryland, which will issue a report on the cause of the damage. The fee may be paid by the cleaner or customer, or both may agree to split the cost. According to the IFI, manufacturers are responsible for the damage in 47 percent of the items the lab tests, consumers for 37.5 percent, and dry cleaners for 15.5 percent. The dry cleaners' share is low because dry cleaners send problems to the lab only when they believe they are not responsible.

If it turns out to be the manufacturer's fault, most retailers will look at the report and either give you a credit or put you in touch with the manufacturer, who will generally reach some form of accommodation with you. I once had a suit that bunched up after being cleaned. The cleaner said it was due to a specific defect in a manufacturing process called fusing. I went

back to the store, which was a retail outlet for a manufacturer. They recognized the defect, knew it was their responsibility, and immediately offered to give me a new suit. A number of Better Business Bureaus offer dry cleaning arbitration programs.

I had one caller who used an IFI cleaner and was having problems, with no response from the cleaners. She called my radio show, and we suggested she actually call IFI. Once she did, within an hour she got a call from the owner of the cleaners, who apologized and offered a full refund.

I also prefer to use a cleaner that does the work on their premises. They'll have immediate access to spot-removing chemicals and will be able to test a stain immediately. If the work is done on-site, the clothes don't go anywhere, so there's less of a chance an item will be lost.

If clothes are cleaned on premises, ask how often the cleaning fluid is distilled. You have no way to know if they're being truthful, but it's a good idea to ask anyway. A good cleaner should distill the solvent daily, because clothes cleaned in dirty solvent can become dingy and discolored. You wouldn't wash clothes in dirty water, and a dry cleaner shouldn't use dirty solvent.

If you notice that an item you've had cleaned has been damaged, go back as soon as possible and show it to the manager on duty. A lot of times they'll ask to clean or press it again or to repair a button or zipper. Or a manager may want to show it to the owner. That's fine. But if the item is still bad after that second cleaning, it's time for the cleaner to take responsibility and come up with some money.

If an item has been destroyed in the cleaning process, the cleaner does not owe you the amount of money needed to replace the garment. The company owes you a depreciated value based on the expected life span of that item. If it's a shirt you would normally keep for five years and you've owned it for two years before it is destroyed, you deserve 60 percent of the value of the shirt. If you normally keep an item for two years and it's damaged in the second year, you may not be entitled to any money at all, since it was near the end of its useful life. You'll have to negotiate with the cleaner over how much you deserve as compensation for a ruined item.

Sometimes, you might have a cleaner that has been doing a good job up to that point and takes responsibility for the damage, but doesn't seem able to cough up any money. You could cut a deal for some free cleaning service in exchange for the loss suffered on that item.

One heavily advertised solution to the cost of dry cleaning is do-it-yourself kits. Dryel is the most well-known, but it's one of several competitors on the market. It seems to work fine on very basic stains, but in tests I did for a TV report, we found repeatedly that it did not work on very tough stains. That disappointed me, because I was hoping this was going to be the bargain-basement method of cleaning. It's very inexpensive, less than a dollar per garment. But for the tougher things, keep going to the cleaners.

Also, one of the things people get with cleaning is pressing. With any of these self-service methods, you get a garment that may be cleaner and smell fresher, but you're going to have to do the pressing. Many people don't want to do that.

## TIPS ON DRY CLEANING

◉ Choose a dry cleaner that will do a good job of cleaning your clothes and will be fair to you if problems ever develop. Price is less important.

◉ Consider a cleaner that is a member of the International Fabricare Institute. If there's a dispute over how a garment was damaged, the cleaner can submit the item to IFI for testing.

◉ If it turns out to be the manufacturer's fault, most retailers will look at the report and either give you a credit or put you in touch with the manufacturer, who will generally reach some form of accommodation with you.

- If an item is destroyed in the cleaning process, the cleaner does not owe you the amount of money needed to replace the garment. The company owes you a depreciated value based on the number of years the item is expected to last.

- Self-service cleaning kits are okay for minor stains, but don't do well on major stains.

## CONTACT

IFI Garment Analysis Laboratory
800-638-2627
www.ifi.org

# FRANCHISES

People see franchises as a quick way to go into business for themselves, without having to build the reputation of a business from nothing. Buying a franchise isn't necessarily bad or good in itself, but it requires planning. Any time you're thinking of going into a business or industry you know little about, don't immediately set up shop or buy a franchise.

The best approach is to go to work in the industry, either for an independent operator or the franchise you're evaluating. Work in it for at least six months, preferably one year. I don't care if it means you're taking out the trash. Go in with your eyes and ears open so you can learn as much as possible. By doing this you'll learn two things. First and most important, you'll find out if it's a business you like.

Second, you'll learn enough as an insider to know if promises made by a franchise are genuine. You'd be amazed how many people do this and then completely drop any thoughts of getting involved in the business.

Before I went into the travel business, I went to work in an agency for six months. I did everything you do as a lower-level employee in a travel agency, including writing and delivering tickets. The only mistake I made was doing it for only six months. A year would have been better. But because I did that beforehand, my own company started turning a profit in only its fourth month of business. It was terrific to start making money that quickly.

If you find after working in an industry that you like it and want to buy a franchise, think about these questions:

209

**210**

Is the name readily recognizable in your area? Does the name brand have a good reputation in the general community and in that trade? Does the franchisor truly provide the support its glossy literature promises?

The best way to find out about franchise support is to call franchisees in another town. People in your own town may not be truthful because they may see you as a potential buyer for their business. You also need to evaluate the cost you pay for that support, including the up-front fees and the percent of your sales you'll pay the franchisor. Make sure your business will be able to support that level of royalties.

Another thing to evaluate is territory. Some franchisees, just as they become successful, are stunned to find out that the franchisor is placing another franchise right down the street from their business. A famous sandwich shop chain has made many of its franchise holders unhappy by opening too many of its stores close to others, making it difficult for them to be profitable.

Other franchises have been criticized for spending too much effort to open new stores and thus generate up-front fees, or letting corporate leadership lapse because a founder sells out or becomes less involved. Some say the Wendy's hamburger chain enjoyed a resurgence because founder Dave Thomas became a more visible leader.

One of the big advantages of a well-recognized franchise name is that your company is easier to sell if you decide to leave the business. It's much harder to sell an independent, non-branded location. However, the fact that a franchise remains on one street corner for years does not mean it's successful. Often a franchisor will buy back a troubled franchise and run it until a new owner is found, rather than let anyone know it has failed. The industry rule of thumb is that 90 percent of franchises succeed. But one franchise consultant I've spoken with believes a third of franchises at any given time are successful, a third are getting by, and a third are failing.

**TIPS ON FRANCHISES**

◉ Before buying a franchise, go to work in the industry, either for an independent operator or the franchise you're thinking about buying. You'll learn plenty about the business and may decide it's not for you.

◉ Find out the answers to these questions: Is the franchise name readily recognizable in your area? Does that name brand have a good reputation in the general community and in that trade? Does the franchisor provide strong support?

- Call franchisees in the next town and ask them what they like and don't like about the business.

- Evaluate your territory and make sure the company won't put another location close to you.

# MULTILEVEL MARKETING

If you're thinking of going to work for a multilevel marketing organization, beware of all the hoopla and be on guard for possible illegalities.

Multilevel marketing organizations recruit individuals to sell a variety of products, including such things as household cleaners and diet aids.

You make money in two ways in a multilevel marketing organization. The first is by serving as a combination retailer and sales representative — you buy products from the company and resell them to customers. The second way is by recruiting people into the organization and earning a commission off their sales. That's where the term multilevel comes in. If I recruit you and you recruit a friend, I get commissions off both your sales and your friend's sales.

Multilevel marketing organizations want you to believe that, with very limited expense on your part, but a great desire to win, you can become wealthy.

A multilevel marketing presentation is something like a high school pep rally. You'll hear testimonials from people who say they were near the financial abyss and found the ticket selling purple oranges. Now they're rolling in money and have a fancy car and a retirement home at the beach.

You'll also see this at the company's Web site, where you'll be amazed to learn that you're the last person to find out about the easy millions that are yours for the taking. The company sites are incredible enough, but people who are involved in this have set up their own independent sites, which have even more outlandish claims.

If you go to a search engine and enter the name of any hot multilevel organization, you'll see dozens of independent, or unauthorized sites, from people who are trying to add salespeople into their own commission structure.

If you're thinking of joining such an organization, consider whether you have any sales skills, whether you believe in the product, and whether the product is priced fairly. You should be confident you will be able to go up to a stranger or an acquaintance — because you're going to exhaust your friends and relatives very quickly — convince them of the virtues of the product and get them to buy. A lot of

211

people can't or don't want to do that.

Some of the companies overcome this reluctance to sell to strangers by offering to help you set up a Web site, which they say will generate plenty of sales on its own. If there's anything we've learned about e-commerce, products do not sell themselves. You still have to have sales skills to succeed at this.

If you're going to sell a product, it should represent a fair value. It's no fun to justify why you sold someone, particularly a friend, a product that's more expensive than a similar product they could buy at the store. As consumers, they won't want to and shouldn't buy something that's overpriced.

I don't recommend joining any multilevel marketing organization that requires you to pay a substantial up-front fee to participate.

It's also very important to determine if the emphasis of a multilevel marketing company is on selling its products or on recruiting other people into the organization. If you hear a lot about the virtues of the products, the organization is on a sound footing. However, if the main purpose of the organization is rounding up new recruits, it may be an illegal pyramid. One caller told me about a meeting she went to in which the product was never mentioned. All they ever talked about was recruiting.

My staff and I helped authorities close down an outfit called WealthBuilders, which set up offices in churches and took money from people using a pyramid scheme. The pitch was that people who signed up would make lots of money from home doing customer service work.

WealthBuilders sold each victim a computer for an outrageous amount of money. When victims signed up friends, they'd recoup some of their sign-up cost. The organization pushed recruiting hard, because that's where the money came from.

A pyramid organization can succeed only as long as it recruits new members, but as it does so it requires more and more members to support its ever-expanding base. Normally, it will just collapse. But let's say, hypothetically, it is remarkably skilled at recruiting and has no difficulty signing members. Eventually it would run out of people in the United States or on the earth and would then collapse. Pyramids are illegal because only the scam artists who start them make any money.

One more word of caution about multilevel marketing. If you're an outstanding salesperson, you probably would do better by selling through a traditional sales channel, where you don't have to split your commissions with others in the organization.

One advantage of multilevel marketing, though, may be that it helps you discover a talent you didn't know you had, and you can then graduate to a true, full-time selling position. One thing you don't want to do is quit your regular job to join a multilevel organization. I've heard horror stories of people who've quit jobs only to find that, either they weren't success- ful, or the multilevel organization left town and left them unemployed.

### TIPS ON MULTILEVEL MARKETING

◉ You make money in two ways in a multilevel marketing organization: you buy products from the company and resell them to customers, and you recruit people into the organization and earn a commission off their sales.

◉ Don't join a multilevel marketing organization unless you have sales ability, you believe in the product, and the product is priced fairly.

◉ Don't join if the main purpose of the organization is rounding up new recruits. Such an organization may be an illegal pyramid.

◉ If you're an outstanding salesperson who would do well at multilevel marketing, you probably would do better by selling through a traditional sales channel, where you don't have to split your commissions.

213

# RIPOFFS

**You really** have to be on your toes to avoid the ripoff artists, because they're all around and looking to take your money. Many of the calls I get each week on my radio show are from people who have been ripped off by a phony loan company or telemarketer, or who are suspicious that something they've heard about is not legitimate.

Most scams appeal to your dreams or your vanity. The common cons operate on the premise that you will make a decision quickly and emotionally, instead of doing the legwork to verify information or to develop your own knowledge. If you rely exclusively on what you're being told by someone else, you become a sitting duck. Often when you are taken you have no recourse, because the ripoff artists are clever enough to avoid committing a crime.

I especially hope that you beware of a sales technique called the "No Be Back," which you'll see often in high-pressure sales schemes. It turns up in health clubs and timeshares and whenever a salesperson wants you to buy something that isn't a good value. In the "No Be Back," the salesperson forces you to buy right then, because if you're able to leave the high-pressure sales environment, go home, and think about it, odds are you'll realize it's not a smart decision and you won't waste your money. The salesperson would rather have you say no than leave as a maybe.

One thing I'm not as worried about is the danger of someone stealing your credit card number while you're buying a book or a sweater via the Internet. That's a much greater danger when you use your credit card at a store or restaurant, and you're dealing strictly with people. In one case, there's an electronic barrier that some hacker will have to try to pierce. In the other case, there is no barrier. There are plenty of opportunities for crooked clerks to steal your credit card number and use it for fraudulent purposes.

There's so much at stake for online retailers to get this right that I'm not that worried it will go wrong. Just take a look at your credit card bill each month when you pay it. If an unauthorized transaction appears, notify the credit card issuer right away.

In this chapter, I'll tell you about many of the most common ripoffs and help you to avoid being taken.

IDENTITY THEFT

EXTENDED WARRANTIES

CREDIT LIFE INSURANCE

CHARITIES

HEALTH CLUBS

TIMESHARES

INVENTION SERVICES

BUSINESS AND EMPLOYMENT SCAMS

MODELING SCHOOLS

JUNK CALLS

# IDENTITY THEFT

I'm sure you've heard the expression, "Imitation is the sincerest form of flattery." But it's no compliment in the case of identity theft, a fast-growing crime that causes tremendous anguish for victims.

Criminals who practice identity theft literally take your name, Social Security number, and good credit rating, and use them to fraudulently purchase thousands of dollars worth of merchandise. They obtain instant credit and credit cards, buy merchandise, write checks, rent apartments, and buy cars, all as if they were you. It's remarkable. Using sophisticated equipment and software, criminals can print perfect-looking driver's licenses with what-

ever photo and signature they choose, and do it all in minutes in a van. Then they just drop someone off at a store with the fake ID, go store-to-store, and load up the van.

About two months after the identity theft occurs, the problems start for you. Bill collectors start calling to ask why you haven't paid for the furniture or big-screen TV you supposedly bought.

The first thing you should do when you realize you've been a victim of identity theft is to get a police report from your local police department. Surprisingly, some police departments are reluctant to provide police reports for identity fraud, but they are required to do so under the federal Identity Fraud and Assumption Deterrence Act of 1998.

Next, you should contact all three credit bureaus — Equifax, Experian and Trans Union — and have a fraud alert added to your credit report. After that, you're going to have to spend a great deal of time working with each store or company that issued credit, and each party that accepted a check, filling out affidavits of fraud. Unfortunately, you'll need to keep these affidavits and your police report for the rest of your life, because people have short memories, and they'll often sell the unpaid debt to a collection agency, which might come after you five, ten, or fifteen years later on a debt that never was yours in the first place.

There's a good Web site, www.privacyrights.org, that takes you step-by-step through the process of cleaning up your reputation.

If you're a victim of identity theft, it's going to be a hassle for you to buy a car or a home — all the things the crook was able to do easily — because your credit score and your checking account are going to look terrible. Even if you do all these things correctly, it will take about two years to get your credit rating back because of a horrible lack of coordination between the credit bureaus and credit grantors, and even separate departments within the bureaus. The credit bureau's fraud department may acknowledge the fraud, but another department may continue to issue incorrect reports. The most important

thing is to document everything.

Part of the problem with identity theft is that law enforcement doesn't see you as the victim of the crime. To them, the victim is the store that was defrauded of its merchandise. But you're the one who's left trying to get back your good name.

One thing you normally don't have to do is cancel your credit cards, because the thieves are using a new account they've opened, not your existing account.

The most difficult situations involve the checks that the crooks write in your name, because most states treat writing a bad check as a criminal offense. Many victims of identity fraud have faced arrest because of this. A woman I interviewed for a TV report had to stay at friends' houses for weeks because the local police department had six warrants out for her arrest for six different bad checks, none of which she had written. Someone had broken into her home and taken, among other things, her checks. Ironically, she was a paralegal working for a law firm, and even the law firm had difficulty trying to straighten out the mess and keep her from being arrested. Eventually, after our TV story, the police backed down and agreed not to arrest her. Another woman in Savannah, Georgia, spent 18 months in jail because of identity theft. She got lost in the system, and they just left her in the county jail.

There's virtually nothing you can do to keep thieves from stealing your

⚠ 217

**218** ⚠

identity, because the 1974 Privacy Act allows the three major credit bureaus to invade your privacy at will, and gives you no control over how they make your Social Security number and personal information available.

There are a few simple things you can do that will help slightly. One is not to carry a checkbook, because the worst problems we've heard about always involve checks, and if you don't carry a checkbook, there's less of a chance it will be stolen. I pay with cash or credit card.

When you use a credit card, don't leave the receipt behind. I often fill my car with gasoline to find that the person before me left his receipt at the pump. Some gas stations obscure the credit card

number, except for the last four digits. But others leave the full number, name, and expiration date of the card, all the information a thief needs to buy things as if they were the real card holder.

In addition, I don't carry my Social Security card. And if your state uses your Social Security number as your driver's license number, ask to have it changed to a random number when you renew. If your driver's license has your Social Security number on it, that gives a crook everything they need to take over your identity.

Finally, I shred credit card receipts and other documents before throwing them away. You can buy an inexpensive shredder for about $20.

### TIPS ON IDENTITY THEFT

◉ If you're a victim of identity theft, get a police report from your local police department, ask each of the three credit bureaus to place a fraud alert on your credit report, and fill out affidavits of fraud with each company that issued credit in your name. Keep these documents forever.

◉ Don't carry a checkbook. Pay by cash or credit card.

◉ Don't carry your Social Security card with you or use your Social Security number as your driver's license number.

### INTERNET

www.privacyrights.org

### CONTACT

Equifax
800-525-6285 (fraud alert)

Experian
888-301-7195 (fraud alert)

Trans Union
800-680-7289 (fraud alert)

# EXTENDED WARRANTIES

One of the things people worry about most when they buy a new computer or VCR is what to do if it breaks. Repairs can be costly, and manufacturers' warranties are notoriously short. That's why extended warranties, or service contracts, have been such a successful ripoff.

Buying an extended warranty on a computer is the worst money you can spend. Because technology changes so quickly, the computer you bought three years ago is worth nearly nothing today. You shouldn't buy a warranty on an item whose value will drop so sharply.

The same rule applies to consumer electronics, which are better made and less expensive every year. Who would have imagined a few years ago that you could buy a four-head VCR on sale for $59? Don't waste money on an extended warranty. If a VCR breaks, you're better off buying an inexpensive new one than buying an extended warranty or paying to have it repaired.

For appliances, there's a more basic reason that extended warranties are a bad deal — they rarely pay off. Only 12 to 20 percent of the money paid for extended warranties is used to pay for repairs or claims. That's far less than a typical insurance policy, which pays out 70 cents of every premium dollar in claims. So extended warranties are remarkably profitable for the retailer.

There are several reasons the claims rate is so low on extended warranties. People often lose the contracts, or they move, or they forget they purchased the contract in the first place. The usage rate is even lower than the breakdown rate of the appliance.

In any case, you are better off taking the money you would have spent on extended warranties and putting it into a repair fund, although admittedly this takes quite a bit of discipline. If your refrigerator or washing machine breaks, you can use the money in the repair fund to have it fixed. Over time you'll come out way ahead by not buying service contracts and self-insuring appliances this way.

When you make a purchase, the salesperson may pressure you to buy the extended warranty. Because extended warranties are so profitable, salespeople risk being fired if they fail to sell enough of them. In fact, many times the

⚠ 219

**220** ⚠ warranty is the only profit on the sale, because of the razor-thin margins in appliance retailing and the comparison shopping done by consumers.

Best Buy, one of the few retailers that doesn't push extended warranties, improved its financial performance several years ago simply by asking customers if they want one.

Consumers are hit with extended warranties most often when they buy appliances, rather than cars, because they make these purchases more frequently. But a car is where the decision represents the greatest amount of money. For more on cars and extended warranties, read the section on trade-ins, financing, and extended warranties in the Cars chapter of this book.

 **TIPS ON EXTENDED WARRANTIES**

◉ Don't buy an extended warranty on electronic devices such as a computer or VCR. The value of a new computer will drop to nearly nothing in just a few years, and a VCR can be replaced very inexpensively if it breaks.

◉ An extended warranty for an appliance is a bad deal because warranties rarely pay off. Only 12 to 20 percent of the money paid for extended warranties is ever used to pay for repairs or claims.

◉ People often lose the contracts, they move, or they forget they purchased the contract in the first place. The usage rate is even lower than the breakdown rate.

◉ You're better off taking the money you would have spent on an extended warranty for a refrigerator or washing machine and putting it into a repair fund.

# CREDIT LIFE INSURANCE

Credit life and disability — also known as croak-and-choke insurance — is a terrible buy for you, but a big money-maker for those who sell it. Not surprisingly then, people who want you to buy credit life are almost everywhere you turn.

Your bank or mortgage company will try to rip you off with credit life and disability, as will the lender that finances your automobile. When you buy a major appliance, the store will also make an attempt to sell you croak-and-choke.

This is the most worthless product that has ever been dreamed up by the insurance industry. Croak-and-choke pays off your loan balance if you die or if you become disabled. But it protects the lender, not you. By buying it, you are paying to protect the lender.

People agree to buy credit life in the mistaken notion that they're protecting their loved ones from their debts. Let's say you have an outstanding mortgage balance of $50,000 and you're concerned that your family will lose the house if you die. The better thing to do is buy a term life insurance policy that pays your loved ones directly. Then they can decide how to use the money. It may be better for them to keep the mortgage in existence and use the insurance proceeds to pay for living expenses. But if you have this ripoff credit life and disability, all it does is pay off the loan on the home or car and your family has no choice in the matter.

Credit life insurance is far more expensive than legitimate life insurance. By buying term life instead of credit life, you pay a lot less for the same amount of coverage. Or, if you spent the same amount on insurance, term life would provide a much larger death benefit.

For example, a 40-year-old could buy $100,000 worth of term life insurance for as little as $150 per year, or $1.50 per $1,000 of coverage. By contrast, I received a quote on credit life insurance of $660 a year (or $55 a month) to cover a mortgage of just $66,000. That's $10 per $1,000 of coverage, or nearly seven times the cost of term life.

To make matters worse, the balance of any installment loan will decline as the consumer makes payments, but the cost of credit life doesn't decline, making credit life even more expensive. If you pay $9 a month for credit life on a $15,000 car loan, you'll pay the same $9 a month a few years later, when you owe just $5,000 on the loan. You pay the same amount for less coverage.

Even after rate cuts in many states, Americans who purchase credit life insurance are being overcharged by more than $500 million each year, according to a study by the National Insurance Consumer Organization and the Consumer Federation of America. Insurers have paid an average of just 44 cents for every dollar collected in premiums, the study showed.

In only three states, New York, Maine, and Vermont, are consumers getting a respectable 60 cents in benefits for each premium dollar. To insure a $10,000, 12 percent loan in those three states, it costs $155 over 48 months, including finance charges. But in Louisiana, the worst offender in the study, the cost of credit life for the same loan would be an astronomical $673.

You may not even need to protect your family from a car note or any similar debt. If you die and have a car note under your signature alone, then the responsibility for that car goes to your estate, not to your family. It will be up to the executor or the executrix of the estate to decide what to do. He or she

⚠ **221**

**222** ⚠

can either give the vehicle back to the lender or make arrangements to continue payments on the loan and decide how to distribute the vehicle. If the vehicle was worth less than the amount still owed, the lender would have a right to make a claim on the estate for the difference. Turning the vehicle in could not hurt the credit rating of any member of your family.

Some people believe that they will not be approved for a loan unless they agree to buy credit life and disability, and lenders will lie to loan applicants to make them believe it. But legally that cannot be a determining factor in whether you get the loan.

 **TIPS ON CREDIT LIFE INSURANCE**

⦿ Credit life and disability insurance, also known as "croak-and-choke," is worthless. It protects the lender if you die or are disabled. It doesn't protect you.

⦿ If you're concerned that your family will lose the house if you die, buy a term life insurance policy that pays your loved ones directly. They can decide how to use the money.

⦿ Credit life insurance is far more expensive than term life insurance.

# CHARITIES

How do you know when you're donating money to a legitimate charity? A lot of folks collect money for fake charities, and because criminals have become more clever and technology has improved, it's become a lot harder to tell a true charity from a fake one. The frustrating thing for consumers and small businesses is that many of these groups have names that are very similar to those of real charities.

A good approach is to pick a cause that you're involved in, such as helping the homeless or fighting cancer. That way you'll know it's something you believe in and whether your money is being efficiently spent. If you're not actually involved in a cause, but you still want to give money to charity, request literature from the organization. That's a good idea whether you're solicited in person or on the phone.

Even better, don't make decisions about giving to charity in a haphazard manner. Instead, take one particular time per year and make all your charitable-giving decisions. Some people do that at the end of the year when they have a snapshot of their income tax picture. Then they can make charitable donations with an eye toward their personal finances. When you know how much you can give and make all your donations at one time, you're able to figure out exactly where you want your money to go. If you avoid just pulling out the checkbook or wallet, and instead plan your donations, you'll be much wiser in giving to worthwhile causes. You'll be giving your money in a way that comes from the heart by using your head first.

This works very well for small businesses. If you have your own small business, you no doubt get solicitation calls frequently from charities and quasi-charities such as civic organizations. If you require that they make a written request and explain that you review requests at a set time each year, many of those companies go away and you never hear from them again. The others that actually do write need to be patient and realize you'll consider them during the time of year that you make donations. I recommend that small companies have three employees sit on a committee to decide how the money is handed out. You, as the owner of the business, decide how much money is going to go to charity each year. Then empower the employees to hand it out.

A friend of mine did this in his business, and he said it was the greatest suggestion I ever had. He used to get bogged down with calls from people trying to convince him their cause was worthwhile. Now that requests have to be submitted in writing and they're only considered one week of the year, most of the hassle he went through has been eliminated.

My advice on door-to-door solicitors is never give them one cent. If you want to give money to that cause later on, that's fine. Ask for literature from the solicitor, but do not give one penny at the door. You need an opportunity for perspective, to think about whether this is a cause you really want to support. You're just never going to know whether that person coming to your door is legitimate.

When you're asked for contributions that amount to pocket change, 25 or 50 cents for the Shriners or Salvation Army, for example, just make your own best decision. Do what you feel like doing at the moment — you're not going to miss the quarter. I'm not as worried about people being taken in that way as much as I am the contributions of $5, $10, or more that con artists try to get you to give on impulse.

I did a series for local television that illustrates how much money ripoff artists can make through fake charities. I put on a Santa Claus suit and stood near a highway off-ramp with a collection bucket labeled with a fictional charity, "Homeless Families Fund." I never asked anybody for money, but

△ 223

**224** ⚠

people just gave it to me, one after another. People in one out of every nine cars gave me money. If I'd kept it, I would have made $27 an hour tax-free. Instead, we donated it to a legitimate charity, Habitat for Humanity. Although you may feel better giving money to a roadside fund-raiser, more often than not the money will be going to a scammer.

Ripoff charities that use the telephone definitely are something to avoid. What often happens with these pseudo-charities is you're supposed to make a purchase rather than a contribution. Such groups will call and say they're with the "Handicapped Veterans of America." They'll tell you they don't want charity but would like you to consider buying their "long-life light bulbs," which supposedly last eight times longer than normal light bulbs. If you buy, they'll tell you, you'll be helping the veterans stay off welfare. These types of pitches are thinly disguised con games. This is not the way to give to a cause. If you're interested in helping the disabled find employment, then give to a vocational or educational training program. Don't buy overpriced light bulbs.

I've noticed an increased aggressiveness from charities that pretend to work on behalf of police officers, firefighters, or other public safety organizations. These groups are not charities, and virtually without exception are using professional fundraisers. They're so aggressive that, if you agree to make a "contribution," they'll send a courier to your house or business to pick up your check. Unfortunately, the chance that your money will go to a real charity are near zero.

There are organizations that report on the performance of charities and can tell you exactly what portion of your money actually goes to those in need. The National Charities Information Bureau publishes a list that rates charities. Or you can get some great information at their Web site, www.give.org. The Better Business Bureau also has a Web site, www.bbb.org, that provides information on charities.

If you follow my system of determining how much to give each year to charity and use this list to help decide which charities will get that money, you'll feel really good about your system for giving money. You'll be confident that you've served society well with your dollars.

Interestingly, I don't get a lot of calls from people complaining that they've been ripped off by a charity. Perhaps people just write it off to experience. But what these ripoffs do is prevent people from giving to worthwhile charities. If somebody has been burned by a phony charity, they're reluctant to open their checkbook the next time for a legitimate cause.

In any case, never allow anyone — the solicitor, your employer — to pressure you to give to a charity. The money you give to charity should come from your heart.

 TIPS ON CHARITIES

◉ If possible, pick a cause that you know personally so you know your money will be spent efficiently.

◉ To help verify that a charity is legitimate, always request literature from the organization.

◉ Plan your charitable giving, making all decisions at one time each year.

◉ If you own a small business, decide how much to give and have a committee of employees hand out the money.

◉ Never give any money to door-to-door solicitors.

◉ Watch out for phony charities that telephone and ask you to buy a product at inflated prices.

◉ Never allow anyone to pressure you into giving to a charity.

## CONTACT

National Charities Information Bureau
212-929-6300
www.give.org

Better Business Bureau
www.bbb.org

# HEALTH CLUBS

Most health clubs are interested more in your checkbook than your health. And signing a long-term contract with one can really hurt your financial fitness.

When you go into these high-pressure health clubs, you're greeted by a commission salesperson, not a health expert. Her job is to strong-arm you into signing a long-term membership, typically for three years.

Callers have told me they're not even shown the facilities during a sales presentation. If they do see the facility, it's a very limited tour. The salesperson concentrates on making oral promises that are not in the contract and doesn't

⚠ 225

**226** ⚠ bother to show you the contract until very late in the presentation.

Salespeople use all kinds of "closer" techniques, words, and phrases designed to pressure you into signing. For example, a salesperson might say, "Don't you think today is the day you should start building a healthier body?"

People usually go to a health club with the best of intentions. Sometimes they go to get healthier, or more often than not, to get thinner. People often sign a health club contract because they believe they're doing something to improve themselves. But signing the contract doesn't do anything except obligate you to a long-term commitment to pay a lot of money, usually with hefty finance charges attached.

The enthusiasm of a new health club member often wanes quickly. For the first few weeks after you join, you'll probably visit the club several times. Then you start going twice a week and then once a week. Suddenly, you're going every other week, and before you know it, usually within three months, you're not even setting foot there. You're feeling so guilty that you're driving a different route home so you don't have to see the place.

At that point, the deal starts to look very unfair. You're getting a bill every month from a health club that you're not visiting, and you don't want to pay any more. But if you don't pay, they're going to come after you, either with their own collectors or with a third-party collection agency. I often get calls from people who can't qualify for a mortgage because of something on their credit report. A major reason for that — No. 1 as far as my callers are concerned — is a past-due bill for a health club.

Once you enter into a health club membership, you own it — with one exception. Most states give you three business days from the day you sign the contract to cancel your membership with no consequences. You must follow the exact procedure in the contract for canceling. Don't telephone and tell the club you're canceling. Don't drop by and hand them a note. Usually you'll have to send a letter by certified mail, return receipt requested. Keep a copy of that letter and your certified mail slip forever. You never know when someone's going to get amnesia about the fact that you canceled properly. One day you may need to provide proof.

If you've waited beyond the allowed number of days to cancel, you have little choice but to keep paying. If you stop paying, the club will ruin your credit, making it difficult for you to buy a car or a house, or obtain a credit card. Normally you'll get a notice from the club or their finance company. Later you'll be turned over to a collection agency. The collection efforts will continue, often sporadically, through the years. Eventually, when you try to establish new credit, the delinquent membership will jump off your credit report to bite you. At that point, you will have to come to an accommodation with the health club.

Ripoff health clubs often operate right on the edge of the law, and their goal is to get money out of you no matter what. I had one case involving a 17-year-old boy who signed a health club contract, then went home and realized that he was pressured into it by a salesperson. In his state, a contract signed by a 17-year-old is voidable, but it's not automatically void. He tried for months to cancel his contract but the health club kept stalling. He called the day before his 18th birthday. Once he turned 18, he could no longer void the contract. So I had to walk his father through the steps to make sure the boy didn't get taken at midnight that night. It would have been an unfriendly birthday present.

Another thing to watch out for with a health club is "free membership" contests. Health clubs offer free memberships to gather names and addresses of possible new members. When you sign up at the yogurt store to win the one-year membership, and win a free 30-day membership instead, you know you're just being taken in for a sales presentation. Normally they won't give you your membership card until you've been on the sales presentation, and by then, they expect to have sold you a membership. Every single person who enters the contest at the yogurt store wins the 30-day membership.

Reputable health clubs do exist, and if you're looking to join one, here's what I recommend. First, look for a club that allows you to pay as you go.

Very few health clubs will tell you outright that you can sign up on a month-to-month basis, but if you're persistent and are willing to pay a little more per month, several clubs probably will cut you that kind of deal.

I heard of one club that charges $10 a month more for month-to-month membership, and it requires that you authorize a monthly draft from your checking or credit card account. That's not a great offer, but it's better than a three-year contract.

Another had a no-pressure approach and a membership that included a $150 initiation fee and a two-month minimum. A third asked for a $150 down payment. These are just some examples. Health clubs come and go and offers change. But you can find acceptable deals out there if you look.

It's okay to sign a three-year agreement with a health club if the agreement has a buyout clause, and as long as you don't pay in advance. With a buyout clause, you're protected if you are transferred to a new job or move to a different area. A fair buyout is two months of membership fees. At least it gives you a way to get out early.

A job transfer might move you only five or 10 miles away, but that might be too far for you to want to stay with the same health club. If five miles is too far, make sure the contract lets you terminate if you move five or more miles away.

Because people travel, many clubs now are offering multicity memberships, which allow you to use the club's facilities

⚠ 227

in other cities for free or a minimal fee, usually $5 or less a workout. If you're on the road a lot, and you want to work out as you travel, find out if there is a multicity membership available.

Don't ever pay a health club in advance. In some states, membership money isn't held in escrow or by bond. So if the club closes its doors and you've paid in advance for a full year, you lose all your money. It's a real danger because health clubs close all the time.

I remember one club that had been offering very inexpensive one- and two-year memberships. The club kept collecting cash from members right up to the day it closed its doors. All of those people got stuck without a membership and without refunds. When you pay in advance for a health club, you do so at your own risk.

Some states do provide greater protection. New York, for example, requires health clubs to post a bond of up to $150,000 if it signs members to long-term contracts. The money is used to reimburse the club's members.

If you finance your membership contract and the club closes, you no longer have to make any payments to the finance company. If your club has closed, send the finance company a certified letter telling them the club has closed and that you owe no more money on the contract. However, some states may require you to attend another location of the club that remains open.

If your club does close, competing clubs nearby may take you as a member at little or no cost. They do it for good will, and they figure you may sign up with them when your original membership expires.

If you think a particular health club may suit you, call the local consumer agency in your state to see if there are any unsatisfied complaints about the club. If the club passes that test, go and take a look. Visit during the busiest time of the week — usually early in the week in the evening. Ask for a tour and look at the condition of the equipment and how crowded the facility is. If you wanted to use a stair step machine, is there one available, or do you have to wait in line to use one? Go into the locker room and see how clean it is. Watch an aerobics or other fitness class and see whether or not the instructor seems knowledgeable. Then, talk to some of the participants after the class. Interview a fitness trainer. See how long he has been there and ask what his training recommendations are for you. That will tell you how interested he is in you and how knowledgeable he is. Nobody in just a brief conversation can let you know exactly what your weight program will be, but you'll be able to tell how much he really knows.

If you like the club, ask for a copy of its contract that you can take home. Do not sign the contract while you're at the health club, but ask for time to read it carefully. If there's anything you don't understand, put a question mark next to it. Then call the club — don't go back in — and get answers to those questions. The reason you don't go back in is you may not get any answers, or you may get false answers, and you'll feel pressure to sign when you're back in the club's environment. If you're calling, you maintain the balance of power.

Don't agree to anything you don't understand. If there's anything a club salesperson can't explain to you, put a slash through it, put your initials by it, and sign the contract without that clause included.

If the health club does not allow you to leave with a copy of the contract, do not sign and do not join that health club. Any reputable business will give you an unsigned contract for you to review, I don't care what you're buying.

Don't listen to what the salesperson says unless she includes it in writing. I had one caller who was thinking about moving to another state and wondered what would happen to his membership if he moved. He was told that it would be no problem, that all he had to do was provide documentation — say, a copy of his new lease — and the club would let him out of the membership. Well, that wasn't true at all. The agreement he signed keeps him obligated no matter where he lives.

Another fellow was told he could either use his local health club or transfer his membership to another place. That was wonderful because he loves to play racquetball. But the membership was not truly transferable, because although he could play racquetball at facility No. 1, at facility No. 2, the membership was good only for general health club use. The racquetball portion was an extra $500 a year. Here he was obligated to a membership that was useless for what he wanted.

Any promises that are made about facilities, terms and conditions of the agreement, or potential termination promises must be included in the language of the contract.

## TIPS ON HEALTH CLUBS

◉ Don't sign long-term contracts for health club membership or pay for more than 30 days in advance. Month-to-month deals are much safer.

◉ Don't fall for "free membership" contests that are really sales pitches.

◉ Take the contract home with you and read it thoroughly. Don't sign the contract at the club.

◉ Get any promises made by the salesperson included in the contract, or they don't mean a thing.

◉ In most states, you have three days from the day you sign a health club contract to cancel with no consequences.

⚠ 229

**230** ⚠

- If you finance your membership and the club closes, you have no further obligation to pay.

- If you think a particular club may suit you, call the appropriate consumer agency in your state to check for outstanding complaints against the club. Tour the facility and ask questions.

## TIMESHARES

The timeshare business, once the playground of small, unknown companies, is being taken over by respected companies such as Marriott and Disney. The sleazy operators are still there, but the entry of the big players has given the industry a bit more respectability.

But no matter who's selling them, timeshares are a very bad deal.

Timeshares appeal to those of us who would love to own a house in the mountains or at the beach, but can't afford one. When you buy a timeshare, you get the right to use a vacation property at a particular time each year, or during a particular season, usually for one week. It sounds like a decent idea, but because it's almost impossible to sell a timeshare, it turns out to be a financial burden from which there is no escape.

In addition to the cost of buying a timeshare, usually $8,000 to $10,000, you have to pay an annual association fee of about $400 for each week you get to use the timeshare. That's a lot of money for something you already own. And if you get tired of spending your vacation at the same place every year, or if your budget tightens and you have to skip a vacation, you still have to pay the maintenance fee.

A timeshare differs significantly from a vacation home in that there is a ready market for vacation homes. If you have a vacation home and you decide to sell it, you hire a real estate agent, the house sells, and your obligation to it is over. But you can't sell a timeshare because no one will buy it from you. I get calls every week from people who would gladly give their timeshares away. Nobody will take them, because they don't want the obligation, either. Once you own a timeshare, it's with you forever.

One way to give up ownership of a house is through foreclosure. You can't do that with a timeshare because developers won't take it back. If you don't pay, they'll send you to a collection agency and eventually sue you. Your obligation continues no matter what.

Even if the upfront cost was zero, the burden of paying the annual fee makes owning a timeshare a bad idea. In fact, if you ever inherit a timeshare, I recommend that you disavow your inheritance of it. Otherwise, the obligations of the deceased become yours. Generally things you inherit are to your benefit. A timeshare is to your detriment.

People are so desperate to sell timeshares that they get conned by timeshare brokers, people who say they can successfully market a timeshare. These folks will charge a listing fee of about $300. Once you write a check for that listing fee, you can kiss it goodbye. I have never heard of any caller who has ever been able to sell a timeshare through a broker.

Even though you pay a maintenance and association fee, you don't have control over what happens if a timeshare is not well maintained. You don't have the rights you would have with a condominium complex, where the owners of the condominium units run the association that takes care of maintenance. Timeshare agreements are always done so the timeshare operator has the power even when you have the ownership. So you could wind up with a property that's poorly maintained, even run down.

If new operators like Marriott and Disney think timeshares are such a good deal, why don't they offer to buy them back for the selling price?

At the high end of the market, developers sell the units by allowing you to stay at the resort for a few days or a weekend at an extra-low price. Then you attend a sales presentation

while you're there. If you want to go for the weekend, it's okay, as long as you promise yourself you won't buy, no matter how good it sounds. If you really do like the place, after you have a chance to go home and think about it, and you really want to buy it, buy not from the developer but from a timeshare owner who wants to sell. You'll be able to buy at a huge discount, usually 80 percent below retail.

If you're an owner who wants to sell your timeshare, go stay there, and look for a buyer while you're there. The secondary marketplace is the place to buy or sell, at big discounts for the original price. Be prepared to sell your $10,000 timeshare for about $2,000.

Most of the cost of a timeshare goes into an elaborate sales and marketing effort. First, you'll be called by a telemarketer, whose job is to convince you to come to the presentation. That person is paid based on how many people show up for the timeshare presentations, so he'll tell you anything to get you in the door.

The biggest lie he'll tell you is it's a short presentation; in reality it will last about three hours. The idea is to immerse you completely in a carefully orchestrated event.

The prizes you're offered as an incentive to attend a presentation are almost always overly glorified. For example, you'll be told you're going to receive two free tickets to Hawaii, with a retail value of $1,200. Later, it turns out that you've won a certificate

⚠ 231

allowing you to purchase a trip to Hawaii. You get the free tickets only if you agree to buy 10 nights at a specific hotel. Before you know it, the hotel and free tickets cost more than it would have cost to buy the air and hotel from someone else.

This certificate program is a common tactic in high-pressure sales schemes. The timeshare operator can obtain these "free airfare" certificates for $5 each. If a company is selling these certificates for $5, it's obviously not going to redeem them for free airline tickets to Hawaii.

When you show up for the timeshare presentation, the first thing they do is check to see if you're qualified to be a timeshare owner. If you have good credit, but aren't wealthy enough to buy your own beach house, you're probably a good target.

If you qualify, you're brought into a very impressive-looking reception area. A salesperson will then take you through an elaborate presentation, normally followed by a film. Next you'll be shown an actual model of the timeshare unit, fully built and beautifully decorated.

This is one of the No Be Back sales. It isn't a sensible purchase, and they know that once you leave their high-pressure environment, you'll never buy.

During the film segment of the presentation, there will be a product endorsement of the timeshare by someone who appeals to the potential buyer. I went to a timeshare presentation for a

property in Myrtle Beach, South Carolina, in which a stock-car driver made the pitch. The endorser could be any of a number of different people, depending on what market segment the timeshare is targeting.

The message is seductive. "Just imagine yourself once a year with us on this beautiful stretch of sand." They're selling an illusion, a piece of the American dream. A lot of people figure maybe they can't afford to have the whole dream, but this seven days they can have.

Most people have to stretch to come up with $8,000 to $10,000, and generally they have to finance it. Even with financing, people just don't have an extra $100 or more to throw away each month.

After the presentation and film, you're brought into another room, and all kinds of psychological tricks are used to get you to buy. For example, every time somebody buys, they pop a champagne bottle. The sales reps stand up in unison and start applauding. There's a festive atmosphere. The buyers smile, their picture is taken, and champagne is poured. Then the sales rep will say something to you like, "Do you see the joy in their face? Don't you want to be able to experience that joy of ownership yourself?"

If you don't agree to buy, a closer is brought to your table, a professional who knows how to hit people where they're weakest. At one presentation I went to, the closer was alternately trying to humiliate me, trying to be charming, and trying to be threatening. They'll frighten you into thinking you're letting a wonderful opportunity get away. Or they'll put you down by saying you don't have the money to do it. The idea is to get you to prove you do have the money by signing the deal. Many people do buy the timeshare after the closer comes to the table.

When you finish and don't buy, just wait until you try to get your prizes. It's not easy. I went to hear a timeshare presentation in Orlando once, after an offer for some free tickets to a Florida attraction. Of course I didn't buy. The salesperson realized this pretty quickly, but the closer got really angry when I told him I came just for the free tickets. I was able to get the tickets, and I figure it was worth my time to go. The tickets were worth $70, and I was there about two hours, so I was compensated for my time at about $35 an hour. But I had to put up with some aggravation while on vacation.

Some people don't mind. I had a caller who told me he and his wife, while on vacation, used to go to a different timeshare presentation each morning for a different Orlando attraction. They'd go to the timeshare presentation in the morning, and Sea World or Disney World in the afternoon. But you have to know yourself and know you can resist the sales pressure to do that, and not many people can.

Unless you're certain you can say "no," I recommend you avoid going to timeshare presentations at all. There's too much of a chance that you might be tempted or intimidated into buying something that will turn out to be a very big mistake. It doesn't matter what your income level is or what your level of education, you can fall for these false pitches.

## TIPS ON TIMESHARES

◉ Timeshares are worthless and cannot be resold.

◉ Prizes that are promised are usually overblown and of little value.

◉ Don't attend timeshare presentations because you might be tempted to make a huge mistake and buy.

⚠ 233

# 234 ⚠ INVENTION SERVICES

There's been an explosion of interest in the United States in inventing. People are tinkering in their basements and garages, hoping to strike it rich with a new, commercially successful product. They want to create the next big hit, like the founders of Apple Computer did.

Enthusiastic would-be inventors have become perfect prey for a group of ripoff artists who promise to help take these inventions to the marketplace. Instead, they steal hundreds of dollars from each inventor, without ever providing any help.

The ripoff "invention services" attract folks by offering a free evaluation of inventions. Inventors call the 800 number, send in some application forms, and inevitably receive a call from a salesperson who raves about the invention and its potential. But to do further research, the salesperson says, the organization needs $500 from the inventor. Many people quickly send a check.

After a few more weeks, the company will start the second phase of the scam. They'll send a second, more complete information kit, and tell the inventor that his idea is now ready to be prepared for the marketplace. They'll ask for a larger amount, usually $5,000 or $6,000 "to conduct a thorough market analysis." Many inventors send in a second check, only to learn weeks or months later that the ripoff invention service did nothing but take their money.

One of these companies, Invention Submission Corporation, entered into a consent agreement with the federal government in which they agreed to disclose that less than 1 percent of the ideas people submit ever make it to market. These companies are not in the business of bringing ideas alive, they're in the business of getting rich off of you.

The reason these phony organizations continue to operate is that it's very hard for law enforcement authorities to prove that their actions are criminal. So authorities have taken civil action to try to win restitution for victims and, through greater disclosure, try to warn others to stay away. Unfortunately, con artists who have little fear of going to jail will continue what they're doing.

The Federal Trade Commission has information about invention promotion firms at its Web site (www.ftc.gov). And the U.S. Patent and Trademark Office has done a fantastic job on its Web site, www.uspto.gov, of explaining how the whole process works, for would-be inventors.

If you believe you have a good invention idea, there's legitimate help at the local bookstore or library. I like two books in particular: *Patent It Yourself*, by Nolo Press, and *The Inventing and Patenting Sourcebook: Desktop Companion*, by Richard Levy. Not surprisingly, *Patent It Yourself* describes the process of patenting an idea. The Levy book addresses how companies select products to market and how inventors can increase their chances of getting an audience for their ideas.

To have any chance of success, inventors must have a working prototype, Levy says. Companies won't buy sketches; they have to see a working model of the product. So if you've tinkered and drawn, start building.

Inventions fall into three basic categories: weak ideas that don't have a chance, ideas that are good but can't generate enough demand for them to make money, and the small number of good ideas with potential for profit. So inventors have to be both lucky and good.

One of the most helpful parts of Levy's guide is his explanation of the role played by brokers in bringing ideas from inventors to large corporations. Their job is to help separate the good ideas from the weak ones. Most large companies prefer to deal with established brokers, rather than speaking directly with inventors.

There's one other alternative available to help you in many medium-size and large cities around the country. They're called nonprofit inventors clubs, and their members share information that can be very helpful. In a real nonprofit inventors club, you won't be asked to sign any licensing agreements. It's a shared self-help organization, with people encouraging and advising you along the way, and you sharing your information and success stories with others.

Inventors as a group are unusually paranoid, with a tremendous fear that everybody is going to steal their idea. There is some justification for that fear, and who you can trust is a difficult question. My advice is to seek a patent to protect your concept before you present your idea to a corporation.

### TIPS ON INVENTION SERVICES

● Most ripoff invention services use a three-step program to steal money. They offer a free evaluation of the inventor's product through an 800-number, take $500 or so to fund "research," and later request another $5,000 to $6,000 for more extensive "market research."

● One such company was forced to disclose that less than 1 percent of the ideas people submit ever make it to market.

● Turn to the local bookstore or library for legitimate advice on how to bring inventions to market.

● It's important to create a working prototype of your idea, because companies won't buy ideas from sketches.

⚠ 235

⊛ Your best bet is to find an invention broker to propose your idea to a company.

⊛ Nonprofit inventors clubs, which can be found in many cities, also are excellent for sharing ideas and providing encouragement.

### REFERENCE

*Patent It Yourself*
by Nolo Press

*The Inventing and Patenting Sourcebook: Desktop Companion*
by Richard Levy

### INTERNET

www.nolo.com
www.ftc.gov
www.uspto.gov

# BUSINESS AND EMPLOYMENT SCAMS

More and more people are working out of their homes, either by freelancing, telecommuting, or doing consulting work. Their success has encouraged the ripoff artists who want to convince people that there's money to be made stuffing envelopes or starting an unfamiliar business.

People who succeed in working at home do it by marketing proven skills and building on established relationships. A paralegal might decide to work at home, knowing she can count on one or more law firms as clients, and a public relations consultant may have a list of potential or established clients as well.

Even if you don't have one of those skills, scammers will try to convince you that there's money to be made, if you'll give them some money first.

You can steer clear of these with a little common sense. In most of these cases, someone is supposedly willing to set you up in business without having interviewed or screened you in any way. And if you have had a lot of trouble finding a job, why would you suddenly be able to earn several hundred or several thousand dollars a week doing a job in your home?

Most of the business opportunity scams I'm hearing about involve computers and technology. For years I've heard about one in which you're sold lesson books and software that supposedly will allow you to process medical claims for doctors' offices. It's always been complete nonsense. Most doctors use their own employees to process their claims, or they use independent processing companies. But the scammers used to try to get thousands of dollars for the software out of each victim. Now the average is $200 to $500.

When you hear about a scheme like this, one of the best ways to check it out is to call someone in the profession it involves. In this case, you should call doctors' offices and ask the office managers if they are interested in this service and, if they are, what fees they would be willing to pay to have claims processed.

The high number of corporate layoffs in recent years has provided fertile ground for the growth of ripoff employment recruiters. Particularly vulnerable are those people who worked in a job for a long time and thought they were going to work for that company for a lifetime. Suddenly, they have found themselves unemployed and suffering a dramatic loss of confidence.

Because of this sense of loss and hopelessness, they are easy prey for organizations that promise to place them in a job. The organizations claim to have special contacts or special influence that enables them to find jobs. That's just someone taking advantage of the unemployed.

Nobody can guarantee they'll find you a job and — unless you have a very special skill — none have special influence with employers.

I urge you not to do business with any employment organization that requires you to pay an up-front fee. If you are really timid about your job search and you want to use a placement service, it should be one whose fee is paid after you are hired. Your preference should be that the employer pays the fee or that the fee is split between you and the employer. It's obviously less desirable for you to pay the full fee.

If you do have an unusual skill that is highly desirable to employers, you may benefit by turning to a recruiter with expertise in your field. People who would be helped by a specialized recruiter might have skills in engineering, medicine, or the sciences. But such areas are by far the exception, and for these job candidates the employer would pay the fee and would never have any up-front charge.

If you believe you need help looking for a job, I have several recommendations. A number of informal networking organizations exist that don't charge a fee and meet in local churches. I heard about one group that meets at a cafeteria once a week. These groups gather people who are looking for jobs to share ideas, leads, and contacts.

Almost all jobs found in America are found through direct contact with employers or through friends and relatives. The number of jobs found through classified ads or any form of advertising

⚠ 237

**238** ⚠

is less than 15 percent of the total openings. Because most people are passive in their job search, the overwhelming majority of people end up competing for the very limited number of advertised jobs. Very few people are out there looking for the vast majority of jobs through informal and formal networking.

The Internet has become a good resource for job searchers, both in looking for openings and researching potential employers. Ask people in your trade or profession for ideas on which Web sites may be helpful. Use whatever method you can to become familiar with people who might be making hiring decisions.

If you've lost a job, you may become passive and even have trouble getting started in the morning. One of the ways people can pick themselves up, build confidence, and move toward getting a job is by treating the job search as a job. Give yourself specific assignments every day: People you're going to see and things you're going to do. One of the first things you should do is sit down with three-by-five index cards or a computer and list every single person you know. It may sound like busywork but actually it's not, because there are many people you know or knew in the past who may be able to help you in your job search. By going through the mental exercise of making this list, you give yourself a very helpful tool with which to start your job search.

One major word of caution: When you start contacting people who are potential job leads, don't call and ask if they know about work, because people hate that. Ask for advice or information, not for a job. People love to be asked for their advice. People hate to be asked for a job.

 **TIPS ON BUSINESS AND EMPLOYMENT SCAMS**

⦿ Work-at-home offers almost always are scams. If you have had a lot of trouble finding a job, it's unlikely you suddenly would be able to earn several hundred or several thousand dollars a week doing a job in your home.

⦿ If you think you need help looking for a job, try an informal networking group, or find a group on the Internet.

⦿ Placement offices can't guarantee that they'll find you a job, and — unless you have a very special skill — none have special influence with employers.

⦿ Don't do business with any employment organization that requires you to pay an up-front fee.

INTERNET

www.hotjobs.com
www.headhunter.net

# MODELING SCHOOLS

This ripoff appeals not only to a person's vanity and dreams, but to parents' dreams for their children. Modeling scams give individuals and families false hope of a brilliant new career and then shatter those dreams by just taking their money.

They tend to target parents with young children, but they're willing to take anybody's money. Other common victims are young men and women in their late teens and early 20s.

I call them modeling road shows because these groups take the con on the road. They'll come into a city and advertise their modeling tryouts or seminars. If you think you or your child has what it takes to be a model, they want you to come to their show — usually in a hotel ballroom. By showing up, you're prequalifying yourself to be taken.

When you arrive, there will be a large presentation, kind of like a pep rally. Then they'll meet with each person individually or in small groups.

Let's say a parent goes in with three children. To increase the credibility of the modeling road show, they'll take only one child. It'll sound something like, "We think your daughter Letitia has great talent and we'd like to see her some more, but the other two children aren't ready yet." Or, "We like Mark but Sara is too young. Maybe in another year or two." So they pretend they're eliminating people when all they're really doing is setting you up for a squeeze play. The squeeze usually will come in some type of listing fee, modeling fee, lessons charge, or photography charge. They also have something they call a placement fee. Typically they'll take a victim for $200 to $300.

A real modeling agency makes its money off the bookings it gets for you. They're paid a commission for having placed you in an ad. Only fake modeling groups take these road shows all around America. Any time you're hit for money up-front from a modeling organization, you should know something is not right.

One of my callers agreed to pay $180 to one modeling company, including a $50 application fee, $25 for an orientation program, and $105 for a photo session. Interestingly, the contract

⚠ 239

**240** ⚠ mandated a $200 penalty for rescheduling the photo session, certainly an exorbitant charge.

She had regrets almost immediately and called me for help. A road-show contract would have had a three-day cancellation option, but because it was a local company, a three-day option wasn't required. The company did agree to let her out of the deal and return her money after my staff and I interceded. But she was lucky; they could have kept the money and she would have had no recourse.

One legitimate charge you will have to pay if you want to become a model is for a photo portfolio. To get that, you'll have to go to a professional photographer and pay a fair amount of money. You shouldn't get a portfolio unless a legitimate modeling agency, one that is looking for actual talent, gives you an encouraging evaluation.

I've seen pictures supplied by my listeners who have been taken by these phony modeling agencies and there isn't a chance at all that these kids are going to be models. The problem is the parents absolutely believe their child is the most gorgeous creature who ever walked. Moms and Dads should believe their child is gorgeous, but by that definition, every child is gorgeous. Granted, there are certain "real-people" looks that modeling agencies want, but for the most part, they want people who have a special look.

Once the modeling road shows have collected their cash, they leave town. It's impossible to go after them because generally they deliver what they promise, usually modeling lessons. They never promise any modeling work, so they haven't done anything illegal. Breaking hearts isn't against the law.

If you're interested in modeling or acting, one of the best places to learn more is through one of your local theater companies. Many have classes that can help you learn needed skills and break into the industry.

 **TIPS ON MODELING SCHOOLS**

- ⊙ Do business only with legitimate, in-town modeling agencies and never pay up-front fees. Stay away from traveling modeling recruiters.

- ⊙ If you think you or your child has modeling potential, seek an evaluation by a legitimate agency.

- ⊙ Get a photo portfolio done by a professional photographer, but only if a legitimate modeling agency advises you to take that step.

# JUNK CALLS

How many times have you sat down for dinner with your family and been interrupted by a telephone sales call?

Telemarketing has become a truly intrusive industry. If I get a piece of junk mail, I can choose to throw it away without even opening the envelope. But if a human being has me on the phone, I'll probably listen to the pitch to avoid being rude.

For many marketers, it's actually cheaper and more effective to have a human being call you than it is to send you a piece of junk mail. That's why the telemarketing industry spends more than $80 billion a year, and accounts for nearly 40 percent of spending on direct marketing, according to the American Telemarketing Association.

Telemarketing has divided itself into two different categories — legitimate businesses and charities, whose calls are annoying but not otherwise worrisome, and fraudulent telemarketers, who are out to steal your money.

You can avoid both by using Caller ID. Many telemarketers block Caller ID, so while you may not know exactly who's calling, you'll get a message such as "Out of area" or "Private call." You can elect to let those calls go unanswered and avoid a lot of telemarketers. If the caller turns out to be a friend, they can leave a message and you can call back.

The other side of the coin is that, when you call a person or business, there's the possibility that they can use Caller ID to see who you are and learn your telephone number. If you don't want that, ask your phone company about how you can block someone else's Caller ID.

Another way is to use an answering machine to screen your calls, particularly around the dinner hour, when telemarketers are most bothersome. With an answering machine, you can hear who's calling and pick up the receiver if it's a call you want to take. You can even tailor your message so friends and family will know what you're doing and telemarketers will know you're not interested.

Dishonest telemarketers, besides being annoying, are dangerous. Because mail and telephone lists are so easily obtained, illegitimate businesses have no trouble getting your name and number. Con artists have found boiler room operations (the name comes from the cheap office space they rent) to be the most efficient way to steal money. They call you from these boiler rooms and try to get you to buy a product or service. If anyone attempts to sell you something on the telephone and says you must make a decision right then, don't have anything to do with it. Ask phone solicitors to mail you information; otherwise, don't do business with them.

In the worst cases, the con artists

⚠ **241**

**242** ⚠ get you to provide your checking account number or credit card number over the telephone, and use it to steal from your account. The most ironclad rule I can give you is never give out your credit card number or your checking account number on the telephone, unless you make the phone call, because you will live to regret it.

I got a call from a fellow who was solicited for an $800 vacation trip on the telephone and, somewhat reluctantly, agreed to give out his credit card number. As soon as the call was over, he changed his mind and called back to say he wasn't interested. The telemarketer told him the $800 charge already had been posted to his account.

If you're calling a mail-order company such as Land's End, and you know it has an outstanding reputation, then it is okay to use your credit card. In fact, in that instance, using a credit card is preferable to sending a check. That way, if something goes wrong, you can get a refund from your credit card company under the chargeback process.

I urge you especially not to give out your checking account number because that's all criminal telemarketers need to withdraw money from your account. The hoodlums simply present your bank with a draft from your account and within 24 hours, they have your money. It's unbelievable what they do in these boiler rooms. They'll have a check encoding machine right there, and as soon as you give them your checking account number, they'll walk over to

this machine and create a very professional-looking bank draft.

These schemes work in two ways. Sometimes they get your credit card or checking account number and immediately draw money out of your account. Other times, they'll sell you a product or service and get your account number for the purchase. You may receive the merchandise or you may not. But while you're distracted, they tap your account. By the time you realize what happened, they've left town.

Money can be taken from your account without your knowledge or consent because of the banking system's failure to have any meaningful safeguards. Banks are supposed to pay a draft only when it has been authorized in writing by you. But most banks have no internal security system in place to verify the accuracy of a draft. The bank is fully liable for any money it pays out in unauthorized bank drafts. But why should you have to sue your bank to force it to live up to the law? It's better for you to help prevent a crime by not giving out your checking account number.

Banks are failing miserably in their responsibility to prevent fraud. Often when you call the customer service center to report a fraud, they tell you that your rights to do a chargeback are explained on the back of your statement. Here's what's wrong with that. Let's say the charge posts on your next statement. You then write the bank and protest the charge. From the date of your original complaint, as many as 60 days pass before the bureaucrats at the bank send your protest through to the criminals' bank. By that time, the criminals have stolen a bunch of money. The banks look at this fraud as a cost of doing business. That's wrong and foolish. It gives an open invitation to the hoodlums.

The banks' security departments should consider it their responsibility to limit losses. The security departments should be notified whenever a consumer believes he or she has been hoodwinked. The credit card issuers generally don't care because the criminals' bank ends up being stuck with the chargeback, not the consumer's bank. Instead of realizing that these losses hurt the whole industry, the banks tend to blame the customer for not being more careful and try to find some reason not to honor the chargeback.

I had a caller who had learned that his credit card was sent to someone else and used fraudulently to purchase $1,200 worth of goods. It seemed clear that this was part of a larger scheme to create phony credit cards. The bank agreed to remove the fraudulent charges from the caller's account but didn't want to be bothered to look into the scheme.

One more thing about telemarketing. If you work for a telemarketer, you should be concerned about whether you're going to get paid. I've heard case after case of people who have showed up for work to discover that the telemarketer had packed up and left, without paying them for their final week. So if you work for a telemarketer that doesn't seem legitimate, or you're thinking about such a job, understand that you, too, may lose.

## TIPS ON JUNK CALLS

- ◉ Use Caller ID or an answering machine to screen your calls, particularly around the dinner hour.

- ◉ If anyone attempts to sell you something on the telephone and says you must make a decision right then, don't do business with them.

- ◉ Never give out your credit card number or your checking account number on the telephone, unless you make the phone call. With these numbers, con artists can steal from your accounts.

⚠ 243

## CONTACT

National Fraud Information Center Hotline
800-876-7060
www.fraud.org

# WORKBOOK

The Workbook section includes tools to help you in your consumer battles.

Keep the worksheets in the book, tear out the pages as needed, or make photocopies and keep them with your important records. You can also copy them from my Web site, www.clarkhoward.com. Some of the letters, like the "drop-dead" letter, can be quickly customized and mailed. Just fill in the collector's name and your account number and sign it.

## 246 ✐

# PROBLEM DOCUMENTATION SHEET
(To get results, document your efforts to solve the problem. Take people's names and make a note of what they promised to do. Letters are more effective than phone calls.)

## THE PROBLEM

_____

_____

_____

## ACTION LOG

Date of letter or call          Name of person you contacted

_____          _____

What action was promised or taken          _____

_____

_____

## ACTION LOG

Date of letter or call          Name of person you contacted

_____          _____

What action was promised or taken          _____

_____

_____

## ACTION LOG

Date of letter or call          Name of person you contacted

_____          _____

What action was promised or taken          _____

_____

_____

## ACTION LOG

Date of letter or call          Name of person you contacted

_____          _____

What action was promised or taken          _____

_____

_____

# "DROP-DEAD" LETTER TO COLLECTION AGENCIES

Date
_____

To whom it may concern:

I have been contacted by your company about a debt you allege I owe.
　　I am instructing you not to contact me any further in connection with this debt.
　　Under the Fair Debt Collection Practices Act, a federal law, you may not contact me further once I have notified you not to do so.

Sincerely,


_____

Account No. _____


................................................................................................................................

Date
_____

To whom it may concern:

I have been contacted by your company about a debt you allege I owe.
　　I am instructing you not to contact me any further in connection with this debt.
　　Under the Fair Debt Collection Practices Act, a federal law, you may not contact me further once I have notified you not to do so.

Sincerely,


_____

Account No. _____

247

## 248 ✐

## MODEL LETTER OF COMPLAINT

Date _____

John Jones
Regional Vice President
ABCD Company
500 Main Street
Suite 1000
Anywhere, USA

Dear Mr. Jones:

I regret having to write to you about an unpleasant experience I've had with your company. I prefer to contact a company only in praise of an employee or the company's actions.

Unfortunately, my situation is such that it is necessary for me to forward a complaint to you.

*(Give the specifics of the complaint. Say who you've spoken with about the problem, what attempts you've made to solve it, and what specific action you would like.)*

_____

_____

_____

_____

_____

_____

I look forward to hearing from you.  I hope you can respond within 30 days so that we are able to resolve this problem in a speedy fashion.

Sincerely,


_____

# GETTING YOUR NAME OFF MAILING LISTS

Date _____


Mail Preference Service
Direct Marketing Association
P.O. Box 9008
Farmingdale, N.Y.  11735


To whom it may concern:

I am writing to register with your Mail Preference Service.

Please inform your members that I do not want my name sold to any company
for the purpose of placing me on a mailing list and sending me advertising mail.

In addition, I would like my name removed from existing lists.

Thank you very much for your help.


Sincerely,


_____


Name _____

Street _____

City _____  State _____

Zip Code _____

✐ 249

# SAMPLE CREDIT REPORT

## Personal Identification Information

Your Name                                    Social Security Number              123-45-6789
Your Current Address                         Date of Birth                       Day Month Year
City, State, Zip
Previous Address(es)
Your Previous Address
Last Reported Employment        Your Position and Employer

## Public Record Information

Bankruptcy filed on 02/97 in City of Atlanta with case or other ID number 123456789012341
With Liabilities of $5,000, Assets of $60,234, Exempt Amount of $60,000 Type of Personal, Filed Individual, and status Voluntary Ch-7

Lien filed on 03/9:Fulton CTY:Case or Other ID
Number-32114:Amount-$26667:Class-State:Released 07/93:Verified 07/93

Satisfied Judgment filed on 07/94:Fulton CTY:Case or Other ID Number-898872:Defendant-Consumer:Amount-$8984:Plaintiff-ABC Real Estate:Satisfied 03/95:Verified 05/95

## Collection Agency Account Information

Pro Coll (800) XXX-XXXX

Collection Reported 05/96:Assigned 09/93 to Pro Coll (800) XXX-XXXX Client ABC
Hospital:Amount-$978:Unpaid:Balance $978:Date of Last Activity 09/93:Individual
Account:Account Number 787652JC

## Credit Account Information

| Company Name | Account Number | Whose Account | Date Opened | Last Activity | Type of Account | High Credit | Terms | Balance | Past Due | Date Reported |
|---|---|---|---|---|---|---|---|---|---|---|
| Macy's | 12341234 | Joint | 02/94 | 01/97 | Revolving 90 Days Past Due | $4235 | 50 | $243 | $0 | 02/97 |
| Citibank Visa | 12341234 | Joint | 02/97 | 05/97 | Revolving Pays as Agreed | $10000 | 50 | $243 | $0 | 06/97 |
| Rich's-FACS | 12341234 | | 02/94 | 05/97 | Lost or Stolen Card | | | | | 02/97 |

## Additional Information

Foreclosure reported 02/97 by Firm Name verified on 02/94
Checking Account reported 02/97 opened on 04/83 closed for reason: non-sufficient funds with amount $500

## Companies that Requested your Credit File

| | | | |
|---|---|---|---|
| 02/15/97 | AR Sears | 02/13/97 | ACIS 712000003 |
| 02/13/97 | Richs/Facs | 02/11/97 | Equifax - Update |
| 01/16/97 | Macy's | 01/13/97 | Equifax - Disclosure |
| 11/18/96 | AM Macy's | 10/16/96 | PRM - Citibank Visa |

### THE FOLLOWING INQUIRIES ARE NOT REPORTED TO BUSINESSES:

**PRM** - This is a promotional inquiry in which only your name and address were given to a credit grantor so you could be solicited you with an offer such as a credit card. (PRM inquiries remain on file for 12 months.)

**AM** or **AR** - These inquiries indicate a periodic review of your credit history by one of your creditors (AM and AR inquiries remain on file for 12 months.)

**EQUIFAX**, **ACIS** or **UPDATE** - These inquiries indicate Equifax's activity in response to your contact with us for either a copy of your credit file or a request for research.

**PRM**, **AM**, **AR**, **INQ**, **EQUIFAX**, **ACIS** and **UPDATE** inquiries do not show on credit files that businesses receive, only on copies provided to you.

## YOUR ACCOUNT NUMBERS: THE ESSENTIAL LIST

### Credit Card Accounts

| Creditor | Account number | Credit limit | If lost, call this No. | Interest Rate |
|---|---|---|---|---|
| _____ | _____ | _____ | _____ | _____ |
| _____ | _____ | _____ | _____ | _____ |
| _____ | _____ | _____ | _____ | _____ |
| _____ | _____ | _____ | _____ | _____ |
| _____ | _____ | _____ | _____ | _____ |

Your maximum liability if a credit card is stolen is $50 per card. You have no liability for charges made after you report the card as lost or stolen.

### Bank Accounts

| Institution | Type of Account | Account No. | Balance as of |
|---|---|---|---|
| _____ | _____ | _____ | _____ |
| _____ | _____ | _____ | _____ |
| _____ | _____ | _____ | _____ |
| _____ | _____ | _____ | _____ |

## WHAT TO DO WHEN YOU'RE IN AN AUTO ACCIDENT

1) Wait for a police officer to write a report.

2) Exchange information with the other driver about yourselves and your insurance companies.

3) Get the names and telephone numbers of as many witnesses as you can.

4) While the accident is fresh in your mind and you're waiting for the police, draw a sketch of the accident scene.

5) As soon as possible, report it to your insurance company, even if you don't plan to make a claim.

6) Contact the other driver's insurance company.

251

## 252 ✐

# REQUEST FOR REPAIRS TO RENTAL PROPERTY

Date _____

To whom it may concern:

We are distressed that you have not responded to several requests to make repairs on our apartment.

*(Briefly describe nature of the problem and what action you would like the landlord to take.)*

Please take care of this in the next 48 hours, or it will be necessary for us to hire a repair person ourselves and deduct the cost of their services from our next rent check.

Thank you.

Sincerely,

_____

Apartment No. _____

# YOUR INSURANCE INFORMATION: THE ESSENTIAL LIST

## LIFE
Company:
Agent:
Phone #:
Account No.:
Policy Type:
Benefit Amount:
Beneficiary:

## DISABILITY
Company:
Agent:
Phone #:
Policy No.:

How long after disability does coverage take effect? _____

How long does the policy remain in effect?_____

What is the benefit amount?_____

## HOMEOWNERS
Company:
Agent:
Phone #:
Policy No.:

Features:

Does the policy include protections against inflation? _____

## AUTO
Company:
Agent:
Phone #:
Policy No.:

Features:

Liability coverage:
Collision coverage:
Comprehensive coverage:

Other features:

Is there reimbursement for towing or car rental expenses? _____

## THE PHONE BOOK

**254**

(Web sites are listed if available)

Academy of Family Mediators
800-292-4236
www.igc.apc.org/afm/

American Century Investments
(Formerly Twentieth Century Investments)
800-345-2021

American Institute of Architects
(For a remodeling contract, ask for the
standard form of agreement between owner
and contractor: A101, A111 or A201)
800-365-2724
www.aia.org

American Institute of CPAs
888-777-7077
www.aicpa.org

American Society of Home Inspectors
800-743-2744
www.ashi.com

Bureau of the Public Debt
Division of Customer Services
(Ask for the phone number of the Federal
Reserve branch office closest to your area.)
202-874-4000
www.publicdebt.treas.gov

CardWeb.com Inc.
800-344-7714
www.cardweb.com

Center for Auto Safety
(auto recalls)
202-328-7700
www.essential.org\cas

Consumer Reports
(Auto insurance shopping service)
800-224-9495
www.consumerreports.com

Council of Better Business Bureaus
Autoline
800-955-5100
www.bbb.org\bbd (Online complaint form)

Direct Marketing Association
P.O. Box 9008
Farmingdale, N.Y. 11735
www.the-dma.org

Equifax Information Service
800-685-1111
800-525-6285 (fraud alert)
Internet: www.equifax.com

Experian
Experian National Consumer Assistance
Center
888-397-3742
888-301-7195 (fraud alert)
www.experian.com

Federal Trade Commission
Publications Division
(For a copy of the brochure "Fair Debt
Collection Practices Act")
202-326-2222
www.ftc.gov

Fidelity Investments
800-544-6666
www.fidelity.com

Ford Consumer Assistance Center
(Auto arbitration, Ford vehicles)
800-392-3673

Funeral Consumers Alliance
(For a directory of memorial societies in
your area)
802-482-3437
www.funerals.org/famsa

International Fabricare Institute
Garment Analysis Laboratory
800-638-2627
www.ifi.org

INVESCO Funds Group
800-525-8085
www.invesco.com

IRS Taxpayer Advocate
800-829-1040
www.irs.gov

Janus Capital
800-525-3713
www.janus.com

MasterCard International
800-307-7309
www.mastercard.com

Morningstar Inc.
312-424-4288
www.morningstar.com

Mortgage Banker's Association of America
(Mortgages and refinancing)
202-557-2700
www.mbaa.org

National Association of the Remodeling
Industry
703-575-1100
www.nari.org

National Association of Securities Dealers
(Investments)
800-289-9999 (Disciplinary history)
301-590-6500 (Licensing information —
refer to your state when calling)
www.naspr.com
(You may request information online)

National Charities Information Bureau
(Performance ratings on charities)
212-929-6300
www.give.org

National Foundation for Consumer Credit
Counseling
800-388-2227
www.nfcc.org

National Highway Traffic Safety
Administration
DOT Auto Safety Hotline
800-424-9393
www.nhtsa.dot.gov

National Pest Control Network
Washington, DC
800-858-7378
http://ace.orst.edu/info/nptn

The Remodelor's Council of the National
Association of Home Builders
800-368-5242, ext. 216
www.nahb.com

Charles Schwab Corp.
800-648-5300
www.schwab.com

The Scudder Funds
800-225-2470
http://funds.scudder.com

Stein Roe
Young Investors Fund
800-338-2550
www.steinroe.com

T.Rowe Price Investor Services
800-638-5660
www.troweprice.com

Trans Union
P.O. Box 200
Chester, PA 19022
800-888-4213
800-680-7289 (fraud alert)
www.transunion.com

Twentieth Century Investments (See
American Century Investments)

USAA Life Insurance Company
800-531-8000

USAA First Start Growth Fund
800-841-6489

Vanguard Group Client Services
800-662-2739
www.vanguard.com

VISA International
800-847-2911 (Lost or stolen credit cards)
www.visa.com

## 256 ✎ CLARK HOWARD'S FAVORITE WEB SITES

(For more, go to www.clarkhoward.com)

### ATM LOCATIONS
www.mastercard.com
www.visa.com

### AUTO SAFETY
www.alldata.com
 (To check for recalls or potential
 problems with your car)
www.autosafety.org
 (Center for Auto Safety)
www.nhtsa.dot.gov/
 (National Highway Traffic Safety
 Administration)

### BANKS
www.occ.treas.gov
 (Complaints about banks)

### BETTER BUSINESS BUREAU
www.bbb.org
 (Charity reports and buying jewelry)

### CAR BUYING
www.consumerreports.com
 (Car prices, quality)
www.edmunds.com
 (Car prices)
www.carorder.com
 (Buy a new car online)
www.carsdirect.com
 (Buy a new car online)
www.greenlight.com
 (Buy a new car online)
www.autobyteldirect.com
 (Buy a new car online)
www.eloan.com
 (Car loans)
www.kbb.com
 (*Kelly Blue Book* used car prices)
www.carfax.com
 (Mileage rollbacks, lemons)
www.imotors.com
 (Used car buying service)

www.carlemon.com
 (Lemon law information)
www.autopedia.com
 (Lemon law information)
www.autotrader.com
 (Used car information)

### CAR INSURANCE
www.consumerreports.com
 (Ratings of insurers)

### CAR RENTALS
www.alamo.com
www.drivebudget.com
www.dollar.com

### CHARITIES
www.give.org
 (National Charities Information Bureau)

### COINS AND STAMPS
www.collectorsauction.com
www.stampsonline.com
www.money.org
 (American Numismatic Association)

### COLLEGE SAVING
www.savingforcollege.com
 (College savings: 529 plans)
www.collegesavings.org
 (College savings: 529 plans)
www.tiaa-cref.org
 (College savings)

### COLLEGE SCHOLARSHIPS
www.collegeboard.com
 (Estimate costs of college)
www.fastweb.com
 (Scholarship information)
www.nasfaa.org
 (National Association of Student
 Financial Aid Administrators)
www.finaid.org
 (Guide to financial aid)

## CREDIT CARDS
www.cardweb.com
   (Credit card rates)
www.the-dma.org
   (Direct Marketing Association)

## CREDIT PROBLEMS
www.nfcc.org
   (Consumer credit counseling)

## CREDIT REPORTS
www.equifax.com
www.transunion.com
www.experian.com
www.fairisaac.com
   (Explains credit report scoring)

## DRY CLEANING
www.ifi.org
   (International Fabricare Institute)

## E-MAIL
www.yahoo.com
   (Free e-mail)
www.hotmail.com
   (Free e-mail)
www.juno.com
   (Free e-mail)

## FUNERALS
www.funerals.org/famsa
   (Funeral planning)

## HOTELS
www.hoteldiscount.com
   (Hotel discounts)
www.roomsaver.com
   (Hotel coupons)
www.hotelbook.com
   (Hotel discounts)

## HOUSES
www.ashi.com
   (American Society of Homes Inspectors)

www.iicrc.org
   (Carpet and upholstery cleaning
   information)
www.nrca.net
   (National Roofing Contractors
   Association)

## IDENTITY THEFT
www.privacyrights.org
   (How to resolve problems with
   identity theft)

## INTERNET ACCESS
www.altavista.com
   (Free Internet access)
www.netzero.com
   (Free Internet access)
www.bluelight.com
   (Free Internet access)
www.juno.com
   (Free Internet access)
www.dslreports.com
   (To see if DSL service is available in
   your area)
www.cable-modem.net
   (To see if cable modem service is
   available in your area)
www.alladvantage.com
   (Pays you for surfing the Internet)
www.virginconnectme.com
   (Web appliance)

## INTERNET ESCROW SERVICES
www.iescrow.com
   (Internet escrow service)

## INTERNET FRAUD
www.ifccfbi.gov
   (Internet Fraud Complaint Center)
www.fraud.org
   (National Fraud Information Center)

## INVENTIONS
www.ftc.gov
   (Federal Trade Commission)
www.nolo.com

257

**258** ✎
(Inventions, wills, legal information)
www.uspto.gov
(U.S. Patent Office)

## INVESTMENTS

www.morningstar.com
(Mutual fund information)
www.quicken.com
(Investments, mortgage calculator)
www.fundalarm.com
(Links to dozens of other investment sites)
www.investorama.com
(Stocks, general)
www.hoovers.com
(Business Information)
www.bloomberg.com
(Business information, mortgage calculator)
www.fdic.gov
(To see if online banks are legitimate)
www.bankrate.com
(CD rates)
www.sheldonjacobs.com
(Investment strategy)
www.sec.gov
(Securities and Exchange Commission)
www.freetrade.com
(Trade stocks for free)
www.rothira.com
(Roth IRA information)
www.aaii.org
(American Association of Individual Investors)
www.mfea.com
(Mutual Fund Investors Center)
www.ici.org
(Mutual fund information)
www.investingonline.org
(Guide to discount brokers)
http://finance.yahoo.com/?u
(Yahoo Finance)
www.steinroe.com
(Stein Roe Young Investors Fund)
www.calcbuilder.com
(Financial calculators)
www.indexfunds.com
(Index fund information)
www.unclaimed.org
(Recovering unclaimed property)

www.missingmoney.com
(To locate lost money)

## JOBS

www.hotjobs.com
www.headhunter.net

## LEGAL INFORMATION

www.nolo.com
www.freeadvice.com
www.lawguru.com
www.findlaw.com
www.uslaw.com
www.abanet.org
(American Bar Association)

## LIFE INSURANCE

www.ambest.com
(Insurance company ratings)
www.quotesmith.com
(Life insurance quotes)
www.masterquote.com
(Insurance quotes)

## LIVING WILL

www.aarp.org
(American Association of Retired Persons)

## LONG-DISTANCE SERVICE

www.dialpad.com
(Free long-distance over the Internet)
www.telephonechoice.com
(Inexpensive 'dial-1' long-distance)
www.bigzoo.com
(Inexpensive prepaid long-distance)
www.broadpoint.com
(Free advertiser-supported long-distance)
www.fcc.gov
(Complain about long-distance carriers)
www.speak4free.com
(Free long-distance over the Internet)
www.phonefree.com
(Free long-distance over the Internet)

## MEDIATION

www.igc.apc.org/afm/
    (Academy of Family Mediators)

## MORTGAGES

www.quicken.com/mortgage/
    (Quicken mortgage information)
www.countrywide.com
    (Countrywide Mortgage: online
    mortgage application)
www.mortgage.com
    (Mortgage calculators, loan information)
www.e-loan.com
    (Consumer loan information)
www.iown.com
    (Mortgage loans)
www.hsh.com
    (Amortization schedule, consumer loan
    information)
www.lendingtree.com
    (Mortgages, credit cards, other loans)

## MOVING

www.homefair.com
    (To get information on your new city,
    including cost of living and schools.
    You can also create a checklist of things
    to do before moving day.)
www.moving.org
    (To find a legitimate moving company)
www.homegain.com
    (Home sales information)
www.virtualrelocation.com
    (Relocation tools and information)
www.moversresource.com
    (Moving information)

## REAL ESTATE

www.realtor.com

## TAXES

www.irs.gov
    (IRS Taxpayer Advocate)

## TELEMARKETING FRAUD

www.fraud.org
    (National Fraud Information Center)

## TRAVEL

www.travelocity.com
    (Booking airfares)
www.expedia.com
    (Booking airfares)
www.onetravel.com
    (Booking airfares)
www.thetrip.com
    (Booking airfares)
www.dot.gov/airconsumer
    (Complaints)
www.passengerrights.com
    (Complaints)
www.travel.state.gov
    (Warnings about overseas travel)

## WEB SITE REGISTRATION/HOSTING

www.namezero.com
    (Free domain name registration)
www.geocities.com
    (Free Web site hosting)
www.ohgolly.com
    (Build your own Web site for free)
www.econgo.com
    (Free e-commerce site)

## WILLS

www.aarp.org
    (Information on wills and trusts)

## WIRELESS TELEPHONE

www.decide.com
    (Wireless coverage areas)
www.point.com
    (Shopping for a wireless service)